The Bedside 'Guardian' 28

'*I wouldn't worry, sir, – I believe that at this very moment Geoffrey Howe is working on a scheme to enable you to buy the train.*'
24 May 1979

THE BEDSIDE
'GUARDIAN'
28

A selection from

The 'Guardian' 1978–79

Edited by

W. L. Webb

With an introduction by

John Cleese

Cartoons by

Gibbard and Bryan McAllister

COLLINS
St James's Place, London
1979

William Collins Sons & Co Ltd
London · Glasgow · Sydney · Auckland
Toronto · Johannesburg

First published 1979
© Guardian Newspapers 1979
ISBN 0 00 216195 8
Set in Monotype Imprint
Made and Printed in Great Britain by
William Collins Sons & Co Ltd Glasgow

Foreword

Sorry about this. I said I'd do it because I was flattered to be asked, and then I panicked and told my secretary to ring the next day and say I couldn't do it after all, I'd made a mistake, but she forgot and by the time I realized she hadn't got me out of it it was too late, and so I've got to do it now although I haven't anything to say, except 'I like the *Guardian*', which as a theme for 1,000 words is a bit thin, especially when you're preaching to the converted.

So I really do apologize. It won't happen again. It's just that when you're a comic, people shout at you in the street, things like 'Come on, say something funny' or 'Give us your silly walk then' or 'Where's Sybil?' and you're feeling all cheap and degraded, and then someone rings you up and asks you to do something important like writing the Introduction for a nice class of book like this, or opening a fête, or accepting an O.B.E., and you just jump at it, without thinking what a fool you'll make of yourself.

So please don't read any more of this, just turn on a few pages, and start reading. Here are some suggestions:

1 Really interesting piece about Tony Benn by Simon Hoggart (p. 153)
2 Very funny piece about cricket by Ian Peebles (p. 207)
3 Sterling stuff about German democracy by James Fenton (p. 59)
4 Very silly leader about President Carter's piles (p. 43)
5 Moving bit about Bhutto's execution by Peter Niesewand (p. 78)
6 Mysterious contribution by Nancy Banks-Smith (might be criticism; (p. 44)

All this, and more, in this, the 28th *Guardian* Bedside Book. I hope you enjoy it.

Oh, please don't follow me on to this page. Look, why don't you read Peter Jenkins on India (p. 8)? A really marvellous writer at the top of his form. Just leave me alone here to get on with the Introduction. Thank you.

Pom, pom, pom.

Now let's see ...

Preface

It's a bit of a cheat, but I did manage to get hold of an old copy of *Teach Yourself to Write the Introduction to the Bedside Guardian*, so I'm going to use it. Apparently it's not difficult. You're supposed to start with a funny story about C. P. Scott, or one of the Press Barons, or H. L. Mencken. However I don't know any. Except for the one about Mencken being told that Calvin Coolidge was dead and saying 'How can they tell?', which doesn't really fit in, so I'll just have to leave that section out. Then you're supposed to say something about the *Guardian* offices, or at least the corridors, but unfortunately I've never been there. Alastair Hetherington said in 1974 that the new ones were noisier but I hope things have got better now. I expect they're quite nice really.

Then you have to say something about the rest of Fleet Street being awful. Well, they *are*, aren't they? I mean, did you see the last election? The *Guardian* was the only daily that didn't read like a propaganda sheet. It was the only chink of hope in that whole benighted, God-forsaken affair. If it wasn't for Peter Jenkins (even his slightly skittish bits like 'Away from it all' – p. 24) I don't think I'd have got through it. And Simon Hoggart. I derived quantifiable spiritual nourishment from his pieces too, especially those on Keith Joseph and William Whitelaw. Fascinating that Whitelaw really does speak to voters like that (p. 151; I'd seen him doing it on television but assumed the film had been edited by political opponents.

Where was I? Oh, the rest of Fleet Street. Well, being on the box and therefore, by definition, desirable column fodder, I've met a lot of journalists now, and a sizeable proportion, well, *frankly* they take your breath away. The very worst of course are the gossip columnists. Telling you about these demented minor

6

public school creatures is like shooting fish in a barrel, but I still have 500 words to go so . . . One of my informants tells me they hold an annual dinner. It's not well attended because they all get the place and the date wrong, and in any case it's the one time in the year when they have to pay for their own food and drink. Did I say food? Well, the ones who do attend drink the loyal toast quite early in the proceedings – no one is allowed to vomit until after it – and the wording of the toast is 'To Dr Goebbels, our guide and mentor'. What they all admire about Dr Goebbels, of course, is not so much his politics, as his accuracy. 'If he could get to the top with little fibs like that,' they all reason, 'why not us?' Well, I can now reveal why not. For the same reason the good Doctor would never have hired them. Because they'd never bothered to check that the lies were untrue before they printed them, that's why not.

The *Guardian*, naturally, doesn't have a gossip column. If it wants to be naughty it does it in its leaders, like a man. See the amiable bitchery about the hole in Prince Charles' roof, or the A.A.'s weather reports, or In the Nico of Time.

Introduction

Actually, I seem to have made a mistake and put what should have been the Introduction in the Preface so all I'll say here is that the *Guardian* writers seem to me – this is the serious, sincere bit – to be open-minded and literate and funny and to care about whether they get it right, not like journalists at all. In fact, the sort of people you wouldn't mind having in your own house, for dinner. Come to think of it, after what Barry Norman told me last week about how the *Guardian* pays, perhaps they would like some dinner. If so, just fill in the form below. Bill Webb's got my address.

> I . . . . (BLOCK CAPITALS,
> PLEASE) write for the *Guardian* and could
> use a good meal. Please call me at
> . . . . (OFFICE) or . . . .
> (HOME) to fix a time suitable to both of us.
> I am/am not vegetarian.
> Signed . . . .

John Cleese

Cold coming to Westminster

The route was blue with policemen, blue policemen sharing the common cold with 25,000 marchers. Up from all parts of the country, the NUPE, COHSE, TGWU and GMWU contingents were awed that they commanded so much attention. Police were a dotted line flanking them all the way from Hyde Park to the House of Commons, bus-loads of reserves lurked round corners, traffic police radios set up a chorus that vied with the spasmodic chanting. No one, it was agreed, had ever seen so many policemen.

To the rhythm of the Calverton silver band and the trill of police whistles, the marchers flowed into Park Lane. A circus come to town and led by a pretty police van with chequered dome and flashing lights. The doorman of the Dorchester seemed a circus master waiting in the wings as the column tripped by, bright banners enlivening a dull day, marchers speckled with slogan stickers, press photographers performing acrobatics up lamp posts. The young Left peddling their *Militant, Socialist Worker, New Worker* and *Socialist Challenge* were sideshows.

'What do we want?' roared self-appointed cheer-leaders. 'More pay' they roared back. 'When do we want it?' 'Now!' And the placards told the rest: All Out Against Low Pay, declared the hospital workers. End Low Pay, echoed NUPE. Low Paid Workers Need A Minimum Wage, shrieked Day-Glo posters. And bobbing along among them all Nye Bevan, an old, old photograph dusted down to put over an old, old message. Why Nye? 'Didn't he start the health service or something?'

There were cold stares from the fur coats outside the hotels of Park Lane, joggers jogging against a mean wind in the park spared sidelong glances, van drivers joked as marchers dabbed stickers on their windscreens. There were good natured exchanges between marchers and police escorts. Could have been worse, might have snowed. Long way to come.

From offices white collars waved, were rewarded with bursts of chanting. 'What do we want?' 'More Pay.' 'When do we want it?' 'Now.' From the windows of an army officers' club, stiff upper lips acknowledged chants by gently inclining white heads. Over her shoulder in a bookshop Lauren Bacall cast her sultry look, another old, old photograph doing duty.

The marchers ranged from the wizened old to children who'd come with Mum. There were a few dogs, sporting stickers, and a NALGO couple who couldn't find a NALGO banner to march under. 'They said they were all coming . . .' From Tiverton, council carpenters argued their case for a craftsman's wages, or sixty quid a week anyhow. They were getting £42. Any overtime? Oh, yes; but overtime should be an option. You shouldn't *have* to do it to get a living wage. From Newton le Willows, from Wales, from the North of England, from the Midlands, from London . . . 'What do we want?' 'When do we want it?' 'Now, now, now!'

It was too cold for high spirits, too calm to get the adrenalin shifting. It began to feel a long way and the wind was rising as they neared the Thames. Those beautiful banners (some of the finest were from the London Division of NUPE and the TGWU Region One) began to misbehave, leaping like unwieldy kites controlled by a committee. Contingents of bearers slowed to master them. The police van slowed to wait for them. Everything got slower and colder, and marchers had nothing to watch but monotonous ranks of policemen.

Marchers get the boring side of the placards. They get full benefit of the fumes of patient traffic. They get hungry. Someone offered a new chant. 'What we want is lunch.' They laughed, but a contingent made a break for a sweet shop where they queued behind a man choosing whether to spend £13 or £15 on a box of cigars. He picked the £13 box. Times are hard.

It was no surprise that a band of marchers slipped into The Surprise, but startling that a fur-coated woman outside the pub should harangue them. 'Get back to work.' 'Boo.' And more boos at the staff of a small hospital where it was business as usual. Counter boos from inside, and then laughter. A placard snaps noisily on a lamp post and is discarded. Some banners had never been unfurled, but were cosseted. Placards were dispensable. Next time, they hoped, another slogan would be needed. A placard was dropped. The column moved on. When there are 25,000

'There's one small amendment, no one will be able to buy their own council house with a loan from Keyser Ullmann.'
15 May 1979

people behind you you don't bend down to pick something up.

And then police loudspeakers were warning that the end was nigh, and placards were not allowed in Parliament Square. Outside the Tate the fine banners and the disposable placards were gathered up by union officials. Police loudspeakers directed deputations to the House of Commons one way, the rest towards the Central Hall. 'Follow the police cordon.' The marchers did, no longer marchers once robbed of their banners, just a straggle wending its way through a labyrinth of back streets. A red-nosed policewoman in pearl earrings looked at her wristwatch. It was nearly over and there had not been any shouting.

There were 25,000 demonstrators, pinched with cold, from

all over the country and lost now in a warren of strange streets. They stopped to ask passers-by the way to the Central Hall. They got conflicting advice and stood in confused huddles in the bitter London streets. Suddenly there was no sign of a policeman.

28 January 1979   **Lesley Adamson**

Managing the managers

Throughout the Confederation of British Industry conference, which opened at Brighton yesterday, the closed circuit TV monitors relayed urgent messages to the delegates – a secretary who had to be phoned, a managing director demanding immediate attention, a luncheon appointment to be confirmed. Sometimes there were so many of these messages being flashed at once that they obliterated the speaker's face on the television screen.

Since the captains of British industry are in such urgent demand elsewhere, one asks what on earth they are doing at Brighton? There can be nothing pressing about the debates, which appear to be the most boring ever heard at an important conference. Great waves of narcolepsy billow like knock-out gas from the platform over the heads of the delegates, leaving them peaceful, somnolent, wholly unreceptive to any cerebral stimulus.

Occasionally someone titters, now and then a vague susurrus which might be a vestigial cheer can be heard. At the end of an especially vigorous attack on the unions, one man attempted a single-handed standing ovation. After a few moments, red-faced, he sat down, sucked inexorably back into the mire of boredom which surrounded him.

All this tedium, this perverse desire by the speakers not to excite, inform, or arouse seemed strange. Unlike the other big conferences, which are chiefly excuses for an internal punch-up, the CBI conference is openly planned as a huge public relations exercise designed to demonstrate industry's responsible attitude, the need for pay restraint, tax reform, and so forth.

Curiously, even today, some management seems to have a view of its workers which would be familiar to a mill-owner or a district commissioner in the last century. Your typical Johnny worker, they believe, is a docile sort of chap, anxious only to work hard for his master, led astray by trade unionists and government.

A Mr Fane Vernon said, to the whisper of applause which passes for a thundering ovation here, that workers did not want worker participation. 'They want the exercise of management authority and leadership!' A man from Birds Eye Foods said that 'persuasion and an element of coercion are what most people are used to and need – the style that is adopted in good schools'.

Apart from an honest desire to be obedient and respectful, the only other thing that motivates the typical worker is a primitive, cunning design to get his hands on more money. A steel coil manufacturer from Wales explained how he had tried to fiddle the tax on his workers' overtime but had failed. 'We have all become a bunch of fiddlers,' he said, any moral onus conveniently resting on the Government's shoulders.

Worker participation is self-evidently ludicrous. A man from Esso declared: 'When I go on a plane I want the pilot to be an expert; I don't want the baggage handler telling him what to do.' A Yorkshire manufacturer condemned the Bullock Report: 'Who would send Bullock to the top of Everest without training?' The faint ghost of a cheer which greeted this suggested that it is exactly the fate some delegates would reserve for the Master of St Catherine's.

However, the situation is quite different for management itself, not only underpaid but grotesquely overtaxed. Michael Edwardes, the head of BL, explained that the 83 per cent top tax rate was driving people out of the country. Yet he failed to explain why he, a South African, had been driven into the country. Why should managers keep only 17 per cent of the money they are given for extra effort? he asked.

There is a touching belief among the delegates here that all their pay rises are for virtue, hard work, and proficiency. All workers' pay rises merely reflect trade union muscle. Mr Edwardes wanted to 'mobilize the silent majority to get the top tax rates down'. He had the grace to recognize that there was a certain inconsistency in the head of BL wanting to reduce public spending.

One of the great delights has been the number of self-made

men explaining their own immense success in business, and the competition between them for the most humble beginnings. Winner was the manager of Ward Brothers who announced: 'Twenty years ago we started with four lads and an overdraft – all we had was guts.' Now the members of the CBI, thanks to their guts, enterprise, and spirit, have Chester Barrie suits, enormous cars, and the opportunity to eat the £8 a head lunches provided by the confederation.

7 November 1978   **Simon Hoggart**

Healey the Tax

Not the least of Mr Denis Healey's achievements as Chancellor of the Exchequer has been to turn the income tax into a music hall joke. He has developed a popular act. Every day he puts on false eyebrows and dresses up as a grotesque Tax Inspector. As he descended upon Carlisle yesterday housewives fled giggling into the Tesco at the sight of him. 'Ha, ha, you didn't expect to see me did you?'

'Any chance of the loan of a fiver, Denis?' asked a newspaper vendor. 'Sorry,' said the Chancellor, 'I'm here to collect the taxes. Might as well have your money while I'm here,' he said to some more shopping ladies. 'Can I come in and see the VAT books?' he asked the girl at a shoe shop. Wherever he went people fell about laughing. When he stopped outside the Midland Bank the burglar alarm went off.

It is not easy to credit the notion that Mrs Thatcher is about to be swept to power on the crest of an angry taxpayers' revolt when people behave in this good humoured fashion. In view of all that is written about the remoteness of government in Britain it is remarkable how people will walk up to the Chancellor of the Exchequer in the street and show him their payslip or complain about the deductions from their pension.

Mr Healey is going around the country shamelessly anticipating his next budget. As soon as he was off the train yesterday he began talking like Robin Hood. Before he was out of the station he'd slashed income tax and promised to raise the money by taxing companies. He made this sound completely painless. When a pensioner with a part-time job came up to him in the street he promised her: 'In three weeks' time I'm going to raise the amount you can earn without paying tax.'

Carlisle is in the heart of the Whitelaw country. Part of Mr Healey's patter yesterday was to tell people how he had the other day driven through 'one of Willie's forests'. Happily, he added, there was a Labour sticker on every tenth tree.

After his walkabout he gave local newsmen his impressions of the campaign. He had been discovering a growing scepticism and worry about Conservative policies and – he added darkly – about the personalities of Conservative leaders. It was now pretty obvious that their promise to cut taxes had blown up in their faces. This was because it would mean putting up the prices of goods bought by poor people.

So, the emphasis of the Tory campaign had shifted from an appeal to selfish greed to an appeal to rather less respectable emotions of fear and hate. He delivered this little party piece in the most pleasant of manners, the friendly smile still fixed on his familiar ruddy face.

Mr Healey's Herculean displays of extroversion are the result of some diffidence in his character, I suspect. I have suspected this since I heard his mother on a television profile some years ago describing how Denis as a boy would set off alone several paces ahead of the family on their Sunday walks.

He has a great many friends in the streets but few in politics. He is as good as his last budget. No man needs Labour to win more than Denis Healey. No man wants Labour to win more than Denis Healey. His chances of leading his party will be much greater if Mr Callaghan is returned to Number 10 next week. Another year in the job and he might be happy to return to the proverbial farm. Mr Healey's claims to succeed could then scarcely be denied.

In opposition it might be a different story. It would be in Mr Healey's interests for Mr Callaghan to remain a while longer, especially if yet another election appeared imminent. The worst outcome for Mr Healey would be a Thatcher landslide which could send the Labour Party lurching to the Left.

His own career apart, Mr Healey's approach to politics is

far more suited to government than to opposition. He gives the impression of a man with no beliefs other than in his own abilities. But this appearance of ideological nakedness is deceptive, his disguise perhaps; he knows well enough where he would like to go if his stealth can enable him to get there.

He has several times remarked in public how Britain, almost alone, in the Western industrialized world has failed to settle the question as to what kind of economy it should be. Everywhere else there is an agreed mix, a broadly liberal regime for private enterprise backed up by a pragmatic interventionist state. Mr Healey's ambition, I suspect, is to settle that question in Britain too.

27 April 1979   **Peter Jenkins**

Sir Keith's silent majority

Britain's most diffident election campaigner poked his head round the door of the carpet shop and, seeing that it was empty of customers, slid unobserved inside. When the manager appeared he said apologetically, 'I'm not a customer, I'm afraid I'm only a politician.' He then asked a series of rapid questions about who owned the shop, its opening hours, wholesalers' arrangements, and so forth.

Being so diffident, he doesn't wear a rosette and sometimes forgets to say who he is or which party he represents. He would never dream of doing anything so discourteous as to solicit somebody's vote.

The fact is that Sir Keith Joseph, Mrs Thatcher's industry spokesman, her chief economic guru, and one of three men in the Shadow Cabinet she thinks are cleverer than she is (the other two are Lord Hailsham and Sir Ian Gilmour) is not really cut out for this kind of thing. In fact, he hates it. 'One does so regret the intrusion into people's lives,' he confided before a walkabout in the West Midlands this weekend. (The term 'walkabout' is actually Australian, and describes an aborigine practice of a man going into the bush on his own for a few weeks. This would be Sir Keith's ideal election tour.)

We went into a baker's, but since it was full of voters, we walked straight out again. 'We mustn't interrupt here,' he said. The local candidate in Aldridge suggested a visit to a supermarket. 'Do you think it's proper to go in?' he asked. 'I do try to avoid places with customers in.'

When, unavoidably, he does meet someone – perhaps because the local agent has thrust them at him – he does nothing so embarrassing as to suggest that they vote Conservative. Instead, he enquires if they have any questions to ask him. Since very few people get up in the morning and muse, 'I must ask Sir Keith Joseph about the minimum lending rate if I bump into him in Tesco's today,' few people have a question ready.

He plucked up the courage to address a young housewife who said, 'Good afternoon,' quite agreeably. 'People are so polite to me when I interrupt them,' he said in genuine amazement. 'Look at you, you're actually smiling.' He was even more surprised when a man with a Labour sticker failed to sandbag him or hurl rotten fruit. 'I think you're all so polite to us,' he said, in genuine wonder at the sheer niceness of the human race.

Later, we made successful visits to an empty Indian restaurant and a market stall with no customers.

At a printing works he kept approaching people and asking what their skill was. This surprised them, since for the most part the skill seemed to involve watching sheets of printed paper drop out of a machine and into a box. We made the acquaintance of a silicon chip, a rare sighting of the fabled creature. The chip was larger than one had expected, about the size of a small wardrobe. It had the job of printing postage stamps for Mauritius. Sir Keith stared at the chip, and the chip hummed and winked back at Sir Keith, but did not reveal how it intended to vote, or what it had done with the 50,000 Mauritian postage stamp printers it had no doubt replaced.

Sir Keith is happier on public platforms. In fact, he quits the platform and descends with microphone into the audience as if about to sing, like Val Doonican. He has a unique way with hecklers: he answers their questions. This usually shuts them up. He also has a disconcerting habit of departing from the official Tory line. For example, he said firmly in Tamworth that unions could not be changed by law, 'only by education and persuasion'.

And he frankly admitted that the majority of people would not be 'galvanized' by income tax cuts. This is disturbing: one does not expect the chief myth-maker to be an iconoclast.

Even here he can be hideously embarrassed. The chairman read out a eulogy which made him sound like a latter-day Leonardo. Sir Keith buried his head in his hands. At the end of a long hard day keeping one jump ahead of the voters, it was all too much.

30 April 1979   **Simon Hoggart**

'*Arthur Egburt Miller (Conservative) two votes. I therefore declare that the said Arthur Egburt Miller is duly elected as member of the European Parliament for this constituency.*'
12 June 1979

A brush with the art loving public

The best light on the private view of the 211th Summer Exhibition of the Royal Academy came straight through the skylight of Gallery III, vividly illuminating the drinks tables.

Less than a full swig away hung a cloud-fluffed beachscape in three panels by Roger de Grey, RA, basking in the Charles Wollaston Award for the most distinguished work of the exhibition. Called Marenne Estuary. Elderly estuarial folk with veils contemplated it as if from beach chairs.

'So peaceful.'

'Calm as calm.'

'It's the serenity, isn't it?'

Over in the corner the mood was more ruffled, where dense mobs praised The 17th Wedding Anniversary: Our Bedroom at Mole End, a seven-sided tour de force by Anthony Green, RA. It's the kind of picture that induces people to describe it to their companions beside them as if they were blind.

'She's in the nude, yes, mother, except she's got shoes on.'

'Three nudes, in fact.'

'They're all his wife, mother. One's looking at TV.'

'And two men.'

'They're either twins or the same man. One's bringing her coffee, the other one's in pyjamas flying in through the window with a present.'

'Peculiar wedding anniversaries some people do have.'

A young Japanese couple said it was good to break the inhibitions, but if they were to buy something they'd prefer a seashore. With seagulls.

The Lord Mayor, Sir Kenneth Cork, known in the City as 'the undertaker' because he wraps up bankrupt companies, hove to in morning dress. 'See what it's called,' he cried gaily to a burly man in similar togs: 'Wedding Anniversary. Very good, that.'

I complimented the burly fellow on the glittering piece of art pendent from his neck, incorporating the motto *Fortune le veut.*

It was the Sheriff of London, very affable. 'Family motto. Whole design was done by a young girl called Jackie Hodgson in four minutes flat, then a firm in Birmingham cast it in two months, delivery on the dot. Nice to know industry's not falling down on its order dates.'

It was the 1445th work of art on display. Chosen from over 13,000 submissions. By 3 p.m. 3000 painters, critics, friends, Friends of the RA, and people who'd bought pictures in previous years had come to look at them, a crowd growing by compound interest each year. It wasn't going to be easy to winkle out the painters.

A young man with matted hair, and paint-bespattered trousers and canvas shoes. 'Exhibitor? Nah,' he growled. He strode off along the wall like a medieval swordsman, bouncing his comments off the canvases: 'Bad, bad, bad, bad, bad, bad.'

An old bearded man in a wheelchair. No response except to point at his ears. Deaf too.

A tall one with a velvet suit and big bow tie and hair going back as if he'd just come through a wind tunnel. 'Exhibitor? Lord, no. Collector. Sizes? I don't worry about that sort of thing. Prices? Very reasonable. Always are here, because the commission quantity is negligible.'

Actually commission rose this year from 15 to 20 per cent – still only half the galleries' cut. Prices range from about £70 to £32,240 (inc. VAT) for an Eduardo Paolozzi bronze.

The hell with spotting painters. Make do with *jeunes filles en fleur*. Prime one here with fine talent wearing broad-brimmed green hat with fronds.

'That hat? It's practically the last thing Biba sold. I tint it every year. Actually I'm an exhibitor. You want to see my painting? All right. Meet father first.'

Left to father; Sir Roger Bannister, pushing the champers *en famille*. Vigorous exchange with him about art, not sport.

'Daddy, he wants to talk about art, not sport.'

'. . . great new stuff on retarded pubescence.'

Adjacent gallery with Erin Bannister to look at her picture of a doll. Sweet but eerie. An unmarried aunt collected dolls. 'It's Celtic. Mother's Celtic. In my first year at the RA school I've been doing self-portraits. But you get sick of innocence. Dolls are innocent too, but weird.'

Return her to father. Detain a girl in a black leather suit. 'How did you know I was an exhibitor? Show you my painting? All right. This is father.' Mandatory conversation with father - about Ireland. Then off to see Elizabeth Brown's picture Personal Values - valued by her at £350. Post-graduate student from Portsmouth; first time she's been hung; big thrill. The picture is a self-portrait.

Another good-looking woman - must be an exhibitor. Sure enough: Jane Corsellis, who sticks a red tab on her wrist of the kind used to show a painting is sold. Can this grey-haired man in blue denim jacket be father? No, it's John Flavin, another exhibitor. Double top. Both have often been hung before. But waiting for news of acceptance is still agony to her.

'I can't work until I hear. Then if they call me Mrs I know it's rejection, and if I'm Jane I'm in.'

'This is the last great shop window,' he says. 'The man in the street's scared of art galleries, but he comes in here as cheerfully as into the Tower.'

A tiny girl in a silk pyjama suit and pink stockings, with two little stars at the corner of her eyes, is unaccountably not an exhibitor. Hasn't even a father surrogate. End of lucky streak.

But a greybeard in green comes by - James Newton. 'My picture? I'll take you. It's nostalgia for the pulps. It's a bit pornographic, can't think why they hung it. Big metal tits, bondage, you know. It's good, though. Mind you, everything is, except what the RAs put in.'

Then Mel Calman. Typical fate for a cartoonist, they've hung his two in a narrow strip of wall between a corner and a burglar alarm. One is called Private View. 'I always do something snide about art, they like that.'

Hardly room to push a trolley of ice cubes through. The press was like the tube in rush hour. Particularly in the well-named Small South Room, where 158 small pictures were squashed close as memorabilia in a Victorian parlour. Everybody coveted Sheep, a cute triptych by Nicholas Grimshaw. Too late: the red tab said gone, for £100.

Fruit sold well, and chickens, and items like corks and shoes, though nudes were slow.

And portraits. Ah! By the quiet jacket and plump trim of the beard, yes, David Poole. Painted the Queen three times. Has to hand it to HM as a model:

'It's part of the job but it must be tedious for her. She gives five sittings a portrait to three artists a year. For regiments, embassies, all sorts.'

He said business was brisk and companies are giving artists a freer hand with their chairmen. We came to Poole's own exhibit. This was where I came in: The Lord Mayor, in full rig. 'It's more fun than chairmen in suits. With regalia you can let yourself go.'

Mothers with baby-buggies were bruising ankles wholesale. The injured were exclaiming, 'Must whiz now.'

19 May 1979   **Alex Hamilton**

The elements rise up against us

Poland, which has the ideal incomes policy (i.e., you get what you're given), had no difficulty finding people to clear the streets of Warsaw yesterday. Ten thousand people turned out, some of them voluntarily. In Britain, motoring organizations and campaigning newspapers were asking why Moscow (−40 degrees) should be able to grit the roads when London (−4 in some isolated and exposed hilly areas) could not. For Soviet Union, see under Poland. For London, see under work-to-rule; but also, see under dramatic, love of the, and elements, raw, combat with. The AA team, which brought you black ice, bats out of hell, and Freeze-up Friday, was working a skeleton staff on 1 January, so that diabolical was the strongest word to emerge from the superlatives section by 1 p.m. Later in the day, when the regular gloom shift had clocked on (it was a skating rink all the way to work) motorists were being confidently advised to stay at home. Don't move unless absolutely necessary. Treachery looms, blizzards abound. The railways were quicker to respond. This week's reason for non-delivery of *The Observer* was frozen points at Liverpool Street (although large parts of the home counties are served from elsewhere). Essex, the Siberia of the West, was authoritatively said to be cut off by the white hell. Nevertheless the long delays and cancellations of yesterday were slightly fewer than on an average weekday. So normal was life in the capital that the evening papers had to resort to forecasts of more snow to come. Even then they had to admit that it would probably be sleet.

Now all the second-hand New Year weather lore from the motoring lobby was possible only because, it being a joyous holiday, nobody was out of doors to check the facts. It is alleged for example, that all the roads across the Pennines were blocked except the M62 (to be precise, they were skating rinks again, according to the AA). That may or may not be the case. Only a fool would go and see. We are quite prepared to accept that in parts of Scotland and perhaps the North-East driving was likely to require a little more care than usual, but over most of the country it only needs a man to say there are twelve inches of snow against his tool-shed for the whole of Devon and Somerset to be blocked off by twelve-foot drifts. ('And it'll still be there on midsummer's day, mark my words.') Well, everybody loves a legend, and it's all quite harmless. But spare a thought for the Dutchman who tried to thaw his petrol cap with a cigarette lighter. Entire car and garage wiped out, yet 'miraculously', according to a spokesman, no one was hurt.

3 January 1979   **Leader**

A country diary: Kent 1

Towering above the rest of the forest trees in the fresh wet snow the redwood seemed to be on fire. Where the evergreen foliage kept the broad base of the trunk free from snow, wisps of what looked like smoke rose from the fox-red bark. As the sun rose and penetrated the forest glade the rays were reaching patches of dampness and green moss, and evaporating the moisture, making it steam. Where the sun had done its work the fibrous bark was warm to the touch and glowed like a quiet flame. In its original habitat in the High Sierras of the American West Coast the moisture that fuels its magnificent growth is largely derived from winter snowfall so the Wellingtonia, a giant among trees named after a giant among men, looked at home in the wintry weald. The green needles enclosing the twigs like a sheath were bulging with yellow male flowers ready for a new season. Though its growth rate of more than two feet a year has been exceeded by some of the larches in the plantation, the redwood is unsurpassed in its sheer girth. A mere fifty years in the growing and already monarch of that particular glen, it is still in its infancy with another thousand years or more to reach its maturity. I have heard children call it the punch tree because they can punch the thick cushion of bark and not hurt their knuckles. The forester told me that the thermometer had fallen to 14 below zero that week, well short of the 28 degrees of Centigrade frost recorded in 1940 but still severe enough to set my feet stamping at the very thought, frightening off the robins that were viewing us curiously from the nearest bough. Such temperatures would not be to their liking either but a cloud of insects was rising with the sun, supplying food on the wing.

26 January 1979   **John T. White**

Away from it all

My day was spent viewing Mrs Thatcher from the other end of the tube – the wrong end of the tube. What home viewers saw last night was the result of our combined antics in the green grassroots of Suffolk – one planeload and two coachloads of what are these days known as media personnel, most of them willing to play bit parts as members of the local electorate.

First media event of the day took place at Willisham Farm. We arrived at around 1 p.m. For most people this is lunchtime but if film is to be back in London in time for the 5.45 news, lunchtime is peak shooting time. Tory media managers have made the early evening bulletins prime targets as millions of working families watch the box over tea. Mrs Thatcher arrived in her shiny coach with its tinted picture windows. Before stepping down she signalled to Michael Brunson of ITN. Cameras rolling?

She was met by the farm manager, Andy Rutherford. He was full of health, vigour, cornflakes and all that the land can offer;

he was ideally the young farmer to appear with Mrs Thatcher on TV. They moved off together towards the cowsheds. She set the pace, exactly the right one for film crews walking backwards.

First she was filmed looking at the Friesians and then at the Herefords. She seemed to like the Herefords best with their mournful white faces; she let one suck her fingers for several minutes in a rather sensual fashion. They were only calves. 'Now, these are barley-fed plus some concentrates?' she asked knowingly. She was right. She discussed the cost of rearing them, how much they would fetch at market. 'Aren't they behaving marvellously?' she said. 'Normally they do all sorts of things for cameramen.'

Next we went into a field. Why were we going into this field? There seemed nothing special about it. A hand took her arm at the elbow and her patent shoes, two shades of blue, neatly avoided a cow pat. It was nicely done, a skilful piece of campaigning. A small crowd of locals, accompanied by the village constable, looked on from behind a fence. They gazed in rustic amazement as an army of pasty-faced men in London clothes armed with heavy photographic equipment formed a kind of loose scrum in the middle of the cow field. Somewhere within was Mrs Thatcher.

This time she was hugging a calf. In fact she was almost strangling a calf. She was rather alarmed at this. I inspected it knowingly and pronounced it alive. It was only just alive having been born six hours previously. I am unable to say whether its birth was induced by the Hon. Veterinary Surgeon to the Conservative Central Office.

Next Mrs Thatcher lay down on the grass with the calf. She reclined prettily like a milkmaid in an Arcadian musical.

Then we all went back to the farmyard. We passed by the duckpond without incident. Next it was to be lambs. One of them was a black lamb. Mrs Thatcher hugged it. You may have seen her on television last night. Maybe you said, 'Oh how sweet' or – if you were watching the 5.45 news over your tea – 'ain't it lovely.' At the same moment the minds of the Fleet Street caption writers began to work on 'Maggie had a little lamb . . .'

Soon it was time to leave the farm. 'What a pity we can't stay longer,' said Maggie. 'Come along now.' She broke away

'Which button do you push to register your vote?'
3 May 1979

from the young men she had been talking to, either farm labourers or Young Tories. They were wearing crumpled bush hats. She climbed into her bus. A few people were left waving as the crowd she had brought departed with her.

Mrs Thatcher has been practising this style of campaigning for eighteen months or more. She has been rehearsing it at by-elections, perfecting it on her visits to the regions. She is today an excellent performer, a charming and natural tele-campaigner. She has versed herself in the technique and the jargon of media management. The other day she got a cameraman to do a 're-take' of an off-the-cuff speech. Coming out of her Chelsea home one morning she surprised reporters by saying, instead of 'good morning,' 'now I am worried about the London and provincial evenings.'

From the farm we went to Ipswich. There she said to an

insurance employee, Mrs R. Orly, something like this: 'We try to do a number of things each day. We must get out into the countryside, we said. And today we said thank goodness we came. It's so good to get away from the press conferences and all those hundreds of journalists and all those intellectual questions. It's good to see real life for a change.'

Real life as seen on TV. Real life as seen by you if you were watching last night.

19 April 1979   **Peter Jenkins**

Cri de coeur

Sir,

Have things gone too far? My sovereign is a woman; my Prime Minister is a woman; my boss is a woman; and my wife is a woman.

Yours faithfully,
10 May 1979   **C. Grimwood**
Laughton, Sheffield

Always on Wednesday

It is the custom nowadays for women to want to be close. It is another way of achieving independence from men; the implication being, of course, that the clinging, dependent woman still lurks beneath the sturdy breast. The image of man as mirror, confirming existence – or by his absence, denying it – is deep-rooted even now.

Thus substitutes must be found for him. He must be reduced to an unthreatening importance, hitherto accorded a favoured pet. If married he must creep home at midnight to find his wife still out with the girls (correction, 'women'). There are no sexual conclusions to be drawn from her absence. It is not more of the same that woman seeks. Enough is enough.

Open marriage is no longer about sexual freedom. (It can

be no coincidence that the latest blockbuster book contract is for a tome called *Asexuality*.) Orgasms are easy to come by. Emotional and social independence is another ambition altogether.

Women are now learning to treat other women not as make-does for a fallow time but as preferred companions. There is an air of the female St James's to Manhattan these days. The all-women dinner party is supplanting the gatherings of golden couplehood. The most interesting guests and conversations are now to be found at the former.

This is no bowl of soup affair or left-over cold cuts that women used to reserve for one another. 'Let's eat in the kitchen, it's only us,' is a remark from another state of mind. This is a full-blown, best silver, latest *New York Times* recipes dinner. Beware, single men of fifty – you who have dined out for years on your spare status ('just to make up the numbers'): frozen meals now lie ahead.

How strange the way word spreads in New York. Perhaps when the *Times*' Living section writes up this new phenomenon of the women's dinner, they'll be doing it all over Darien, Connecticut. For the moment, it is something women of a certain stage go to and give.

Word has also spread that those women who dress up to eat steamed bass together, also undress to steam together at the East Tenth Street Russian and Turkish Baths. It is the latest way to unwind for those women who wear Calvin Klein suits and Louis Vuiton briefcases or who have just dropped their doctoral thesis off to be typed.

The East Tenth Street Baths are a Lower East Side institution. Once they were a haven for the Jewish immigrant patriarchs, a moment of peace between peddling from barrows along Hester Street and ruling families in airless walk-ups. Six days a week they now cater for those men who run corporations and like to sweat away the day's malevolence, gulp a whisky or two and swap dirty jokes before setting out for some sward-surrounded spread in New Jersey. Wednesday, however, it is different. Wednesday is for women.

Getting to 268 East Tenth is not for the frivolous. The taxis rolling up to the corner of First Avenue are a six-dollar ride away from the Upper East Side studios and Upper West Side homes of those they drop. This is not a neighbourhood to walk in alone after dark. Its perfumes are not Cie, Babe or Cinnebar, but stale garbage and staler sweat.

It looks terrible. The worn steps and shabby façade are not promising. The crayon sign, $7, inside the door is an emphatic contradiction to them. Although gay baths in New York run at $35 dollars (sightseers also risk being beaten up), seven dollars is steep enough to signal that only the privileged enter here.

Al Modlin, whose personality was obviously acquired for the raucous boys-only crowd, stands by the entrance taking money, handing out keys and looking not a little bewildered by the cool crowd of Bloomingdale's specials to whom he is now host. As owner of the Baths, he is evidently used to being treated as a New York character. Six days a week, maybe. On Wednesdays, these women simply overlook him.

Two long lines of beds run down a darkened room with lockers between them. On these beds women gather to talk before going down to the baths in the basement. Protected still by pale blue, heavily laundered wraps, they talk over the week. From one corner, Iran, the Israel-Egypt pact, energy. From another, the tale of a New York adventure, the man picked up in a jazz bar and taken home for the night.

'I don't care if I don't see him again. After five years of an el sicko relationship, it was so good to laugh and have someone be funny and warm in bed.' Man as a piece of fluff; woman as lone operator.

The baths downstairs are tiled and filled with women's bodies of all colours and not so many shapes. Towels are only for wrapping around hair oozing Sassoon conditioner. Agnes stands out immediately. Hovering over her massage table, twenty-one stone of bulbous flesh and cellulite, she wears only plimsolls and a bandage for her varicose veins. Her popular seven-dollar oil massages (forget the words private parts) are interrupted as she ambles over to the door to kiss and greet regulars in broken but expressive English.

'What I love about being with women here,' says a reclining psychologist, 'is that the baths are a great leveller.' Far from it: the slender, lithe bodies with strap marks from Tobago or Jamaica stand in condemnation of those who have fallen into droop and swell. When Agnes started here eight years ago, her customers were old-timers. Today the average age is thirty. High earners, out jogging before dawn, down here steaming after dark. The occasional woman with the predatory eye and carrying voice is subtly ostracized. In the steam room and sauna she always finds space around her. The nuances are those of a cavalry officer's mess. Everyone knows who is not 'one of us'. This is not the intimacy of the therapy group or the clannishness of the political caucus, it is about relaxing in good company.

The forced confidences over spinach salad at lunch tables for two is part of an earlier, more self-conscious drive to be close. There is no sense of daring, no excitement at new parameters, it's just women being together, proving nothing. How ironic that those grandmothers who came here once long, long ago knew instinctively what these MAs and PhDs have only now learned – that women need fellowship too.

'I went to see my grandmother over the weekend,' announces Michelle, 'and I told her I'd found these great baths and how good it is to hang out here. She said, "Michelle, leave me alone; I was going to the East Tenth Street Baths seventy years ago and believe me, we talked about life then too. So what's new?" '

Upstairs, nine o'clock, dressed again, tables of women consume fresh orange juice and dine on the best food along the Lower East Side. There is no hurry to get home. They are home.

18 April 1979   **Linda Blandford**

Features

Mr S's consulting-rooms in Harley Street are plush and airy, with thick new carpets and hessian walls, not a whiff of that pervasive medical smell that haunts every corner of a hospital. Elegant and dapper in a sharp suit and crisp cuffs, I doubt if anyone would guess that Mr S was a doctor.

Mr S is a cosmetic surgeon. Twenty per cent of his time he works for the National Health, doing head and neck surgery in a large general hospital in the Home Counties. The rest of his time is given over to his private practice. He fixes noses, chins, breasts, sagging faces, bulging bodies, flapping ears and almost anything else people might be dissatisfied with.

On this particular afternoon his waiting-room was crowded with men and women of all shapes and nationalities. A couple of women were entirely shrouded in huge black veils, so you couldn't see their noses in any case.

A tall blonde woman in her thirties with a curiously rasping voice sat in the chair beside Mr S's desk in his room. She had a large nose, but hadn't come to him either about her nose or her voice, but for a breast enlargement operation. It had been performed three weeks ago and she was coming back for a check-up. He took her behind the colour co-ordinated hessian screen at one end of the room, where she undressed, while Mr S shone a light on her. It must be said that her small round breasts were magnificent – perfect upright spheres of a kind usually only achieved by porno photographers with the adept use of discreet bits of Sellotape. She had oddly small pale pink nipples.

'We just inserted a silicone bag,' Mr S explained, as he examined her scars with approval. 'It's a wonderful prosthesis, which took years to develop. Of course the actual cost of the prosthesis is about £5 a pair, but they charge £170 to take account of the years of research.' The whole operation cost her £600, with just one night in a private clinic.

'How do you feel now?' he asked her. 'Fine, now,' she said. 'But I found I was very depressed and weepy for a couple of weeks afterwards. I just burst into tears at the slightest thing.' Mr S said this was a very common experience with women undergoing breast enlargements. 'But are you pleased with them now? Are you a satisfied customer?' he asked.

She smiled and said. 'Oh yes, very. My husband, you see, wasn't at all keen for me to have it done, but now he's delighted too.' Mr S warned her not to raise her arms at all in the next two months, nor to lift anything. When she had gone he said she was a transexual, which amazed me; it hadn't even occurred to me. 'You have to be so careful. If you don't treat them absolutely as a woman you lose their confidence completely. One slip of the tongue and they never forgive you.'

His next patient was a young man who had had a nose job. He showed me the before and after pictures. His nose had been broken and was crooked, but I couldn't say that he looked significantly different. 'My nose was a bit blocked before,' he said. 'I had trouble breathing.' Mr S asked if it had been more the breathing or the appearance that had worried him. He said it was the breathing, but that wasn't altogether convincing as he said he was very pleased with the end product but still couldn't breathe well through it.

'My girl-friend likes it,' he said. 'I don't think my other friends noticed, unless I told them.' It cost him £550 which he had saved by doing extra work in the evenings. He hadn't thought of approaching the NHS. He said he felt more confident, though he still seemed a bit shy and awkward.

Mr S turned the young man's face sideways. 'It's a good thing you have a beard,' he said, surveying the man's features as a sculptor might. 'You have a receding chin. The beard helps to balance the effect of the nose. Have you ever thought of having a piece put in your chin?' 'No,' he answered, hesitantly. 'Ah, well, there is a very good chin prosthesis which solves the problem of the receding chin. But perhaps the beard does just as well?'

The next patient was a cheerful young girl who had booked herself an appointment to discuss having a large mole on her chin removed. But surprisingly, when she arrived she said she wasn't worried any more about the mole, but wanted her scarcely visible varicose veins on her legs dealt with.

Two more nose cases came next. The first girl was quite pretty but her nose was still fairly prominent, after the operation. Again I doubted whether she looked remarkably different, but she felt she did. She was delighted and said her attitude to life had changed in the three weeks since the operation. 'I always used to wear very quiet clothes so as not to draw attention to myself. Now I feel better,' she said.

Mr S looked at her, contemplating his handiwork. 'I did talk to you about your high forehead, didn't I? You must do something about it.'

'Oh yes,' she said quickly. 'I'm going to the hairdressers next week to have my hair style changed.'

'Good. Which hairdresser are you going to?' 'Selfridges.' 'Oh, I expect that'll be all right. You really would look a lot better with some hair covering your forehead.'

The next nose job was a particularly beautiful young girl. Mr S almost sighed with pleasure at the sight of her. 'Now you really had a terrible konk, didn't you?' he said. She admitted that she had. She'd had a car accident as a child and her nose was broad and hooked. 'I used to be very self-conscious if I thought anyone was looking at my profile. I always turned and looked at them full-face.' She added that she'd put on a lot of weight since the operation a month ago. 'I think it's just that I don't feel I need to try so hard,' she said.

Earlier that day Mr S had seen a particularly difficult patient. A barmaid came to him asking him to fix a scar on her neck and shoulders, which she had had since a childhood scalding. She said her marriage had broken up, because she would never undress in front of her husband. She always insisted on wearing high necked sweaters all day and all night. 'But when she undressed, there was practically nothing there,' he said. 'The scars were in her mind. It was a phobia. I've sent her along to a psychiatrist, but I doubt if he'll do much good. What she needs is someone, anyone, a friend or relative, to force her, stage by stage, to take her clothes off. Force her to go swimming or something. If she comes back I may do some sort of operation though.'

Mr S's theory about cosmetic surgery is that people often have a warped image of themselves. If you alter their body, even a little, you can sometimes make them quite pleased with themselves, although they may in fact look much the same as before. 'Everyone, in their heart of hearts, would like cosmetic surgery,' is a favourite saying of his. 'We all have bits of us we'd like to improve.'

He says he likes to feel he offers a complete service, especially to the women wanting a face-lift. 'She has bags under her eyes, saggy cheeks and jowls. She's given up her life and part of her identity bringing up her children, and now they've gone. Perhaps her husband now has enough money to go on a glamorous holiday, and she meets the Martini people, but finds she can't dance and has nothing to talk about, no personality.

'She requires complete redesigning. I can deal with her turkey gobbler and her saggy eyes, but I also encouraged her to redesign her clothes, her hair, learn to dance and use a little wit and some jokes. I always think that clothes designers and hairdressers and beauticians can do more in a short time than any amount of psychiatric social workers and what have you.' 'Complete re-styling,' i.e. a face-lift, costs £1500. Eyelids cost £800, a nose about £600.

Mr S has an extremely lucrative practice. He has no shortage of clients and clearly makes a small fortune out of them. (He also runs his own business, but wouldn't divulge its nature.) None of these cosmetic operations are easily available on the NHS. 'Look,' he says. 'To be truly honest, which most doctors aren't, why should I take a client on the NHS when I can make a lot of money making him come to me privately? It would be entirely my decision as to whether to treat someone for a new nose in my NHS hospital, but I always turn them down and say they must see me privately. Anyone can afford it, if they save, as they might for a new car.'

He says he is operating as much on personalities as on bodies. But it seems to me an expensive and painful way of dealing with people's feelings of inadequacy. Looking at some of his before-and-after pictures, I felt he often didn't make a significant difference to his patient's appearance. Wouldn't it have been better to try to persuade them that they are already good looking and they have nothing to worry about?

Unless a face is clearly disfigured or a nose unreasonably grotesque wouldn't it be kinder to reassure his patients and explain that attractiveness, success, and happiness don't, thank goodness, rest in the shape of a nose or the flap of an ear? He admits that quite often he has problems with patients who don't find their lives as radically altered as they had hoped once they've had themselves fixed up.

11 June 1979   **Polly Toynbee**

The Pumas as cubs

During one Olympiad, where I was hired as an interpreter, I had to translate the ardour felt by an Argentinian gold-medal oarsman and a British broadcasting chattel for each other. The poetry, I recall, came from him, the practical drive from her. Their mingling, up to the point when at the bedroom door I said they must now stumble along as best they might without a pilot, depended heavily on me.

At Oxford, waiting for the Pumas to open their rugger tour against Southern Counties, that little episode was the first to come back to me. The second was prompted by an anti-Videla demo there. I could hear again the voice of my headmaster in Buenos Aires, advising: 'When a riot begins, join in. It's always the bystander who gets shot.'

When would the thumping start? Were they meaning to break up the game? Not this time, they said. Strictly leaflets. I read some. Chile, Namibia, Turkey, Zimbabwe, Mozambique, Guatemala, Morocco, Guidimaka . . . A global worry bath. In Argentina, 15,000 disappearances, 4000 officially dead. Plus warnings from Richard Gott on changes towards new forms of illiberalism. Richard on his tod enables you to worry about the whole of South America. What a load of grief, while waiting for the kick-off, with the wind blowing diagonally from corner flag to corner flag, bending the trees at the far end of the ground.

The queue was mildly irked. 'Foul play, Argentina,' cried one of the placards. 'Foul play?' said a burly man quizzically. 'Oh yes, that was two years ago against Wales, wasn't it? Stiff-arm job by Travaglini.' Possibly the best centre the Pumas ever had. *Que barbaro, este!* They've left him out of the tour selection, which is said to have been a dicey process. It's all gentlemen tigers this time. The Travaglini in the pack's his nephew, but no mule-boy, as they say.

It was a very clean game. Almost unnaturally so. I noticed that Iacchetti, an amiable hulk of 120 kg and two metres in stature, and presumably from his blond hair of Piedmontese extraction, doesn't even bother to use his arms in a tackle, leave alone unsheath his claws. He just sort of leans on his opponents. That seems to be enough.

But it wouldn't have been enough for us, in BA. I remember the supporters of the Lomas Club, and their sepulchral chant: 'Blood, Lomas! Blood, blood, blood!' I remember a man being tackled while placing the ball for a kick at goal. I remember most of all my own initiation into the concept of the fair tackle, coupled with the first whisper of the desperate remedy.

This was at the Colegio San Jorge de Quilmes, which shares the Horatian motto *Vestigia Nulla Retrorsum* – no steps backwards with the Guards. It was an Anglo-Argy establishment with a grotesque kinship to English public schools, in as much as violent sporting competition was codified into a house system, and the lictors were chosen off the altar rail. In most other respects they were totally dissimilar. But along with other places with a British strain like St John's and St Andrew's, plus various seminaries and military academies, it's part of the cradle of Argentine rugby. Several 1978 Pumas were reared in them.

Originally, it was against my will that I went there. For most of thirteen years I'd been happy in Brazil, but my father had the idea that I might one day be nationalized, like the railways. My hero was Leonidas, who was to Pele as the Brown Bomber to Ali, but papa was opposed to the culture of the round ball. In thirty years he attended three Brazilian soccer matches: in the first the ref was shot; next time there was a knife fight at one end of a stand which attracted so many participants that the structure collapsed, maiming 300 people; in the last, an unwilling guest of honour as vice-consul in Florianopolis, he was in a riot involving tear gas. For safety he stood between the goal posts, which had ceased to be a focus of interest.

Rugger, he maintained, was more character-forming. But to me Prince Obolenski was as remote as Genghis Khan's cousin. For my first steps in robustness and fair play, I was planted, a timid and shrimpish soccer player, alone in the middle of the field, while the entire College lined up like a Zulu impi, age-range twelve to twenty, and then charged over me. They included David Kerr, later a Scottish trialist and Barrie Holmes, soon afterwards an England full-back. I remember that Kerr had gussets let into his socks to accommodate his calves. The rule was that whoever you tackled below the knee was your ally for the second onset, and so on until the last giants were laid low.

By good luck I trapped a tiny guitar player. '*Che Brasilero,*' he said without heat, '*sos hijo de yegua* – you're the son of a mare.' '*Hodete,*' I replied pleasantly. It was the start of a durable bond. 'Listen,' he said, 'cut out this English tackling. We need tanks, or we're dead. For that, let them think they're through and then bang their ankles together, and shout "Timber". If they go into the San, we're little guys and the nurse will take our side.' It worked.

I shouldn't exaggerate the toughness, though in retrospect some of the incidents seemed toughish. There was usually somebody walking around on crutches, partly because the grounds were so hard.

A certain macho individualism led to the inspirational brilliance, offset by an unfortunate hogging of the ball. Everybody wanted his name on the score sheet. A massive wing called Peludo Hogg, 'the hairy one', who played outside Holmes, was often starved of the ball, to the rage of the crowd who loved nothing better than to see his knee-high action pulverizing the defence. It was interesting to note this week that Sansot, twice with the line at his mercy, gave the ball away. Unselfishness is evidently gaining ground.

Among the bubbling individualists was a scrum-half called Frazer. He took the view that sex just before a match cleared the mind for kicking at goal. Whether or not he was putting his theory to the test, he sometimes trotted out of the pavilion some way behind the rest of the XV. He played for ecstasy, I think, and loved the divine afflatus in others. One club we were playing against, San Isidro, I think, were having a disastrous day with the boot when suddenly one of their second-row forwards, who had never taken a kick in his life, was taken with sublime confidence that he could put a penalty over from half way. '*Dámela, dámela, que la pongo*,' he begged. Bemused, the captain did give it to him. And it sailed over. So they gave him the next one; his boot hit the turf, pulling a muscle in his groin, and he was carried off, to an ovation.

The Pumas' manager, Chaco Kember, who greets the press in a red poncho, an ex-advertising man, and director of the *Buenos Aires Herald*, is one of the legendary figures of college sport. Whisper it not to the shades of the founders, but he was actually a better soccer than rugger player. He has rather blazoned the sexual potential of these Pumas. But somehow at Oxford they huddled together and let their chances slip. The girls who went along sat at tables clutching empty glasses, like people at a séance hoping for outside intervention. Perhaps hopefuls should arm themselves with a ref's whistle if they want action. With such shy clean-living Pumas, it takes more than two to tango. Plainly, they need a little help from their friends.

3 October 1978   **Alex Hamilton**

A leaking royal roof

A man who will eat snake stew for Britain, who is prepared to discourse on subjects as diverse, or as related, as the failings of British management and the decline of individual courage in the West, who travels the world to do all this and more, may well lack the energy to tackle the dry rot in his roof when he gets home. And at a time when something like a million homes in the country are in a serious state of disrepair, the improvement of even one of them is welcome. So we should be grateful to the trustees of Chevening House, who not only take the burdens of domesticity from Prince Charles's shoulders and purse, but set an example to all in the matter of home improvements and repairs. We can even admire them for so understanding the Local Authorities Historic Buildings Act (1962) that they know where and when to slap in a grant application.

Whether Kent County Council should have expressed gratitude and admiration in so solid a manner as a grant of £250 is another matter. The late Lord Stanhope left the nation a house whose main walls were coming adrift from each other and the roof; he also left large sums of money to pin them together, render the place habitable and employ such gardeners, keepers, forestry workers and others as the place demands. The trustees have not only ensured that the place stands solid and picked up a major architectural award for doing so; they have also invested Chevening's money so cleverly that they find they have no shortage of the stuff at all. So £250 is not much to them. It is rather more to Kent amenities and countryside committee, whose total budget this year was only some £15,000. Nor do the people of Kent get more return from the grant than a knowledge that they are contributing to the health of the monarchy – or would be, if

Prince Charles ever decided to live in the place.

No doubt mindful of all this, the trustees are even now debating whether to turn the wretched grant down. Surely the man to advise them in their dilemma is their tenant. After all, £250 is not much to him either, on £75,000 clear a year, excluding housing subsidies, even after he has handed half his total to the Treasury in lieu of tax. As he was telling the Australian Academy of Science only this week, it is the moral factor in man that Western society is so prone to neglect.

28 March 1979   **Leader**

A loo of their own

Dr Richard Feachem is in the happy position of a man whose main enthusiasm in life is about to have a whole decade dedicated to it by the United Nations. Not just a year. A decade. And given the absolute impossibility of the task which faces the organizers of the decade it is more likely to last him his whole lifetime. Dr Feachem, who is Senior Lecturer in Tropical Public Health Engineering at the Ross Institute in London, has an ebullient and infectious enthusiasm for lavatories. Not the kind we use which flush – and thereby use up forty per cent of our household's clean water supply – but all the other kinds which everyone else uses. Or doesn't use. Which is why 1981 will see the beginning of the UN Decade of Drinking Water and Sanitation.

The stated aims of the decade are to provide everyone in the entire world with access to a reasonable latrine and to some kind of clean water supply. The number of people in the world who have neither of these, according to Richard Feachem, is so enormous that there would have to be latrines built for half a million people a day for the next twelve years to cope with the problems and keep up with the rising population. The Decade isn't starting quite yet because, as he says, the implications are so staggering that no one would have a clue what to do right away.

But an initial attempt is being made by a group of World Bank experts, including Dr Feachem, who were meeting in the Ross Institute all last week to look back over two and a half years of intensive research into what most of the world actually *does* when it excretes, and how it can be helped to do it as cheaply and healthily as possible in the future. Richard Feachem was drawn into the project four years ago when he found that what he thought were his original thoughts on the matter were exactly shared by a Swiss called John Kalbermatten who was the Chief Water and Sewerage Adviser to the World Bank, and who was acutely aware of the irony of World Bank projects which provided flushing toilets only for those who could afford them.

'The big fascination,' Dr Feachem explains, 'is the sewerage or nothing syndrome. Western culture knows how to build sewers. We learned it from the Romans, then we forgot about it for 1800 years, then we put them into London in the 1850s and other capitals followed. So when the whole aid industry came into being after the war, the rich countries were only offering sewage systems to the poor ones, it was the only thing we knew. It means large pipes with water running along them, and plumbing, and lots of poor countries are also arid ones which don't have the water to move the excreta along. So lots of sewers were built which served a small proportion of the population, these being the urban rich and the middle class who can afford the rates to pay for them.'

In 1975 Kalbermatten invited Dr Feachem to join a World Bank research project into what solutions lay between sewage and nothing. For two and a half years Richard Feachem, and people like him, went round the world looking at how people coped. 'With a particular interest in the Far East which has a tradition of cartage – cartage being a system where excreta is not mixed with water but gets collected from the houses and carried round. It could be by donkey, with carts, or a man with a leaky basket on his head. The Japanese are going over to sewerage but part of the city of Kyoto still runs on the cartage system, a very sophisticated one using suction tankers. In some countries the collector takes it out of town and it goes straight on to the fields untreated, very hazardous to health. If it doesn't go on the fields it gets fed to fish as in China, and this can be dangerous if you eat partially-cooked fish.'

The alternatives to cartage, which works by emptying buckets or tanks in people's homes, include the pit latrines – or hole in the ground – which can be greatly improved by putting a chimney on the pit and taking the smell out of the hut. However most people in the world have no sanitation system at all. Early morning sees the peasants of Africa and Asia squatting on the roadside or in the fields.

'In Islamic cultures,' explains Dr Feachem, 'where some women are confined to the home, the men go out into the alleys but the women go in the yard or on the roof or in the cattle shed. And if they go in the cattle shed then the cattle eat the excreta with consequent danger of worms when you eat the meat. In pig cultures like New Guinea or Thailand or Burma, pigs are very partial to human faeces. It can be an unnerving experience going out and squatting in the undergrowth in New Guinea and hearing a lot of rustling behind you and there's a big pig just waiting to gobble up what you've produced.'

The survey produced some surprises, the biggest of which was that the alternatives were not only cheaper than sewerage, which everyone knew, but they were *much* cheaper. Taken as a world-wide average the total household costs of sewerage for one year were $400, of a modern, well-designed and ventilated pit latrine, $28.

Now it's implementation time. With the United Nations Development Programme putting in the money and the World Bank carrying out the work, the team will be starting to provide low-cost non-sewered solutions to the latrine problems in four-teen different countries. By using simple technology and being sensitive to local needs they hope to avoid some of the more obvious hazards of the Western flush lavatory – such as break-down of all the different materials people use to clean their bottoms. Earth is very popular, so is sand and stones and, in parts of Africa, maize cobs. But there are other hazards yet unmet. A block of latrines in one Moslem country went unused because its users had to face Mecca as they defecated.

Ironically, it is quite likely that one piece of traditional public health dogma may crumble as a result of all this intensive sanitary activity. It has always been assumed that if you provided clean water and adequate sanitation, dirt and disease would be van-quished, but it may not be so. Dr Feachem's particular interests in the project are public health and evaluation and he is aware of one great failing: that the part of the population most at risk won't benefit.

'Small children are the people most unlikely to use latrines. Their parents don't encourage them, either because they think it's unimportant or because they're afraid they'll mess them up. In most societies, including England, adults believe that children's faeces are innocuous – they're used to handling them – but in fact, the pathogenicity of children's excreta is likely to be higher. Frequency of infection is highest in children and most diarrhoeal diseases occur in children. Because they live on the ground they pick up more worms, bacteria, and so on. So parents are really most at risk from the faeces of their own children. Little may be achieved unless older children use the new latrines and mothers pay more attention to the cleanliness of their babies.'

13 March 1979 **Lesley Garner**

Golden bowls

An improving example has come the Diary's way of the entrepreneurial spirit which we are all struggling to acquire after last Thursday. It concerns the Royal Doulton Simplicitas lavatory bowl, a richly decorated floral object, which the Diary mentioned yesterday and which goes on display at the Victoria and Albert Museum from 30 May.

A Belfast reader had warm nostalgic feelings when he read about the bowl, because he sat and did his duty on one during student days in Richmond, Surrey, twenty years ago. He shared a flat in a divided-up old mansion with two other young bachelors, and the Simplicitas closet was their pride and joy.

They were not particularly rare at that time, he reports, in formerly gracious parts of West London which had slid into multi-occupancy and become bedsitterland. And one of his friends, of whose progress more shortly, turned this fact into a highly profitable venture. Discovering a rich vein of floral lavatories around down-at-heel Westbourne Grove, he posed very plausibly as a local authority official, calling on occupants of the decaying mansions and demanding to inspect their loos.

If he found one of the baroque creations of Royal Doulton, he said gravely that it no longer met sanitary requirements. The tenants were downcast, but cheered up at once when the visitor told them that the council would be pleased to replace the porcelain and to do the work free. A plumber and mate of his acquaintance then followed the private enterprise pioneer round and replaced the Simplicitates with common or garden modern bowls.

The ancient lavatories thus acquired were shipped through a Brighton dealer to the United States at a net profit to our man of some $300 apiece. And he has since risen to become a big bug in Marks & Spencer, the estimable firm which on Tuesday incidentally provided Mrs T with Sir Derek Rayner, her new efficiency man for dealing with Whitehall waste.

Simplicitas itself: a bowl of profits.
10 May 1979   **Martin Wainwright**

Mr Carter's condition

In the absence of the *Sunday Times*, people will have to turn to *Time* magazine for a long and detailed probe into President Carter's fundamental problem, his piles. It is not a piece beginning: 'At 6.23 a.m. on Wednesday, 20 December, Jimmy Carter turned from the window, grimaced slightly, and put his hand behind his back . . .' *Time* scarcely captures the relaxed omniscience of *Insight*, but what it lacks in split-second timing it makes up in good solid quotes. 'Habit,' it says, 'may also be a factor, including the "bathroom as library" syndrome. Explains Los Angeles proctologist Michael Freilich: "We were not meant to sit on toilets, we were meant to squat in the field." ' (Meant by whom?) 'Fearful of the cost and trauma of traditional surgical cures,' *Time* goes on, 'or simply embarrassed, most sufferers medicate themselves. Popular over-the-counter preparations can indeed relieve the symptoms temporarily. So can hot baths and a change in diet and bowel habits.' Mr Carter's own proctological history (a new word to us: it means concerned with the study of the backside) is then gone into: college days, rubber-band ligation in 1974. Possible courses for the future are discussed: 'Still another technique involves dilating, or widening, the anus with stretching devices. Particularly useful for piles near the sensitive anus is cryosurgery. A probe, cooled by liquid nitrogen (temperature —196 degrees Centigrade or —321 degrees Fahrenheit), painlessly freezes the troublesome tissue. But freezing produces a foul-smelling discharge that requires wearing a sanitary pad for a few weeks ...' Anyone for open government? Not every head of state would announce his piles to the world. Mr Carter did so to avoid upsetting Wall Street with a euphemism like lassa fever. Yet according to *Time* half of all adult Americans may suffer from them, which means statistically that three presidents from Truman in 1945 to Ford in 1977 have been concealing the truth from the American people. Mr Carter, in his wholesome way, has also written about his lust, so that piece by piece the world is gaining a fairly full picture of what makes a successful politician. And surely it is fairly cheering? A man who plays fair about lechery and piles can be trusted to keep nothing else back. And can anyone compete with him? For unless General Haig can somehow make out that he contracted gallstones while on duty at SHAPE he's in for a hard campaign.

9 January 1979   **Leader**

Saturday Night People

Twenty-five years after drowning, Bill Bixby returns, untouched by time, to find everyone he knew wearing ill-fitting blue wigs. Though he entered into the spirit of the seventies very commendably, knocking out a nurse and stealing a car, he was clearly disconcerted to be married to a grandmother.

A Twist in the Tale is an American series taken only by London Weekend Television, the rest of the network opting as one man for golf. But I thought it all Terribly True. We, who have sat through *Bruce Forsyth's Big Night* (LWT), know all too well how it feels to regain consciousness after two hours and realize that your loved ones have vanished, your home is scheduled for redevelopment, your faithful old dog bites you to the bone

44

and the sight of your own face in the mirror makes you recoil, as if you had caught your braces in the door handle. And you are the last man left alive wearing braces anyway.

Saturday Night People (LWT), who rise or fall like a ballcock depending on whether the *Big Night* overflows, are more often than not Sunday Morning People. That a film should be haunted is an engaging idea. Several deserve to be. Some seem to be. They snap with a most melodious twang. They are wiped by an unseen hand. Or spied by one. I saw pinned up in the TV Centre recently a most moving plea for the return of *The Lost Valley* which had been shot and, after who knows what privations and expense, flown back to Britain and, rather appropriately, lost.

After six cameras had broken down in eighteen days and knocking had appeared on monitored and cleared material, the producer of *A Sense of Loss: Evelyn Waugh* (BBC-2) put his misfortunes down to the mischievous spirit of Waugh, not a man who appreciated either publicity or the BBC. 'Mr Waugh is not inclined to sacrifice any comfort for the convenience of listeners,' he told the corporation, demanding £8 18s 6d in advance for first-class travel and tips. 'His sense of his own importance makes production very difficult,' says a producer's report on Waugh. But the results, such as a Face to Face with John Freeman, are still full of life.

His perturbed spirit might have been appeased if the commentary had changed 'corrupt and venial school' to 'corrupt and venal'. As Waugh gave fair warning, a fault in syntax brought him trucking forward bulging with wrath. I feel much the same when Bruce's *Big Night* spells Plimsoll as Plimsole and *A Twist in the Tale* is introduced as about 'that strange phenomena the Bermuda Trial'.

A Sense of Loss had many small felicities. A lady connected with the school which Waugh satirized in *Decline and Fall* defended it gamely on the ground that 'the boys were noted for their respect for war memorials'. And I can forgive a programme almost anything when it acknowledges the assistance of The Earl and Countess of Beauchamp and Mrs Doris Gadsden. And so should Waugh.

23 October 1978   **Nancy Banks-Smith**

Lady Rothermere's plan

'At the last minute I said Let's just have baked potatoes and the cheap caviare and we'll scrap Cook's boring menu.' Lady Rothermere, wife of Vere Harmsworth, known affectionately in *Private Eye* as Bubbles, is reliving her latest Molotov cocktail. That's her private shorthand for the informal parties when only 120 people, only 5 ambassadors, turn up at the ring of a phone rather than the RSVP of a formal card.

We are in her family house in Chester Terrace. If Nash was a cissy his stones would have hit Regent's Park easily. It is just past most people's lunch time and the rich smell of roast beef wafts round the house waiting for an essential taxi about to deliver the beloved best friend of Lady Rothermere's tomboy daughter.

Here in the drawing-room the chaos is working its way up from the floor. Three, perhaps four, telephones are scattered around the bright green rugs. Documents are piled high in disordered rows. She and the children are moving to America, possibly buying an English country house.

The windows are totally dazzled by a curtain designer's elaborate concoctions of blue and yellow layers of taffeta. A pair of worn trainers are dumped just here. There, a carton of Coke cans is to hand. Naked wires droop sadly from the walls, where presumably light fittings have been ripped. Upstairs Lady Rothermere's young son still hasn't emerged from his room because he doesn't want to. Downstairs you can hear the servant class is alive and well, clattering.

Contrast this with the elegant, empty calm of the apartment in Eaton Square where our meeting had been planned, arranged by her secretary and by Lady Rothermere's cousin who runs her social engagements. Nobody lives there now, so the porter said, as I hung around the entrance hall, sitting on repro Hepplewhite literally chained to the wall.

Finally the secretary arrived who turned out to be a psychology student temping. Then the cousin. Then a man from Harrods delivering *one loaf*. Lady Rothermere had woken up ill that morning, too groggy to cross London so she talked to all of us on the phone, changing her mind from one conversation to the next about what we were all going to do, giving me ample chance for a nosey look round. This drawing-room is dominated by a five-foot chandelier with a big bow on top matching the green silk everywhere else. I counted twenty-eight family photographs.

Somewhere beyond this room there is a sort of mini Corinthian hall, round, with pillars. In the cloakroom, black as pitch, you can just make out that candles have providently been placed on the basin: if there is electricity in there I couldn't find it. In the corridor on the way out one of us clonked into a decorative foible and a gold knob fell off it noisily. 'Does it matter?' cried the cousin, clearly convinced there were plenty more gold knobs where that one came from.

Back in Regent's Park, with enviable lack of vanity Lady Rothermere eventually appeared in a tight, quilted dressing gown, orange and purple flowers, over a knee-length yellow nightie, a totally different picture from the wide smiles and the Zandra Rhodes of her public appearance.

She loathes her nickname Bubbles. 'It sounds superficial and I'm really the reverse of that. It doesn't sum up anyone intelligent. Though the secret of all women of any intelligence is to hide it. It frightens men off. I think I acquired the name for two reasons: when my husband became chairman of the *Daily Mail* I didn't want to come on the heavy wife and then there was a year when I was chairman of Old Ben, the Newspaper Benevolent Fund, and this marvellous man there said you're going to be exhausted travelling all over the country and I'll always have a bottle of champagne ready for you wherever you are. That was the best year of my life because the people one met in the Old Ben homes were so genuine. They made lovely things for me and the children which meant far more to me than the marvellous things from Gucci that a Hollywood film producer sends me.'

Her favourite charity is the NSPCC where she is truly revered. 'I know some people approach charity entertaining as if it's just an excuse to extract money and it's a bore but I've always felt it should be fun – for me as well as for everybody else.' I wondered if she ever made contact with the children at the receiving end of her endeavours. 'I have been to some of the homes. The children are very cool. They view you slightly like someone trying to be a Lady Bountiful.'

She is disarmingly candid. Often she utterly forgets she's invited people to her parties. 'Then I see them at the door and it's such a lovely surprise. I always enjoy my own parties. Everything's arranged, usually by telephone. The cook and the butler who I bring in will take care of everything and I go and have a bath with Floris and it's as if I'm a guest. All I have to do is introduce people and I enjoy doing that anyway. I have people from varied walks of life because I have so many interests myself.

'I was brought up in the country. I simply never knew London until I was seventeen. Then I was an actress and a model. I love people. I'm particularly interested in creative people. I think of myself as a creative, romantic person. I do understand the business side of life though I think it's rather dry. I can be very businesslike and practical when necessary.

'I almost never provide spirits at my parties. People don't expect you to. I find they're quite happy to choose between red or white wine. Or champagne of course. I wouldn't expect people to drink too much. It's the electricity, the excitement of people meeting each other, not the effect of alcohol that make a good party.

'You have to be terribly aware of vibrations. There was one particular girl who came here and ruined a whole party. She wanted to attract attention to herself and she fell down and smashed things and there is no way I will ever have her back in this house again.'

She certainly keeps a clear head when she has royalty in the house and there is no room for accidents on her guest list then. 'The great thing about entertaining royalty is never to give them any cause for embarrassment. The guest list is picked very carefully with that in mind. People might not deliberately set out to embarrass them but if they were self-conscious then they would. The royal family are very natural, truthful people, down to earth and they don't like anybody pretentious. They don't like phoneys.

'I don't like phoneys either. I don't mean the Oh Darlings. I mean basically crooked people who are out to come to your party because they want to meet so and so and then use them. Phoneys can be fun – you just have to know that they're phoneys. My trouble is that I always want to believe the best of people. Somebody came to this latest party and I heard that they started to criticize me. That hurt a lot but you've got to expect that sort of thing. Let it roll.'

She uses modern slang easily: her accent, as near to the Queen's as any I have ever heard, gives it a new dimension. The worst thing about society life she feels is the abundant hypocrisy. 'So many people are ambitious. There's nothing wrong with that unless they feel the best way to achieve their ambitions is to be deceptive. I'm not crazy about politicians. Their motives are sometimes to promote their self image rather than their so-called principles: they're not quite playing straight.'

So she feels she'd rather be alone than surrounded by ambitious phoneys. 'A great many people are lonely: very famous people who you'd think would be surrounded by invitations. I've been lonely in my life. I was in hospital for a year when I was a teenager with rheumatic fever, taken away from all my friends and then I broke my spine in a riding accident. I think it was being isolated at such a young age that gave me the impetus to go forward in the social world. That, coupled with the fact that my husband used not to come home until nine or ten in the evening. That really inspired me to start a social life of my own with my own friends.

'I think most people are conditioned to living very boring lives, literally paying the rent, keeping their children clothed, schooled, frightened of being different. I'm not, thank God, frightened of anything, at least not for myself. I do not fear for myself. I do fear losing one of my children or one of them being seriously ill. To be honest I also have the emotional fear of being lonely, the kind of loneliness I knew when I was ill.'

She thinks upper-class Englishmen generate unhappiness in thinking women.

'English families have this tradition of packing the boys off away from home at seven or eight. They grow up thoroughly frightened of women. I'm speaking now of my own generation. The young ones are different but the older ones thoroughly distrust women unless they fall into one of two categories –

mother or mistress. Their ideal is to have a wife in the country
and a flat in town for themselves. That was the suggestion when I
married my second husband. A lot of women are very comfortable
with the situation, breeding either children or horses or whatever
but there was no way I was going to fall in with it. I said I was
going to live with my husband and my children were going to
live with us, travel with us, not be packed off.

'The Americans organize things much better.' Lady Rothermere is so impressed with American attitudes that her two
youngest children are at the American school in London. Another
daughter is at a finishing school.

Last summer she shared a party for Andy Warhol. 'I looked
round the room and everybody there was so beautiful. The girls,
I always have pretty girls, nice girls, not hustling types, because
they're decorative like flowers but since it was summer they
looked particularly . . . you know, and the men were so good-
looking that night. I said to my co-host, "We really should have
asked just one ugly person. Just one." '

11 May 1979   **Pauline Peters**

Lance Secretan's empire

One day, an official from the National Meter Reading Force will
knock on your door and check the electricity, gas and water
readings in one short, uncomplicated, unduplicated visit. For
the electric man, the gas man and the water man will no longer
come singly; indeed, they will no longer come at all. One day,
your son/daughter/grandmother – or all three – might be working
for Global Reductions, a major permanent employer of staff
which, while it has no shops of its own, leases its personnel to
stores to cope with the sales rush, moving them from one bargain-
time to another every two weeks.

When these things happen, it will mean that Lance Secretan
has managed to exert a little influence in the service industries.
For the labour market right now is a windy place for employers
as much as workers. Some 300,000 jobs are being kept in being
by government grant and subsidy; declining employment con-

tinues in the shrinking manufacturing sector; and legislation is making it both difficult and expensive for companies to have a workforce which is flexible enough to cope with up-turns and down-turns in production. And the micro-processor will shake up employment patterns even more.

Only in the service industries are more jobs being created. Lance Secretan has found a profitable niche there for the company he heads. Secretan is forty this year. He has short yellow hair and a slimmed-down baby face. And he is simply and ingeniously in the business of employing people, about 70,000 this year, guaranteeing them work and wages, and hiring them out to companies which need extra staff for a limited period. He is managing director of Manpower – that isn't a futuristic fantasy; it is a bold blue fascia which glows in dozens of high streets.

When the American parent company sent Secretan to take charge of its British outlet in the late sixties, it can have had no idea what he was going to do with it. The 'belly up' operation he found here was a traditional employment agency. The pattern hadn't changed for thirty years or more. Secretan wondered why there had been no innovation. So he killed off the placement side, and began to think of something other than supplying temps.

To most of us, a temp is someone who fills in for a day when Mavis goes to see her mother, or when she has a holiday from her typewriter. After that, she disappears, conveniently. The emphasis is traditionally on hiring a person to do someone else's work. Secretan's bright idea was to shift the basis of the agreement to getting the work done, an agreed amount, by an agreed time, to a satisfactory level and with the agency compensating the employer for any mistakes made by the staff it sends to them. And while he's about it, he could offer a contract to do the cleaning and the portering as well.

Secretan thinks a lot about work. Not only the concept, but the word itself, what it means and what it might come to mean. He is not academic but he is interested in what some academics are doing. And so he is intrigued that, according to Professor Elliot Jacques of Brunel University, the word 'employment' cannot be traced back further than 1846. Secretan reckons that the word 'has a new and temporary definition'. And that it might change.

Professor Jacques, an industrial psychologist, believes that demands for a shorter working week will peter out at about thirty-five hours: enough to satisfy our economic and social usefulness; shorter hours would disorient people. Secretan himself puts in between eighty and one hundred hours, though he probably doesn't need to now. When he was a younger man making his way up in Canada – he left this country when he was eight – he worked in the Toronto Stock Market by day and had a second job selling encyclopaedias.

Now he trades in other people's flexibility, for the gold watch as the lure for forty years continuous service with the same company is not as powerful as it used to be.

'About half of those we employ drop out at between one and four weeks, usually they are in between permanent jobs. The remainder, I would say, are just like any other permanent employment group. The staff turnover is between twenty-five and thirty-five per cent. They are covered by sickness insurance, state pension and they get paid holidays.' It is really casualization, which benefits the employer, with the security of normal employment for those on Manpower's books.

He can keep employers happy, too, for he appears to have found a winning formula in reconciling total job security with the need for a flexible supply of labour. For while he is sympathetic to people who want to be accommodated by the labour market other than on an eight or nine to five basis from here to eternity, he recognizes the difficulties of employers. Employment legislation has moved recently and dramatically in favour of the worker, and he fully approves this. Temps hired under normal arrangements start to accumulate rights after four weeks; and if they stay on and on, they are entitled to redundancy pay after two years.

It is just very difficult to get rid of staff if they are no longer needed, because the job isn't there or because they prove unreliable. Secretan's scenario is that because the law is making employment more expensive and less flexible, the wages bill is becoming a fixed cost rather than a variable one. And, he argues, that the relative costs between labour and capital have narrowed and, in some cases, reversed. 'In many industries, this now means that companies will make a decision which increases capital investment, and therefore wealth for itself and for the country, but does not increase the number of new jobs being offered.'

It can come down to a few hairy experiences: 'The employee who was always drunk could be got rid of after a couple of warnings. But now, it is much more difficult to get rid of him. Our role is laying off that cost for a firm. Building in time and cost factor so that you don't have to pick up a tab for £10,000 for unfair dismissal. Effectively, you're buying insurance for that kind of risk.'

As well as unfair dismissal, there is constructive dismissal (being pushed upstairs, or moving an executive into the post-room); there is protective legislation against discrimination on grounds of race or sex; equal pay; equal opportunity. Transferring the burden of seeing that these are complied with from a company which uses labour to the agency from which staff are hired, was part of the bright idea. It also copes with seasonal fluctuations in demand for staff.

Having mapped his way among the legislation, Secretan, whose approach is regarded by the American parent company as 'idiosyncratic, maverick, out of step, innovative, creative', seeks business in unlikely corners. His people clean hospitals at air-force bases; clean Wolfson College, Oxford; they run a second assembly line for a cosmetics firm during rush periods. They spent two years merging the records of two giant insurance companies which amalgamated – Guardian and Royal Exchange. They clean up after oil-spills and fires.

He controls an empire of skills, semi-skills and non-skills: 25 to 30 per cent are office and secretarial; 15 per cent are skilled technical staff; 10 per cent sales and marketing; and the remainder unskilled industrial workers. Manpower doesn't come cheap. Secretan says the bill will be 10 per cent higher than from employment agencies; and maybe 30 per cent more than from what he calls the 'cowboy' operators. It includes wages, national insurance, takes account of holiday pay, administrative costs, and a contribution to Manpower's 'value-added remuneration programme' for its staff. Whatever the bill, the profit is 10 per cent.

If that doesn't sound a great deal, Secretan says it's not bad on a turnover of £20 millions last year. He projects £26 millions for this year and sees limitless horizons. So the company, which is now owned by Parker Pens, will get richer, and so will the staff who stay with it, for theirs is the stake in the 'value-added remuneration programme' which is a trans-atlantic cosmetic word for profit-sharing. But the man who largely built it up is wondering about goals other than personal wealth.

'With my definition and set of values, I'm very adequately provided for, and my motivation is no longer financial. I decided seven or eight years ago what I was good at. I'm not good at tax, so I went to see the best legal and financial advisers I could afford.'

He doesn't think it is necessary for him to have a financial stake in Manpower. He did before the Parker takeover. The holding was peanuts, but he had to pay capital gains on it. Nor does he think that the Inland Revenue saps his commitment: 'I don't believe that taxation is a major disincentive to performance.' When, after several years of building up a company and exploring new markets, you land in the golden bracket, there are ways of ensuring a long and comfortable life.

'A great deal of my income is deferred. Some of the effects of tax can be offset by perks.' Secretan is a little reluctant to explore this and he begins very modestly indeed with 'well, there are the normal luncheon vouchers'. He is, however, not an elaborate luncher and three or four meal-tickets may well cover the daily cost. But for a man who must at least be in the £30,000 a year bracket, there is additionally a significant percentage in benefits. The most spectacular of these is a pension which will equal his full retiring salary. Though it is not index-linked. There is the car, a BMW and a chauffeur and an educational trust which would pay for his children's schooling if necessary.

Several months are spent abroad each year, for he is in charge of operations in West Europe and the Middle East, and there is a tax reduction because of that; there is the travel and the international seminars, paid for by Manpower, which he sets great store by, because 'I'm always learning'.

For tax purposes, he has a large mortgage on his house (£25,000 is the maximum) at Whitchurch in Oxfordshire. It is an eighteenth-century forge, far less grand than the one with a

54

river frontage of 450 yards which he used to have. 'It was too high a profile,' Secretan explains in his slightly unsettling mixture of Anglo-Americanese. 'Now I'm much better at knowing what I really want.'

10 May 1979   **John Cunningham**

In the Nico of time

Dear Edward,   *11 May*
   As you know, the Jays will have to be moved from Washington. Would you be interested? Do say yes. It would be a great strength to the Cabinet to know you're only a telephone call away.

                                                     Yours, M.

Dear Edward,   *13 May*
   I wonder whether you received a note from me the other day about Washington? Take your time, of course, but it will be a great relief to have it settled.

                                                     Yours, M.

Dear Edward,   *15 May*
   I don't want to hurry you about Washington, but apparently the FCO is pushing a man called Henderson. We'd all feel happier with you there. Initially it's a five-year appointment. If it's the money we could talk.

                                                     Yours, M.

Dear Edward,   *17 May*
   About Washington, don't worry about transport. The piano can be air-freighted.

                                                     Yours, M.

'Oh, don't worry about me – I'll just potter around in the background!'
7 May 1979

Dear Edward,   *19 May*

I've talked to Jimmy Carter. He says would you be around to take the White House carol service this year? I've said it would be very convenient indeed for us, but the decision is yours.

Yours, M.

Dear Edward,   *20 May*

We could fill in with a chargé for a few weeks if you'd prefer to sail across.

Yours, M.

Dear Edward,   *21 May*

Thank you for the postcard, received today.

As you know, I've felt for some time that we are seriously under-represented on the Antarctic Whaling Commission . . .

M.

23 May 1979   **Leader**

Voices of the dead

Isaac Bashevis Singer begins with a disconcerting irony: 'I was brought up in three dead languages – Hebrew, Aramaic, Yiddish.' This ironic statement functions as an invocation of those dead who spoke, specifically, the Yiddish of Poland. He invites us to a seance to hear their voices; *Shosha** is a haunting rather than a novel.

The narrator, Aaron Greidinger, a rabbi's son, born before World War I on Krochmalna Street in the Jewish quarter of Warsaw, forms a childhood attachment to a neighbour's daughter, the naive Shosha. Time passes; Greidinger forgets her as he abandons Hasidic orthodoxy for the life of the rootless, neurotic urban intelligentsia. He embraces alienation as comprehensively as he embraces women. There is Dora, the Communist; then Celia, wife of an innocent, well-heeled friend.

57

Celia's apartment is furnished with Jewish antiques: 'It was difficult for me to accept the fact that this intense Jewishness was merely decoration, its essence since lost to many of us.' Celia's other lover, Feitzeljohn, is alienation in its frivolous aspect, with his philosophy of play and his love of a quick buck. Greidinger scribbles a bit; then meets Betty, an American actress for whom he writes a never-to-be-produced play in Yiddish. With the money Betty's impresario lover gives him, he rents a nice flat, sleeps with the maid. One way and another, Greidinger's soul, if not already lost, is well on the way to being mislaid.

Then, on a whim, he revisits Krochmalna Street and finds Shosha, miraculously unchanged. She slept away a year of sickness in 1917, has remained a child both in appearance and in simplicity of heart. She is waiting for him; has never forgotten him, has always been waiting for him. Meanwhile, Hitler prepares to attack. Betty, the actress, offers Greidinger a compromised marriage and safe passage to America, a truly Mephistophelean bargain.

But Greidinger will stay behind, to marry the spotless Shosha. The wedding is an involuntary, a fated act of reconciliation. He will live with her and her mother on Krochmalna Street as the archaic, timeless life of that culture rooted in the Talmud approaches its atrocious rendezvous with history. All is shown, frozen in memory, with a loving terror at the imminence of death.

Although the characters are delineated with a precise realism, they possess a strong, allegorical dimension. Indeed, Shosha herself, the Holy Fool, mentally and physically retarded, whom Greidinger rapes in her sleep on their wedding night, would be a scarcely tolerable invention if she were not credited with a more than human luminosity. Betty, the actress, corrupt, deracinated, self-loathing, seduces Greidinger on the very night that he meets Shosha again yet offers the key to escape, such is her demonic ambivalence. The Communist girl stands for the light that failed.

Greidinger's own quality is absolute and annihilating despair: 'We were fated to play our little games and be crushed.' But this shabby, meagre soul, perhaps redeemed by love, survives. And the reader will find it impossible to escape the anguish of the survivor, also.

A coda finds Greidinger, utterly alone, visiting Israel, the Jewish Land, thirteen years after the fall of Troy. He discusses the inscrutability of God with another living ghost, Celia's widower, who now reveals himself as another Holy Fool. On a bus in Tel Aviv: 'The passengers cursed one another in Yiddish, Polish, German and broken Hebrew.' The saved utilize the dead languages with the gracelessness of the living. The heritage of four thousand years has been redeemed; but the dead stay dead, most eloquent in their absence.

Shosha communicates itself almost as shared memory, shared pain. Schönberg returned to the formal practice of Judaism as Hitler began to murder Jews. *Shosha* makes me think of that. It is as inconsolable as it is serene.

    * Shosha, *by Isaac Bashevis Singer, was published by Jonathan Cape.*

15 February 1979   **Angela Carter**

German democracy and its ghosts

Psychologists call it survivor syndrome. The survivor of some terrible ordeal, a concentration camp, for instance, or an earthquake, may pass several years in a state of apparently normal health, before entering a terrible depression and decline. It is as if the energy spent on readjustment gradually exhausts itself, and the individual gives way to the trauma.

And surely what happens to individuals may happen to countries as well. For years it might seem as if the past can be forgotten, as if Fascism, war, destruction, and defeat can be laid aside, while the country concentrates on its immediate problems – hunger, the reconstruction of the cities, the establishment of a new economy. And then – at precisely the moment when it seems as if, by a little adjustment here, a bit more effort there, the most pressing problems could actually be solved – the blow falls, the trauma is revealed.

It is as if, while the survivors of the Nazi concentration camps are discovering that they are losing the battle against their memories, West Germany has discovered the same thing. The memories of war are like those literal traumas – the old wound that plays up in bad weather, the piece of shrapnel that inexplicably decides one day to work its way to the surface.

At such a moment in history, one might expect the most curious phenomena. It might be, for instance, that the nation begins to move through more than one period at the same time – that in the Germany of the seventies there are people convinced that they are living through the thirties, and others insistent that they are faced with the twenties all over again. It might be that inside the solid achievement of the Federal Republic there lurks a ghostly after-image of both the Weimar Republic and the Third Reich.

Suppose that the German terrorists were people who, like the old ladies at Versailles, had walked back in time. Suppose they were suffering from the hallucination of living under Fascism. This would explain some of their moral certitude. They would be conducting that resistance which ought to have been fought long ago. Or suppose the German authorities were under the impression that they were defending the Weimar Republic – this would explain their zeal and their alarm. Contemporary Germany would thus become a battleground for rival hallucinations, and the whole society would be involved, willy-nilly, in a gigantic misapprehension.

I do not intend to underestimate the actual seriousness of the social crisis in West Germany. The crisis is real and consequential, but it is based on perceptions which it is impossible to share. Try as I might, I cannot see the Bonn government as Fascist. Yet there are those who do. Try as I might, I cannot see how the terrorists could overthrow democracy. But there are many who believe they could. Indeed, the West Germans often seem to expect the end at any moment. One morning, democracy will fail to appear at breakfast, they will go up to its room and find it, sitting up in bed, with the light still on and the curtains still drawn, its spectacles halfway down its nose, its mouth slightly open, a pained expression on its face, and a copy of the basic law clutched in its cold hands. And then what will they do?

Because they are afraid that at any moment it might kick the bucket, the West Germans cosset their democracy, protect it, keep asking it whether it feels all right, give in to its most preposterous demands. They have brought it up like an only child, and now that it is nearly thirty it is neurotic, spoiled, and dependent on constant and costly analysis.

It is quite unlike anything else that goes under the name of democracy. For instance, it is argued that the distinctive feature of a totalitarian state, as opposed to a mere dictatorship, is that it not only demands obedience, it also requires the active endorsement of its subjects. One is not allowed simply to mind one's own business, one has to make continual declarations of loyalty, admiration, and faith.

But this is precisely the way that West German democracy has been behaving of late. It is not enough, it appears, to be without a criminal record. There must be positive proof of one's political reliability. West German democracy has spied not merely on its young students, but also on children and apprentices. It is a stifling democracy. It is intrusive and objectionable.

It remains, nevertheless, a democracy, albeit of a paradoxical kind. There are those who say that democratic Communism is impossible (a contradiction in terms – 'like fried snowballs'). How about the notion of a totalitarian democracy? All the ingredients are there. The system itself was imposed on a defeated people – it was historically compulsory. And it is maintained by a vast military and security apparatus, which is growing all the time.

German democracy is very much like fried snowballs. It is a democracy in peril – excepting in the polls, which indicate that the overwhelming majority of the population wants it to continue along these lines. It is a society threatened by terrorism, but by a kind of terrorism of which the vast majority of the population has no reason to be afraid.

How then did this hysteria come about? Why should the West Germans have so bitterly reacted to the threat of both Communist and terrorist takeover? This is a question which an enormous number of Social Democrat and Free Democrat politicians are asking now. Indeed the press is full of it, the parties are absorbed by it, and a new glut of breast-beating confessions has come on the market.

In particular, there is the question of the radical decree of 1972, by which extremists were barred from public service, and about which there is almost a consensus among the governing parties that it was a mistake. One feature of the radical decree, which dismayed politicians more than any others, was the bad press it has got in the world at large. Indeed if, as seems likely, the whole thing will shortly be dismantled, credit will to a great extent be due to those groups outside Germany, and those foreign correspondents, who made the ugly word '*Berufsverbot*' famous in the world at large.

If there was one thing the West Germans did not want to do it was to add another notorious German word to foreign languages. But the *Berufsverbot* within Germany was like one of those ambiguous figures which you can see either as a vase or a pair of faces, or like Ayer's Rock in Australia, which changes colour as the sun goes down. If you were one of those who believed you were living in the Weimar Republic, the significance of the *Berufsverbot* was obvious.

Weimar was destroyed, you would be likely to believe, by the twin forces of Communism and Fascism – crushed between Scylla and Charybdis. And one of the great things that made this possible was the disloyalty of the civil servants, lawyers, teachers, and professors who thought democracy could be dispensed with. The exclusion of such people from the new Weimar was obviously essential.

If on the other hand you were mentally living in the thirties, you saw the *Berufsverbot* as the equivalent of those Nazi measures which scattered great writers, artists, and academics across the world. You saw yourself, if you were affected, as heir to the tradition of the persecuted 'enemy within' – the Liberal, the Socialist, the Marxist, even the Jew.

It might have been predicted, although intelligent politicians do not appear to have foreseen this, that in the outside world the second view would be more resonant. For a start, the notion that Weimar was crushed between Fascism and Communism is rather less current outside than inside Germany.

There is, to be sure, a notion floating around English politics that Weimar was destroyed by proportional representation. But that is for the specialists. Most people believe, and not without some reason, that Weimar was destroyed by Fascism, and in particular by Hitler.

But the radical decree was not directed against Fascism. True, it claimed to be. And true, any politician supporting it today will always begin by saying: 'Just as I would not want my children to be taught by a neo-Nazi, so . . . etc.' But this is self-evident bilge. The occasion for the radical decree was the rise of the extra-parliamentary Left, its intention to stop the long march through the institutions.

Which brings us to a second reason why the decree was bound to find little sympathy in the West. For, even before the rise of Euro-Communism, the West had got used to living with native left-wing parties of all kinds. However much they might be presented as in league with foreign powers, there was a sense in which they were recognized as genuine home-products.

As Peter Glotz, a member of the Berlin senate, and one of those who has come to regret the radical decree, put it: 'The average Italian perceives the Communist teacher in Naples as a countryman – perhaps as one gone astray. The average German considers the German Communist to be an agent of a foreign power.'

This is a consequence of the division of the country. Many German Communists do indeed look to the East as the focus for their loyalties. It is not surprising that their views make them unpopular – what is surprising is the lack of self-confidence of the democracy which feels it can only deal with these views through legislation.

Other countries were able to absorb (in some cases quite triumphantly) their left-wing movements. West Germany was not. It has to sentence them to internal exile. As Glotz points out, the state was able to reintegrate the Nazis five years after the end of the war. But those who took part in the student revolt are still, ten years after the event, the subject of restrictions.

He puts two questions. Why cannot the Right in Germany distinguish between democratic Socialism and Communism? And why cannot the Left distinguish between the populism of Franz Josef Strauss and Fascism?

The second of these questions seems to me in a way the more

mysterious. For it is by no means simply the Left that sees the resurgence of Fascism where it does not exist. This is a general problem. It is not merely the booming British major who explodes over his pink gin: 'They've done it twice before this century, and they could do it again.' It is also the Germans themselves who, sadly comic, bury their faces in their hands and say: 'We've done it twice before and – oh no – here we go again . . .'

Take, for instance, the recent spate of reports about the Hitler wave. There was nothing wrong with the facts in most of these stories. The taboo on talking or reading about Hitler had come to an end – surely a healthy development.

It was discovered that a lot of children did not know who Hitler was – obviously a bad thing. There was a spate of books and magazines, many of them bad. Joachim Fest produced an excellent biography of Hitler, and a questionable film. The film aroused enormous interest. The nostalgia industry also began cashing in on the Nazi period, which led to some tasteless fads. All this was reported with great interest inside and outside Germany.

There was only one thing wrong: the term 'Hitler wave'. This was coined by the Germans, and eagerly picked up around the world. But it was utterly misleading. There was simply no such thing.

But this did not stop the West Germans from agonizing over the 'problem'. On such occasions, the country behaves like a giant searching for fleas. What all the world heard was the giant's triumphant cry – 'got one'. Not unnaturally, the world rushed to see what had happened.

This ability to see Fascists all over the place is the one thing shared between those who live under the impression that they are in Weimar and those who inhabit the hallucinatory Third Reich. But the two groups see different Fascists. The Weimarians are looking always for the new wave, the new forms of Fascism. The Third Reich inhabitants are looking at the older generation. Nothing has happened. There has been no denazification. Everyone above a certain age is guilty.

And here an important complication arises. For it is obvious that in West Germany those who insist on finding Fascists everywhere will indeed occasionally come across a Fascist, or come across a man with a shady past. Does this mean that the whole establishment is tainted? When Hanns-Martin Schleyer was found, after the kidnapping, to have been a member of the SS, did this provide a retrospective justification for the murder?

To certain people, and not just to the terrorists themselves, it did. Indeed I have been assured that Schleyer's past was known about, if not proved, beforehand, and I have seen student cabaret in Berlin which played mercilessly with the event, without a shred of sympathy for the victim. To the actors and to the spectators of this show, Schleyer was part of the brown comedy of West German life.

This kind of hatred is impossible to share, and practically impossible to understand. But unless it is appreciated in some way, one misses the qualitative logic of German politics.

Consider then the following case, which has recently come to light because of a controversy over Bavaria's new police law. Take Article 44, paragraph 33: 'Firearms should not be employed against people who, according to outward impressions, are not yet fourteen. This does not apply if the use of firearms is the only means of protection for life and limb.'

Obviously any decision over the second part of this clause is going to be fiercely contested, and the Minister of the Interior will need to command a great deal of respect should it ever come to issue. But suppose the Minister of the Interior was a former member of the SA and the Nazi Party. Would that not influence one's opinion of any decision he made?

According to recent reports, Octor Alfred Seidl, the Bavarian interior minister, joined the SA at the age of twenty-three, and another prominent Nazi organization in 1937. His doctoral thesis in law, published the next year, is a classic exposition of Nazi doctrine, which refers warmly to one of the most notorious jurists of the Fascist period.

Now imagine living in a region where Dr Seidl controls the police, where Dr Seidl is in charge of the bureau for the protection of the constitution, which is empowered to investigate political activists and gather material on schoolchildren, where Dr Seidl is calling for the return of the death penalty. Would one be entirely happy, living in such a place?

When Senator Glotz pleads from Berlin for the Left to distinguish between Strauss's populism and Fascism, he is no doubt right. But in such circumstances it may well be hard to avoid being ambushed by the feeling: Nothing has changed, it's all happening again.

The convenient legends by which Germany lived for so long have proved incapable of meeting the present crisis. For instance, if all those who now believe that they played some role in the resistance to Nazism were counted up, it would be impossible to explain how the Third Reich managed to last a single day.

One leading politician, chatting in the early hours, will refer to his exploits in this field. 'I could write a book,' he told a group of journalists, 'about what I did in those days against the Nazis.' One wanted to cry out: 'Well, why the hell don't you write a book then? Go on. Set it all down.' But I think that these exploits will remain legendary.

Another politician had a stroke of bad luck. His efforts to justify his past only resulted in more details emerging. And what was his first reaction? To explain that, so far from being at best an unheroic lawyer in the Nazi period, he had been a member of the resistance. Nobody could tell whether he believed this, but the more he struggled to establish it, the more his friends became embarrassed and his enemies appalled. For a while he seemed to embody not the evil, not the hypocrisy, not the dangerousness, but the utter absurdity of West German politics.

For there is an absurd quality to all these debates, and the latest debate is the most absurd of all. The Social Democrats have decided at last that a man should be considered 'loyal to the constitution' unless otherwise proved, and they have launched a campaign to this effect throughout the country.

This is, is it not, a remarkable discovery to have made? It is rather as if they had suddenly decided that a man is innocent until he is proved guilty.

But then West Germany, as I said, is not like any other democracy. It suffers its history, and division, like a recurring disease. Sometimes the fever returns, and with it the hallucinations. At the moment it seems as if the fever is subsiding. The patient is waking up, and wondering, perhaps, what on earth has been going on.

30 October 1978   **James Fenton**

Waiting in vain for reinforcements

The most symptomatic of recent events in Israel was not the handing over of El Arish, focus although that is of much anxiety and hope, but the astonishing spectacle of the President of the state of Israel pleading for two hours with a handful of Soviet adolescents. These Russian boys and girls, children of Soviet Jews in Vienna transit centres, were in the country for a tour that, it was clearly hoped, might influence their parents' decision whether to migrate to Israel or to the United States.

The increasing failure of Soviet Jews to go to Israel has been a bitter disappointment to the Israel Establishment and its implications have yet to be fully worked out. President Navon, dapper in his dark suit, told his dutiful audience: 'Jews were accused of being nonproductive and lazy. But here we have produced one of the best agricultural systems in the world, and our army has gained the respect of our enemies.'

The Russians told journalists that their parents in Vienna had been put off mainly by 'death, war, and terrorism'. Navon tried to cast the dangers of life in Israel in a more romantic light: 'The choice is in your hands. You can live a life of drinking Coca Cola and sitting in a villa in America – or you can take part in the building of the Jewish state.'

Navon's was the simplest possible formulation of the Israeli myth: the Jew as farmer and soldier, Israel as the Jewish state, and, above all, the contrast between a life of purpose, danger, and dedication against slothful ease and degeneracy ('Coca Cola') elsewhere. One wit summed up the Israeli message to hesitant Soviet Jews as: 'We have nothing to offer you except blood, sweat and tears – and a subsidized flat, and income-tax concessions.' The tape of President Navon's impromptu dissertation has meanwhile been sent off to Vienna, but it is unlikely to change the dismal facts and figures.

Since serious migration began in the late sixties, an estimated 200,000 Jews have left the Soviet Union, out of a total Jewish population there of nearly three million – the largest reserve of discontented and disadvantaged Jews left in the world. It is difficult to exaggerate the hope that was pinned, and is still pinned, to Soviet Jewry by many Israelis.

Of the 200,000 so far out, 150,000 have come to Israel. But that healthy proportion conceals two things: one is that the first immigrants came disproportionately from Zionist activists and from peripheral Jewish communities like the Georgian Jews. Now the emigration is of Russian Jews proper, and the painful fact is that they are not coming to Israel.

The proportion of 'Vienna Drop-outs' – those that go directly from the transit centres in Austria to the US, rejecting Israel without setting foot in it – has risen from a fifth in 1974 to two-thirds in the first three months of 1979. At that rate, Israel will get only a few score thousand of the quarter of a million Soviet Jews expected to leave in the next few years. The Aliyah-ascent – the grandiose Hebrew word for going to Palestine, might even be overtaken by the Yeridah-descent – the derogatory word for emigration from Israel. Statistics up to 1977 showed a total of 300,000 'yordim' (descenders) since 1948, the people that Rabin once described as 'deserters from the field of battle'. The net gain to Israel last year, for instance, was only 5000.

Most of those Russians that do come are 'soft'. Professor Alexander Voronel, a Soviet immigrant himself, says: 'The brutal truth is that most Soviet immigrants are not in the least Zionist and expecting idealism and pioneering sacrifices from them is unrealistic.' A young American immigrant, commenting on the Russians and Persians in his Hebrew class, wrote: 'The majority of them would like to live anywhere else except Israel.'

The vital importance of the faltering Soviet Aliyah is both arithmetical and cultural. It has led to bitter debate in Israel, because it touches on the very foundation of the Jewish state. At the simplest level, the Russians were expected to provide demographic reinforcement in the battle to maintain a workable majority over the Israeli Arabs and, for the Israeli right wing, also over the Arabs of the occupied territory. Then there is the question of military manpower, which since 1973 has been pushed to the absolute limit that the present population can sustain.

Gush Emunim, the extremist settler movement, in its so-called 'master plan' for the West Bank, says: 'We expect great waves of immigration in the next twenty-five years bringing the total (Jewish) population up to eight or ten million.' But the arithmetic, whether real or imaginary, is in the end less important than what one newspaper described as the blow to 'Israel's historic function as an ingathering state' (destined to receive all or most Jews).

The implication of what is happening is thus not accepted by many Israelis, least of all by those that do not want to re-examine their history, in the light of the Russian 'defection', as a minority phenomenon. The escape from that conclusion takes ever darker and more fantastic routes.

If the Soviet Jews are not coming, refuge is taken in the future, a future in which new outbreaks of anti-Semitism will blast the diaspora. A young and able official, a supporter of the Begin government, knowledgeable and even liberal, said: 'There will be another disaster in world Jewry. It could come in South America. It could come in America itself . . . Let me put it this way. If, by the year 2010, the Arabs outnumber us in Israel,' which, in his philosophy, would still include the occupied territory, 'it will be our own fault.'

The idea of a massive reinforcement from the diaspora is thus central for that part of the Israeli elite, represented both in government and opposition, that believes that, autonomy or no autonomy, Israel must and will keep sovereignty over the occupied territory.

It is the key to the amazing 'plans' of Ariel Sharon, the brilliant former general who is now the Minister of Agriculture, to plant 'two million' Jews in a chain of towns, villages and settlements across the territory over the next twenty years. Sharon's plans are dreams not shared or endorsed by most of his Cabinet colleagues. But the idea of the coming 'reinforcements' is hard to relinquish for many Israelis, including liberals, who do not want to put aside their picture of Israel as the major event of modern Jewish history.

Israelis who do not share this complex are not lacking. It was most bluntly expressed by a young man in a Tel Aviv bar who told me: 'America is the Jewish national home . . . Israel is the Jewish national graveyard.' Typically, and understandably, he regretted what he had said immediately afterwards, and used many sentences taking most of it back.

Few would join him in such an abrupt rejection of Israel's 'historic function as an ingathering state'. There are many that recognize it as a myth. Yehoshua Porath, an academic expert on Arab affairs, said: 'People never came *en masse* from the liberal democracies . . . they came from eastern Europe, before they were murdered by the Germans. That is the tragedy of Zionism, that the people for whom it was designed are dead.'

Another academic said: 'Begin still really believes in it and a lot of people can't let it go . . . millions of Jews for the West Bank! Where the hell are they going to come from?' But the recognition that 'Israel's right to exist' is not indissolubly tied to its status as 'national home', is longer in coming. For it means that it must be accepted that what the Russian Jews are doing now – choosing the West over Israel – is precisely what their forebears did. The great event of modern Jewish history, it can be argued, was neither the Holocaust nor the creation of Israel, but the massive relocation of the Ashkenazi nation in the West.

As the Jewish community of eastern Europe, the Yiddish-speaking, Ashkenazi quasi-state that had found its large, if often difficult role, within the framework of three empires, began to collapse in the nineteenth century, the main response of its members was emigration to the West. Like the Russian Jews today, the majority went anywhere but to Palestine. Just as the Jews had solved their problems in the West several centuries before by moving east, so they now retraced their steps.

Another kind of arithmetic proves the point. Of nearly twelve million Ashkenazi Jews, less than an eighth live in Israel. The irony of Israel's history is that it was intended to become an Ashkenazi national home, but instead became the national home of Oriental Jews, of which it now holds more than two-thirds. But that development was the result of the chain reaction that ran through the Islamic world after the establishment of Israel, and the resulting Oriental immigration was largely unplanned and not entirely welcome to the Israeli leaders.

Ashkenazis founded and still dominate Israel, and it is the notion that it was in some sense an accident rather than the work of God or of an ineluctable destiny, that they find so horrifying. That it will not be and never was the first choice of the majority of Ashkenazis is also a concept difficult to digest.

'Zionism,' Porath says, 'was nearly dead before 1967 . . . it was being replaced by an Israeli identity and an Israeli nationalism . . . for Begin, of course, none of this has happened. Begin does not know any Israelis, he knows only Jews.' It is not that such matters are never discussed in Israel. They are – endlessly, and often lucidly. But somehow the various pieces are never put together into one comprehensive picture that would alter the understanding of Israel's role and purpose. Begin is far from alone in his refusal to accept that Zionism has had its day and that the whole history of Israel – and its whole future – have to be looked at with fresh eyes.

28 May 1979   **Martin Woollacott**

First Valkyrie

Clare Hollingworth, at sixty-eight, sits in her office in London watching the war in Cambodia with some impatience. If there was any way at all for her to get in, she'd be there.

She has covered almost every war, on many fronts, since the start of the Second World War. She talks about her past campaigns with almost girlish enthusiasm, describing some of her most hair-raising moments as 'adventures'. She makes a point of sleeping on the floor at least once a fortnight, so as not to get out of the habit. She has enormous physical strength, which she has needed on many occasions, hiking through jungles and swamps. 'Comfort isn't very important to me,' she says. 'I'm fortunate in that I don't mind going without food for five or six days.'

Her dress is notorious – she hates clothes and tends to wear tired jump suits, only buying new clothes when sufficiently bullied by friends.

She comes from a family of boot and shoe manufacturers in Leicester. 'My father didn't really believe in too much education for girls,' she says. But it was her father who gave her a life-long interest in war. 'We always used to picnic in battlefields. We often went to Bosworth and Naseby, which were nearby. My father was very good at describing battles. He had a very C of E

71

attitude to war – if the King said you should fight, then it was a good thing.'

Later she went to work for the League of Nations, married, briefly, and travelled a great deal, especially in Central Europe. She spent some time in the School of Slavonic Studies and the LSE. She also took a course in military history. She took a job in 1939 administering a fund set up by the *News Chronicle* to aid refugees from Germany and Czechoslovakia. She lived in Katowice on the Polish-German border, and helped to get visas to Europe, Palestine and America for fleeing Jews, Catholics, Communists and Socialists. As a freelance she began writing for provincial papers and the *New Statesman.*

It was later that year that she was amazed to be summoned to the editor of the *Daily Telegraph* and offered a job as a correspondent in Poland. He had read and admired her articles. With a piece of extraordinary beginner's luck, she was the first journalist to witness the outbreak of the Second World War. She was also the first person to inform the British government that the war had begun. 'It's my only real claim to fame,' she says modestly. She was in Katowice, where the border with Germany had just been closed. 'But it wasn't closed to flagged diplomatic cars. Things were so different in those days,' she says. So she borrowed the British Consul's flagged car and drove into Germany the day before the tanks rolled in. 'I had a lovely lunch in Gleiwitz in Germany, a delicious bottle of German wine, and I saw, hidden behind some hessian, rows and rows of German tanks. A German soldier saluted me, on account of the car.'

She returned to Poland. 'I was sleeping that night in a house overlooking the frontier. It was a disturbed night, with the animals making a lot of noise. Then, at first light, in the early hours, the planes started coming over and the tanks started moving. The anti-aircraft guns were blazing. I telephoned the British Embassy in Warsaw at once, and I spoke to Robin Hankey, the ambassador. I said, "The war has begun." He said, "Are you sure, old girl?" So I held the telephone up to the window and shouted, "Can't you hear it?" '

She stayed in Katowice just long enough to help the British Consul destroy documents and secure the seals, and to pick up as many refugees as would fit in the car. 'Tanks were closing round the town in a pincer movement,' she recalls. She took only a toothbrush and typewriter. 'We drove into Warsaw, out again, to Krakow and to Lublin. Everywhere I tried to send my reports by telegram. I thought they were getting through, but none of them did, except the first one.' When she got back to Warsaw the Polish forces were in a state of chaos, the other correspondents and diplomats had left. 'I drove past German tanks. God looks after fools. I was so interested and preoccupied in what was going on that I wasn't afraid.' What did she feel about seeing her first real war? 'I learned the great lesson that war is confusion, nothing ever goes to plan.'

She worked in Paris before being sent for the *Daily Express* to the Balkans, working from Bucharest. She was in Greece for the Italian invasion, and went with the Greek army marching into Albania. 'That was hard,' she said. 'It was a long way, and very cold in the mountains. Very few people spoke English, but I enjoyed every minute. The trouble with covering war is petrol, and filing stories. It was very difficult to get stories back.' She was in Greece, Istanbul and then Cairo, where she remained for the next ten years.

From there she wrote for the *Sunday Times*, and covered the Palestine war. If she ever admits to having been frightened at all in a war, she admits a twinge or two of fear in Palestine. 'I was staying in the King David Hotel when it was blown up. The terrorism was appalling. The Stern gang were blowing up everything.'

In Cairo she married her second husband, Geoffrey Hoare who was the *Times* correspondent. She worked for a while for *The Observer* and *The Economist*, a job filled afterwards by Kim Philby. In 1951 they left the Middle East for Paris, where she worked for the *Guardian*, covering the Algerian war. 'That was exciting. I had a lot of adventures,' she says. It was her coverage of Algeria in 1963 for the *Guardian* that won her in the same year both the Granada Journalist of the Year Award, and the top Hannan Swaffer Journalist of the Year Award, with its £500 prize.

She covered civil war in Iraq, two Indo-Pakistani wars, the Russian invasion of Northern Persia, Borneo, Aden, Cyprus and Vietnam. 'I became more and more fascinated by tactics

73

and strategy,' she says. 'The Algerian situation was most dramatic, with the French army officers leaving to join the OAS while the men joined the rebels. I became less and less surprised that in war everyone gets bogged down in orders and counter-orders. It's all fought out in a muddle – the fog of war.'

Her friends accuse her of having no knowledge of fear. 'That's not true at all,' she says. 'I am terrified of being stuck in lifts, really terrified. But I'm never afraid of being shot. I don't know why not. People have been shot around me on patrols but I'm not frightened. I think I always have this subconscious feeling that I'm going to be all right.'

She has never found being a woman the slightest handicap in reporting wars. 'Officers tend to say that other men will rush to protect you in time of danger. I can tell you, that's never happened to me yet, not once.' Nor has anyone shown any reluctance to take her on difficult or dangerous patrols. She always keeps up with the men.

In 1973, by now widowed and working for the *Daily Telegraph*, she went to Peking for three years. 'I asked for three weeks' leave before I went to China to read up about it. All I discovered in those weeks was that I would never, ever know anything about China.'

When she came back in 1976 she became defence correspondent. She is still ready to take off at any moment for a front line anywhere and has her summer and winter combat kit ready at all times. 'It's a pretty good kit,' she says with pride. It consists mainly of clothes that are somewhere between uniform and safari outfits, with plenty of pockets, and rubber soled canvas boots.

Her view of Europe's future is almost despairing. She believes that in eight to ten years, when Russia's conventional military strength is at its height, the tanks will come rattling across the German border, and Europe will be defenceless. The Americans probably will not resort to nuclear war to protect us, and we shall all become Russian satellites. Political pressure inside Russia will make war and conquest a necessity for Russian leaders, to distract attention from growing internal demands for freedom and consumer goods. The NATO forces in Germany, she says, will be mainly preoccupied with getting their own military wives and children out of the front line.

'I often contemplate where would be the best place to cover the next war from,' she says, in a matter of fact tone of voice. 'It wouldn't be a question of getting to the front line. The first TV crews to get the first pictures next time will be nuclear dust. I'll have to choose somewhere safe, not an obvious first strike target.' I can imagine her sitting with her notebook, in her combat kit in the ruins of some city, scribbling away against a background of distant mushroom clouds, still unafraid.

15 January 1979   **Polly Toynbee**

A life hanging by 80,000 words

You can still find some of Mr Bhutto's numerous books tucked away discreetly on the back shelves in Pakistani bookshops. But his most recent work is not on sale, nor likely to be. Composed in prison, *The Rejoinder* is an 80,000-word defence of the former Prime Minister's philosophy, politics, and life. It could well turn out to be his testament. For Bhutto's lengthy trial on a charge of ordering a political assassination is finally drawing to a close, and General Zia Ul Haq, the soldier who deposed him last summer, has said repeatedly that he will not save him from the gallows if that is the court's judgement.

For all Mr Bhutto's glaring faults, it is impossible not to be moved by the picture of the former Prime Minister struggling against ill health, depression, and adverse conditions – it took his counsel weeks to get him a mattress, for instance – to produce this book. Not previously fully reported in the West, it is far from a masterpiece, but it is full of perception, wit, and interesting, often convincing, analysis. There is also much tendentious argument and special pleading, few expressions of regret, moments of self-pity and even paranoia.

The Rejoinder is technically a legal application to the Supreme Court here in Rawalpindi which is hearing Bhutto's appeal against the death sentence imposed on him by a lower court. Claiming that recent White Papers issued by the Government on rigging in the 1977 elections and on control of the media are an attempt to influence the court, he begs to lodge this reply. He is able to demonstrate what is now quite widely accepted; that, while there was much local rigging in the elections, there is no hard evidence of a master plan. Being Mr Bhutto, he skates swiftly over other, better founded, allegations in the two White Papers.

He is far more effective when he goes on, with verve and force, to accuse the Zia Government of the very offences with which he himself has been charged. If the People's Party Government managed the press, writes Bhutto, by such techniques as bribes and the withdrawal of advertisements, then Zia has done the same, and gone further. 'We did not flog journalists, nor did we steal the printing presses of newspapers, or stop publication for a single day.'

If there was rigging in his election, Bhutto says, what is to be said of a man (Zia) who broke a solemn promise to hold elections and now proposes to postpone them until what he calls 'a positive result' can be obtained? As to Islamic reform, 'Islam does not come out of the barrel of a gun.'

But Bhutto soon moves on from these immediate arguments to an analysis of the role of coups d'état and military governments in the Third World and in Pakistan in particular. The 'chocolate Caesars', he argues, are nearly always an obstacle to real development and independence. Stability in Asia may rest with established monarchies, revolutionary national movements, socialist revolutionary governments, or, in a few cases, parliamentary democracies.

The intervention of the military has always been a disaster. In the sub-continent, with 'its long, persistent lesson in mass awakening', the effects have been even worse. Pakistan, he writes, is in danger of becoming 'Coupistan'. If 'the coup d'état becomes a permanent part of the political infrastructure, it means the falling of the last petal . . . it means the end.' The 'suicidal thought of a permanent role for the army in the politics of Pakistan' – a reference to one of General Zia's remarks – will lead to confrontation and civil war.

Bhutto's assertion that the people of Pakistan have been irreversibly politicized during his years in power is one with which many Pakistanis and foreigners agree. 'The common man felt for the first time that he was the pivot of politics,' was one diplomat's comment. Bhutto writes: 'The people are not going to lump in 1978 what they lumped in 1958' (the year of Ayub Khan's take-over). 'One of the fatal realities of 1978 is that the people have realized that martial law is not law.'

Mr Bhutto fails to explain why, in spite of his prejudice against military regimes, he served Ayub Khan and later developed close relations with some members of the Yahya Khan group of generals. And his concern with himself does not often extend to others - like Yahya Khan, for instance, who filed a pitiful affidavit in the Supreme Court claiming that the five years he spent in detention at Bhutto's command had ruined his health and his reputation.

Bhutto's account of his fall lays much stress on the nuclear re-processing deal and, as he has done before, he accuses, without quite naming names, the United States of engineering it and of subsidizing the opposition. But he is more interested in accusing General Zia and his colleagues of throwing away his achievements by gross blunders. Zia, he argues, has lost the nuclear technology which alone would have enabled Pakistan to preserve its equal status with India; has thrown away what was left of the chance to reach an accommodation with Afghanistan; and, by a variety of foolish internal measures, has strengthened separatist forces in the nation.

Again and again in *The Rejoinder* Bhutto's sense of mission, largely concealed in happier days by his elegant and flippant style, is apparent, some would say naked. 'As our jeep left the village,' he writes of one election experience, 'I could hear the sound of *"Jeeay Bhutto"* (Long live Bhutto) ringing in the distance until we had gone beyond the reach of sound . . . Perhaps I have embedded myself too deep in the hearts of the poor of this land for others to comprehend.' Or: 'I was born to make a nation, to save a people, to overcome an impending doom. I was not born for a death cell.'

Elsewhere he relates how as a seven-year-old child he accused the British Governor of Bombay of 'sucking the blood of the people'. Lord Braborne wagged a finger and called him 'a poet and a revolutionary'. He touches again on his well-known fascination with Napoleon and tells how, on his twenty-first birthday, he received, in Los Angeles where he was studying, a five-volume biography of Napoleon and a copy of the Communist

Manifesto. 'From one I imbibed the politics of power and from the other the politics of poverty.'

Finally, he brings together – and for all the man's ego, many would agree with him – his own fate, soon to be decided, and that of Pakistan. 'More than my life is at stake. Make no mistake about it; the future of Pakistan is at stake.'

Towards the very end, he tells the tale of how he was sent by Ayub to Ankara in 1960 to plead for the lives of the Turkish civilian leaders condemned to death by a new military regime. General Gersel told him that the problems of Turkey would be solved by the executions – an argument echoed by many in the Pakistan of 1978. 'Mister President, Sir,' said the young Bhutto, 'the problems of Turkey will begin with these executions.'

The Rejoinder does not touch on the evidence and arguments before the Supreme Court on the murder case proper. Whatever the rights and wrongs of that, General Zia might do well to bear the young Bhutto's remarks in mind if and when he has to decide whether or not to follow that other advice blazoned on the banners that greet him as he travels around the country. *'Bhutto ko pansi do'* (Hang Bhutto), they shriek. It is typical of Bhutto that his latest, and perhaps his last, intellectual effort should provide both sides with their best ammunition.

2 November 1978   **Martin Woollacott**

Law and order in Rawalpindi

The body of Pakistan's deposed Prime Minister, Zulfikar Ali Bhutto – gaunt from his eighteen-month prison ordeal, his neck snapped, the flesh bruised – now lies in the family grave in the hamlet of Ghari Bhutto.

From this remote walled cemetery, Mr Bhutto may pose a greater threat to the military ruler, General Zia Ul Haq, than he ever did in life.

As he stood on the scaffold at 2 a.m. in Rawalpindi prison and the hangman strapped his legs tightly together, Mr Bhutto cried out: 'Oh Lord, help me, for I am innocent.'

The reaction of Pakistanis to the furtive, dead-of-night

execution has been stunned and angry. Employees in government offices wept openly. An elderly woman snapped: 'This is the most disgraceful day in Pakistan's history.' In Lahore, a crowd stoned cars, and set some alight. In Rawalpindi, youths hurled rocks at a bus. A man said: 'Now this country will be like Iran.'

Violent demonstrations broke out in Srinagar, capital of the state of Jammu and Kashmir on the border with Pakistan. Waves of demonstrators attacked the United Nations military observer's office in Srinagar in an attempt to set it on fire, and police opened fire. Two demonstrators were injured.

In New Delhi, the Youth Congress, youth wing of former Prime Minister Indira Gandhi's party, held a demonstration in front of the Pakistan Embassy. In Rawalpindi, more than a thousand women defied martial law regulations which ban political activity and make it an offence to bring into disrepute members of the armed forces. 'Death to Zia and Zia's children,' they shouted, weeping and beating their breasts in Rawalpindi's Liaqat Park. The place was significant. It was here that Mr Bhutto began the movement which brought down General Ayub Khan's Government ten years ago.

Abdul Hafeez Pirzada, Mr Bhutto's former finance minister, arrived at the park and was carried shoulder high by the crowd. They waved People's Party flags, and shouted: 'Revenge, revenge, revenge.' Some women tore their clothes and taunted the police: 'Shame on you, you couldn't save him.'

Police carrying *lathis* (cane sticks, often metal tipped) repeatedly charged the demonstrators and arrests were made. Prayer meetings have been called for this afternoon all over Pakistan. The military regime has ordered that news of these be censored from newspapers here, and has also banned mention of details of Mr Bhutto's burial.

Foreign embassies have been saddened and worried about the implications the execution will have for Pakistan. Ambassadors were due to hold a regular monthly meeting last night, and Mr Bhutto's fate will dominate the proceedings. The Swedish Embassy closed its doors in disgust yesterday, and pulled in its flag.

Most interesting of all will be the reaction of the armed forces. There were known to be deep divisions on the question of hanging Mr Bhutto – both on the issue of whether he was

6 April 1979

really guilty of conspiring to murder a political opponent, and over the wisdom of killing him, even if he was. Now General Zia has cast the die, and the military must face the consequences.

Mumtez Ali Bhutto, a leading lieutenant in the once-ruling Pakistan People's Party and the dead Prime Minister's cousin, said: 'Bhutto is dead, but the problem for them has been magnified a million-fold. Let us see how they deal with it.'

The hanging of Mr Bhutto was an affair more squalid than executions usually are. Mr Bhutto, who had been kept in filthy conditions for the past eleven days, was denied his final meal from friends outside. Officials refused to take it in. Close relatives were called to meet him on Tuesday, not knowing for certain whether it was to be the final visit, but when they arrived, gaol officials turned them away. The military regime was determined to keep the hanging secret, and they abandoned prison regulations to do it. Only Mr Bhutto himself, and the two family members who were under house arrest – his second wife, the Begum Nugrat, and his daughter Benazir, aged twenty-five – knew that the execution would take place at 2 a.m.

While Mr Bhutto was being taken from his stinking, ant-infested death cell for a last bath, and was being given verses from the Koran to read, a senior spokesman for General Zia was at dinner assuring correspondents that there was no possibility of an execution the following day.

Mr Bhutto was writing his will when, just after midnight, armed troops took up position around the gaol.

The will was signed in the presence of the magistrate who would shortly watch Bhutto die. Then, with his arms tied behind his back, he was taken in slow procession to the scaffold.

His body, the head hooded, dangled from the noose for thirty minutes before the hangman cut him down, and he was laid out in a simple coffin. An army truck waited in the yard to carry it to the nearby Chaklala air force base, adjoining Islamabad international airport. Just before 4 a.m. a military aircraft took off for the town of Sukkur in the province of Sind, and another truck drove the coffin to Mr Bhutto's birthplace.

Here, according to the official statement, the body was handed over to his 'near relatives', and Mr Bhutto's first 'traditional' wife, the Amir Begum, who wears the veils of purdah, was told that he had been hanged.

5 April 1979   **Peter Niesewand**

Passage through India

BOMBAY – Dawn is the busiest moment in the life of the city. Its people mostly live still to the rhythm of the countryside. Family life is acted out on the pavements. Children are peeing into gutters, parents brushing teeth from tin mugs, gaily-coloured blankets are neatly rolled and pillows puffed; these street dwellers are not for the most part destitute, they live above the lower depths of the shanty slums which line the road from the airport.

Some of these people are living near to their places of employment, some conduct street businesses however humble, some of the males are commuters who return at weekends to their villages and families. The porchway of a bank is a safer abode than a mud hut during the monsoon; communities form in streets and alleys; straying children are known and minded; life is intensely social; villages are re-created but at night there are lights.

Shaving is an intimate function. The shaver and the shaved squat cross-legged before each other, their faces almost pressing. The razor is wielded fondly. Some of the classier barbers perform their services in boxes the size of large packing cases. We think of barbers' shaves as an old-fashioned luxury, scarcely surviving except at Trumper's, but in India the labour cost is cheaper than the capital outlay on a razor. It is not easy to adjust the mind to such considerations. It is why discrimination by caste barbers is high on the list of grievances among the *harijans* or untouchables.

'Look at this place, skyscrapers surrounded by shanties' says a businessman, despairingly. It is said that 45 per cent of a population of around eight millions are living at or below the poverty line. It rubs it in to drive in an elegant lady's car with a chauffeur in white duck uniform and cap, 1930s Hollywood style. Bombay like Manhattan can't grow out, only up; not only the unemployed are unhoused but vast numbers of the proletariat. Like fat cat New Yorkers, the Bombay rich love and complain about their city; law and order is breaking down, all cab drivers are criminals, politicians are crooks and the crooks are politicians . . .

Standing on the Apollo Bunder one imagines arriving here by sea. The Victorian would not have seen the Gateway of India for it was built to commemorate the landing of George V and Queen Mary in 1911. They would have seen the high tower of St Thomas's though, which was added to the early eighteenth-century church in 1836 when it became a cathedral. For many it must have seemed the symbol of a graveyard. Inside it is plain and cool; the white walls are smothered with memorials to the dead, so many of them young. 'Struck down in his prime . . .' 'his life cut off by cholera . . .' 'he succumbed to the hardships of his duty'.

POONAH – Is this the place to be holding the annual Indo-British Exchange? It is as if we were to invite the Indians to a conference at Newmarket. We are put up at the Turf Club House. An L-shaped verandah half-frames a manicured lawn at the bottom of which is the white running rail of the racecourse. The club secretary, Brigadier James (Retd.), puts up notices concerning the playing of 'billiards, slosh or snooker'; there is porridge for breakfast and old-fashioned marmalade; the early morning tea pot wears a monogrammed cosy; pegs are still served in the permit room, chota or burra; the racing from Bombay or Bangalore comes over the blower; has nothing changed? My bearer and his several assistants unpack my bags. The contents of my sponge bag are lovingly deployed. But where is sahib's shaving brush? Gentlemen do not use aerosols.

This Indo-British get-together – the Indian Königswinter, we call it – is the inspiration of Labour MP Rod McFarquhar and editor, publisher and columnist Romesh Thaper. This year's theme is 'The Problems of Caste, Creed and Colour'. I am seated next to Professor M. N. Srinivase, whom a terrible fate befell at Berkeley in 1970. Thirty years of notes gathered on the Hindu caste system in rural India were burned in a campus riot. Poor Professor Srinivase – whose subsequent book was aptly called *The Remembered Village* – received a personal note from President Nixon which commiserated with him as from one scholar to another.

Caste is a topical subject in India. Throughout the Hindu belt, which runs like a broad sash across the north of India between the Punjab and West Bengal, there is a backlash going on against the positive discrimination which is exercised in favour of former untouchables and other backward classes. Higher educational places and public service jobs are allocated on a quota basis. Recently there were violent riots in the University of Marathwada in the state of Maharashtra, where we are, in protest against its renaming after Dr B. S. Ambedkar, an untouchable who rose to be Minister of Law in Nehru's government.

He educated himself by eavesdropping outside the schoolroom window. When he became a barrister, an astonishing achievement, clerks working in his offices would drop papers at his feet rather than risk hand-to-hand contact. Crimes against the *harijans* ('children of god' – Mahatma Gandhi's name for the outcastes) have risen sharply. According to a newspaper report, 5968 were reported in 1976 during the Emergency, 10,879 in 1977, and more last year.

The mysteries and subtleties of the Hindu caste system are almost impenetrable for a Westerner. Originally there were priests, warriors, merchants and farmers, labourers – four castes;

anybody who arrived too late to be born into the system was, literally, an outcaste, the lowliest of whom were regarded as untouchable and – in the south – some even as unseeable.

It seems that the politicians have used caste networks as a means of organizing electoral support in rural India where 80 per cent of the population is to be found. This is done through an elaborate system of favours and influence reminiscent of old-style, corrupt machine politics in American cities. The losers are the 45 per cent or so of the population who fall outside of the caste system and are much less well organized politically.

The educated English-speaking Indians sitting round our table – professors, politicians, journalists, businessmen – are fascinated and repelled by the subject of caste, especially untouchability. This has been illegal in India since the Constitution was enacted but discriminations take place. The discussion reminds me of similar ones with conscience-torn American whites.

These are civilized men, dedicated to the upholding of standards, especially academic ones; yet at the same time they are unable to accept or morally justify the principle of inequality on which Indian society is organized. 'Scratch an Indian and you will find a caste' one of them says but another says: 'Twenty years ago you could have identified us from our dress, from what we wore on our heads. Today I cannot tell to which caste any of us belong. That is the democratizing influence of the London School of Economics.'

BHUAUM – 'This is a most underdeveloped place,' says our guide. 'Look, the ladies and gentlemen are both working on farming.' This is one of 550,000 typical Indian villages. We pause on the road to await the dawn. Richard Buckle, landing on the Normandy beach on D-day, is reputed to have exclaimed: 'My, dear, the noise and the people.' You could say the same about the Indian countryside.

The sounds echo across the land – crowing and mooing and bleating and farting; the cries of children and of birds; cow bells ringing and cowherds hallooing. The noise level rises with the sun which once it has peeped over the horizon shoots into the sky like a fiery ball from a Very pistol.

The village is fifteen kilometres from Poonah, is said to have a population of 6000 but seems very much smaller than that. We are told that one quarter are *dalit*, which is the local version of *harijan* and then we are told that there are twelve *harijan* families. Their houses are built apart. They have their own temple, which looks more like a cowshed, but is also used as an hotel. The place is desperately poor. The top man has five and a half acres. The *dalits* have thirty-five acres of uncultivated, barren land under some Government scheme. The village has two wells which have a history as follows:

Until about two years ago when social workers came to the village the Mahrattas had one well and the formerly untouchable *dalits* another. The *dalit* well contained water for only six months of the year and when it did contain water it was inferior. When it was dry they begged from the Mahrattas. The social workers said this wouldn't do. Now the *aalits* are allowed water from the good well but they are not allowed to draw it themselves.

An old man goes into his house, returns, shows us a coloured photograph printed on paper of Dr Ambedkar sitting in his library.

My driver makes the four-hour journey from Poonah to Bombay seven days a fortnight, sleeps in his car, and drives back the next day. The trip costs 152 rupees, about £10, of which his employer pays him 25 rupees. He's been doing it eight years. His father had a Government job in an ordnance factory. His brother he says is a Ph.D who is unemployed, unable to obtain a job in the civil service because of preference given to 'scheduled castes' *(harijans)* with lesser qualifications. He is indignant for his brother's sake. He has a wife, two sons, and a daughter. When I tell him I have three daughters he gives me a look of infinite pity.

CALCUTTA – The idea of the place is frightening. One has been warned to expect horrors. Coming out of an expensive restaurant to step over a dying baby in the gutter is proverbially the quintessential Calcutta experience. It is dark already as the plane arrives. A dense black smog makes the night darker than it should be. At this time of the year the climate conspires with the pollution.

A double decker bus on Chowringhi Road is weighed down by

clinging bodies until the platform is barely an inch above the street; from the other side it emits soot so thick that visibility is lost to oncoming traffic. Dinner - tourist tandoori – on Park Street. Coming out of the restaurant I step over a seven- or eight-year-old boy with no legs; he scuttles around the pavement on his hands like an agile insect.

My guide for the next day is Mani Sankar who combines being a best-selling Bengali novelist with public relations man for Dunlop of India. Satyajit Ray has filmed two parts of his Calcuttan trilogy the most recent of which was that beautiful film *The Middleman*. We begin in the markets of Gariahat in the southern part of the city. This is a fairly prosperous area and there are customers for hilsa, a luxury fish like a salmon, which sells at 16 rupees (about £1) a kilo.

Millions in the city struggle to earn 4 rupees a day. Rice, wheat and cooking oil are rationed and price-controlled in designated areas of the city of which this is one; a Government shop lists the official prices as wheat R1.45 per kg., rice R1.70 and oil R7.00.

A vast profusion of vegetables are on offer, all neatly bundled and scrubbed as for a horticultural show in the Home Counties. The Indian greengrocer is also a doctor and chemist. The latest craze is for garlic as a remedy for high cholesterol or flatulence. It is best taken raw before breakfast but if that is considered anti-social an extract is now available in powder form.

Mani takes me, next, to a lake where a girder bridge is – he says – a peculiar monument to the British in India. It joins an insignificant island on which stands an insignificant mosque. The British had learnt the lesson of the Mutiny and when cutting out this artificial lake preferred to build an expensive bridge than risk destroying a place of worship. Then we go to Number 10 Sudder Street where, from the first-floor balcony – now a boarding house kept by a large Parsee lady, Mrs P. M. Sidhwa - Rabindranath Tagore saw the sunrise and decided to be a poet. Today he would look out over a seedy area given over to porn shops and hippies. The increasingly sad and depressed Anglo-Indian community also lives around here.

For lunch I insist on Bengali food which creates a problem for it turns out there are few genuine Bengali restaurants in

86

Calcutta; the traditional cooking is to be found only in the countryside or in the home. However, Mani suggests the canteen of the All Bengal Women's Union, a feminist organization formed in 1932 to combat prostitution.

We order what turns out to be a delicious meal, mainly fish. The matron sits at our table and tells me: 'The girl who is serving you is a pathetic case. She came to us destitute. We brought her up and arranged a marriage for her. Then her husband went mad so she was sent back here. Her two sons are in our children's home.' When we left the girls said to Mani: 'Thank the English sahib for coming to us rather than eating at the big hotels.' The entire meal cost about 40p for two.

During lunch we talked about begging. Mani tells me that being brought up very properly he was taught never to refuse alms. It was bad manners to say no to a beggar, the old custom was to dispense a handful of rice. Nowadays, most people tried to give something each day, however small.

Some of the beggars were highly organized professionals. They worked in rings and the master beggars were many of them quite rich. From begging you could graduate to petty crime, for example picking pockets. That could be dangerous because if you were caught the crowd might have torn you half apart by the time the police arrived. There was a high degree of specialization among thieves. For example, among car thieves there were people who specialized in particular parts, windscreen-wiper men and so on.

Many would rather commit suicide than have to beg and there were many who did. But begging was not looked down on in a religious sense. As a brahmin boy, Mani's parents had given him his symbolic begging bowl in the form of half a coconut shell and he had to say to his assembled relatives: 'Oh gentlemen, give me some alms,' and they had thrown some rice into it.

Ashok Mitra sits at his desk in the Writers' Building on Dalhousie Square beneath a blown-up photograph of Karl Marx. This late Victorian building, named after the clerks or 'writers' of the East India Company, was the Whitehall of India until the capital was transferred to Delhi in 1911. Now it houses the Marxist government of West Bengal of which Ashok Mitra is Minister of Finance.

Mitra is an academic economist who has spent some time in the United States and Britain, served a term as economic adviser to the Government of India in Delhi and in his spare time written a column about Calcutta for the influential *Economic and Political Weekly*. He is a fast-thinking, fast-talking operator in his forties with a somewhat arrogant air of intellectual impatience; I have met several of his type in Cambridge, Massachusetts.

He quickly slaps down my suggestion that the Communist Party of India (Marxist), a breakaway from the CPI, is to be compared with Euro-Communism. 'We have not abandoned Marxism-Leninism, we remain a revolutionary party,' he declared.

I consulted him about Indira Gandhi, he having worked for her in Delhi. He said he thought her comeback would prove short-lived. Most of the political elements in India were determined not to see her back in power. Once the country got used to the idea that she was no longer there, the populist elements would regroup around his own party, he hoped. Mrs Gandhi did not simply threaten one-party rule but one-family rule; she believed that India belonged to the Nehrus for ever.

We talked chiefly, however, about Calcutta and West Bengal. They were suffering, he said, from all the symptoms of general economic regression including deplorable civic facilities. West Bengal had never really recovered from partition in 1947 when seven millions arrived from Pakistan and fewer than one million emigrated in the opposite direction. The collapse of West Pakistan had brought another influx in 1971. Since the mid-60s industrial output in West Bengal had actually declined by about 40 per cent whereas in India as a whole it had risen by about the same amount.

The British legacy had been one of mercantile, and not industrial capitalism; the ethos of Calcutta was in favour of making money not goods.

The population of metropolitan Calcutta is around the seven million mark. Only about half a million of them live in self-contained houses or flats. About one-and-a-half million have no homes and live in offices, factories or the streets. Nearly two millions live in hovels of mud or unbaked brick or in bamboo shacks. The greatest number, some three millions, live in multi-occupied houses of baked bricks, most of which are overcrowded, unhygienic slums. So when Milton McCann, a business executive, decided to devote his spare time to helping alleviate the misery of life in the Calcutta slums he had plenty to choose from.

That was in 1968 and he selected a totally forsaken pocket of the south-east city called Sapgachi. There is more open space than I had imagined, although most of it is derelict; trees manage to grow and children risk their health bathing in stagnant cisterns around which the washing dries bone-white in the sun. There are industries too but mostly nasty ones, polluting and hazardous – tanneries, rubber factories, alkali plants.

The slum has its own class structure – landlords, merchants, craftsmen: it is a kind of city in its own miserable right, a self-contained hell hole.

When Mr McCann first went to Sapgachi, he told me, the responsible mayor didn't realize that the miserable place came within his jurisdiction. The water supply consisted of two tube wells, there was virtually no drainage, no roads; most of the people were unemployed and the children covered with the skin diseases which result from malnutrition.

Today McCann's organization feeds 500 babies, provides mid-day meals for 2000 aged three to twelve, distributes three slices of bread a day to another 1400 and milk to 1500 aged three to six; it runs a school with 900 pupils, a small hospital and outdoor medical service, a metal-working shop, a hand-weaving centre and a tailoring department. There are now sixteen tube wells and three filtered water lines, latrines, electricity and some roads.

The emphasis of McCann's work is on what he calls 'gracious rehabilitation', that is helping people to help themselves and each other; for example, by teaching selected mothers hygiene and childcare he hopes to spread the word around the slums. The Bengal Service Society has more than four hundred people working for its projects, all but twenty-five of whom are from the slum itself.

McCann is desperately short of medical supplies. He tells me he used to receive valuable consignments of drugs from War on Want but then suddenly they stopped without explanation. Help the Aged stopped sending blankets and Oxfam ceased to help at the time of the Bangladesh disaster. McCann wants to develop his work in rural Bengal. The poverty there is worse still and is the source of the influx into the city. McCann says: 'I believe that you get better results, quicker, through small autonomous organizations such as this one.' He is a remarkable and admirable man. To visit Sapgachi is to be moved by the spirit of human hope and dignity. The address is: Milton McCann, Bengal Service Society, 4E Sapgachi 1st Lane, Calcutta 700 039.

The Bengal Club has survived by selling off its lawns for real estate. The final copy of *The Times* gathers dust on the table of the Reynolds Room. The Raj lingered on here: the names of past presidents are listed on a board of honour – T. C. Hornsby, A. D. Ogilvie, J. M. Parsons . . . The first Indian took over only in 1968 with D. P. M. Kaga.

At the Victoria Memorial you still get some feel of what it was like. Riding in a bullet-proof limousine can be nothing to riding on a ceremonial elephant. It is strange wandering around this great Edwardian mausoleum to hear the words Queen Victoria in the mouths of Bengali school children. How many English children have heard of her? The defiant black statue of her outside the museum was built to last a thousand years or more.

The Anglo-Indians are a dwindling but ever more pathetic community. When I ring up to ask for Mr O'Hara a voice says, 'I'm afraid Mr O'Hara is off station.' That is Anglo-Indian for out of town. People do still talk about 'home'. They fantasize about aristocratic forebears. They go on bringing their children up English. Mrs Duncan says, 'You see our whole outlook was of the British heritage. It was there in everything we learnt and read. I can remember doing my lessons in the Colonial Exercise Book.

'I can remember the coronation of George VI in Calcutta. He was our king. The papers were sent out from England. My family were railway people. We don't know who my Indian ancestor was.'

The Mary Cooper Home, run by the East India Charitable Trust, is a last home from 'home' for the Anglo-Indians. Most of the residents are women long ago widowed, the wives and the daughters of railway officials or soldiers, alien leftovers dying in their own land.

BENARES – The Holy Hindu City. A repellent holy man pursues me through the bazaar to the Golden Temple which must be one of the filthiest wonders of the world. Non-Hindus may not enter but, peering through the gate, I glimpse a cow shitting. Gandhi was greatly shocked when he came here to open Mrs Besant's university.

The streets are vastly more crowded than Calcutta's. People here are a 'very problem' says a rickshaw driver. The beggars are especially undeserving. At dusk the Ganges is like an ocean, the far bank invisible. Cow bells meld with the distant cacophony of bicycle bells and cymbals.

In the morning the guide explains: 'First they will do some ritual things, then they will take the holy dip.' He is used to giving orders; he says he was an instructor with the Northamptonshire Regiment. As the sun shoots into the sky over the far bank of the river, the 'holy dip' commences.

Most of the Rajah's palaces are closed and deserted, kept going by one or two servants. Monkeys roam their parapets. The brahmins squat on their platforms under big umbrellas. They remind me of Silver Ring bookmakers. Touts sail out to us in boats. There is no escape. Holy India. Back to the hotel for breakfast. A telegram from the editor. England needs me.

3 March 1979   **Peter Jenkins**

Keeping tabs on pilgrims' progress

The word 'Bicester' is murmured with reverence these days in the Hajj research centre of King Abdulaziz University at Jeddah. The Oxfordshire town has come up with a cure for the university's hated annual task of pilgrim-counting.

Every year increasing numbers of Moslems trek to Saudi Arabia to pay their respects to the Kaaba and related holy places in Mecca. The trip is the high point of a Moslem's life and last year an estimated 1,500,000 worshippers went. But Mecca and Medina, where Mahommed was equally active, have grown less and less able to cope with the reverent crowds because of unreliable statistics.

The Hajj centre staff, the foremost Saudi authorities on Islam, used to work out the number of pilgrims by taking aerial photographs of the vast crowds round the Kaaba and doing a headcount. Then earlier this year, engineering lecturers at Jeddah read about a new fogwarning system on Britain's M1 motorway in which micro-processors connected to electronic circuits monitored the traffic. Enquiries led the Saudis to Bicester, where the Golden River company has been pioneering the use of microchips in traffic counting. Discussions established that a machine could be made for monitoring pilgrims and a hasty bit of exporting was organized. Installed in a hut on the road from Jeddah to Mecca, which most pilgrims travel, the micro-chip surveillance began.

The electronic classifier's great talent is in distinguishing pilgrim buses from all other traffic. Every time one sways past, with its burden of up to 120 Moslems, the chip registers and sends a message by land line to the Hajj computer at Jeddah. The researchers then simply multiply the number of buses by their likely payload and enter the day's tally in a book.

Mr Michael Dalgleish, the managing director of Golden River, said: 'The essence of the whole operation is that it is so discreet. You wouldn't want turnstiles in a religious ceremony.'

6 January 1979   **Martin Wainwright**

Collaring a godless dog

'Secret passion of the amorous pastor: Married minister who fell for mill girl' – it is a good five months since this archetypal headline appeared in the *Daily Mirror*, and although we would not claim to have monitored everything the paper has said in the meantime we would certainly have noticed anything approaching 'a deliberate policy of denigrating the Church'. Such a policy, according to the Bishop of Crediton in his diocesan letter, has been adopted by one of the national newspapers, but he does not say which. A pretty conundrum.

It can't be the *Sun*, the *Express*, or the *Mail*, which are models of daintiness in this if not in other matters. The *Guardian* is

'None of this would have been allowed to happen on the old wave-lengths.'
5 December 1978

unfolding no such policy; it is not even at the memorandum stage. *The Financial Times* does not go in for campaigns, except on behalf of fork-lift trucks, and the *Morning Star* can presumably be excluded from the reckoning because, although it could not fairly be described as a clerical newspaper, its stand on the subject is known and would not force the bishop to cloak his accusation in the mysterious language he chose. Is it one of the Sundays? Not the populars, presumably, because the scandals they regularly print are printed not for their own sakes but as examples of affronts to the godly which the press has a high duty to expose. *The Observer* is apostolic in tone if not in content. If the *Sunday Times* has a campaign going it must be deep in some unread sub-section of a little-known supplement, and the *Sunday Telegraph*, like its daily companion, is the nearest thing that scrupulous Anglicans have to an *Osservatore Romano*. That leaves *The Times*, and although there is undoubtedly a whiff of popery about it, a hankering after indulgences and relics, it is not anti-Church as such. Only this week one of its contributors was remarking, though admittedly in an oblique way, that there might be an Ultimate Purpose.

So the evidence is scant. Prime Minister Wilson used to entertain conspiracy theories about political correspondents and they did him no good. The bishop should learn from that experience. He would be well advised to take a month's leave and then see if things look any different. If not, of course, it will be his duty to name names, but if he then comes up with the *Socialist Worker* it will be the episcopal con of all time.

29 September 1978 **Leader**

Not in front of the parents

One of the many crunches of parenthood comes when you have to face the fact that though your children may not actually be lying to you, they are certainly not telling you the truth, the whole truth, and nothing but the truth. They are, in other words, keeping things from you.

Initially, they are not very good at it, which is how you know it's happening. Long silences behind closed doors, in-jokes and meaning looks, the whole, 'Where are you going? Out. What are you doing? Nothing,' syndrome – all indications that your children are beginning to have private lives within which mysterious terrain you are persona non grata. Suddenly you find yourself mouthing time-worn phrases like, 'You treat this place as if it were a hotel' – signs that this exclusion is hard to take.

No wonder. Just the other day, it seems, you knew every single thing about them, things no other human being will ever know in quite the same excruciating detail. Every day you washed and dressed them, noting every blotch or scratch upon their bodies, cutting nails, wiping noses and bottoms, watching every change of mood, monitoring every mark of growth. They were transparent, you could hold them up against the light and see right through the pink flesh to their innermost selves.

And then, like a mirror too closely regarded, they begin to mist over, become cloudy and, eventually, almost impenetrable. It is not an easy transformation for a parent to accept; it is not nice to be nudged, however politely, from the front seat of the Dress Circle to the Gods, behind a pillar. It is particularly disagreeable if you have always rather fancied yourself as tolerant and understanding, in touch with the world and its ways, and therefore sure that your children cannot find it as hard to confide in you as you found it to confide in your parents. What secrets can they have that you could not be privy to, help with, or laugh about with them?

The answer, of course, is that the essence of a secret is its secretiveness, particularly from you. The child is busy creating a separate identity for itself, setting up a private life in which privacy itself is the most important ingredient. Somebody once said that the first lie a child tells is a milestone in its development because it shows an awareness of the possibility of that necessary separation.

Understanding this should bring acceptance, a willingness to sit back on the sidelines and wait until the child has become an individual sure enough of itself to readmit you. But how often does this happen? All the time I hear adults talking of their parents and I am forced to realize that many of those parents know less about their children than friends, casual acquaintances, or colleagues, less even than a neighbour or the local laundrette lady.

There seems to be something about age that makes a lot of children embark upon the long slow journey that ends, when their parents are elderly, in total censorship. And I am not talking of families alienated from each other by distance or quarrels – I mean parents and children who see each other frequently, love each other, and still manage never to communicate anything that really affects their lives.

A daughter is unhappy with her husband. A grandchild is caught shoplifting. Another is seriously in debt. A son is anxious about losing his job, worried about his health. Do they mention these problems to their parents? No. On what grounds? 'I wouldn't want to worry them.'

'I think you've reached the point in your life, son, when you've got to decide whether to join The Special Patrol Group or end up in one of The Chief Constable of Manchester's penal camps.'
15 June 1979

Much smaller things are also kept secret. A row with a friend that causes depression. Some book that has interested and absorbed. The whole area of work, which takes up half of life. Even political ideas, religious beliefs, the way you decide to vote.

Do parents contribute in some way to this blanket censorship? One man justifies his refusal to confide thus: 'My mother loves me and so it would upset her to hear such-and-such about me – I'd rather tell friends who can be more helpful because they don't care so much.' What an indictment of love, that its so-called 'caring' disqualifies it from anything as useful as concrete advice and help.

If parental love really is the bedrock we all pretend it is, why does it so often fail so badly when confronted with any slightly unsettling or downright upsetting reality? We may know from bitter experience that parents would, indeed, make matters worse by crying and wailing and beating their breasts in a thoroughly unhelpful manner and then, of course, we cannot be blamed for keeping our own counsel. But I believe it is more deep seated than that. It seems that to keep that counsel is now an absolute convention in our society, a definite policy aimed at excluding older people from life, under the protective cloak of 'kindness'.

One woman I know went on pretending to her mother that she and her husband were happily married when they were actually right in the middle of divorce proceedings. She did it because everyone expected it of her. Her mother was old, after all.

Another woman who writes once a month to her mother-in-law told me that of course she had not mentioned a miserable thing that had recently happened to one grandchild. Why of course? I asked, and she looked startled. I mean (I added), you don't know her that well, do you? You can't be sure how she would react. You tell her all the good things and you say you think she's a calm and sensible sort of woman. Why didn't you tell her? Well, for goodness' sake, she said. My mother-in-law is eighty-two, you know.

I can't say I look forward to being eighty-two myself, but I look forward to it even less if I must face the knowledge that no one, including my nearest and dearest, will tell me anything of what actually affects them deeply. Rose-coloured glasses are all very well but surely they shouldn't be handed out automatically just because your hair is whitening? Surely someone could ask your permission before they force them on your nose? Or does some sea change occur as you grow old that makes you want to sacrifice all truth in order to waltz, untroubled, into a perfect, B-movie, one hundred per cent artificial sunset?

3 May 1979   **Jill Tweedie**

A country diary

North Jutland: The vast deciduous wood is interspersed with dark stands of conifers and intersected by a multitude of paths. Under the trees May lilies and chickweed wintergreen were in delicate white flower, with lilies of the valley and tall Solomon's seal. For some time we listened to the chipping calls and peculiar varied 'song' of crossbills but, although the birds were obviously very close to us and quite ignored our presence, they remained invisible in the dense black tops of the conifers. A great spotted woodpecker climbed up the trunk of a spruce and a buzzard rose from the ground at the edge of a forest pool. Beside the wood a hen sparrowhawk was hunting over a field of knee-high grass, flying only a yard or so above the ground. Beyond the meadow, the short turf and even the shingle down to the Limfjord was spangled with bright low-growing flowers – purple thrift, biting stonecrop and bird's-foot trefoil like pools of gold, white sea-campion, sky-blue germander speedwell. A big hare cantered away from us over the flowers. A chain of shallow fresh-water pools lies between the low sandhills and the sea, and the distressed calls of a pair of ringed plover, as they flew around us, led us to their chick, a tiny atom of grey down already showing the white eye-stripe of its adult plumage, crouched motionless at the waterside.

26 June 1979   **L. P. Samuels**

Separate rooms

Cathleen Nesbitt celebrated her ninetieth birthday yesterday. She made her first appearance on the London stage in 1910. She met Sarah Bernhardt. Name any English or American actor or actress of the last seventy years, and she has worked with them. She knew the Lunts before they knew each other. She still takes all the work she is offered. This summer and autumn she played at the Chichester Festival. When we met at her flat in London a few days ago she had just returned from the retake of some television thing about which she declined to talk, saying she didn't want to be libellous.

As a little girl she went round the world on the tramp steamer of which her father was captain. She remembers herself, aged eight or nine, sitting with her back against the warm funnel reading *Little Women*. She always had her head in a book, and was never seasick. By the age of ten she was a well travelled girl. She remembers seeing Constantinople by moonlight. When she first saw Paris she thought: 'How like Buenos Aires.'

Back home at school in Belfast she shared the history prize of £20 with Helen Waddell, who was to become a celebrated medievalist, and took herself off to Paris to learn French. Later she became an au pair at Lisieux. Her arrival there, in the dark, sounds like something out of *Villette*. Back in London at drama school, she suddenly felt one day that she had authority as an actress. She was playing the part of a French children's nurse. She *knew* she looked as a French nurse should. Even now, she says, when she has been at it for seventy years, if she feels she is absolutely right for a part it gives her a confidence which communicates itself.

She certainly had confidence, though she was shy. In 1911 the Abbey Players came to the Court (now the Royal Court) in London, and needed understudies for an American tour. With the rashness of the very shy, Miss Nesbitt approached Lady Gregory, saying, 'I am an actress.' She recited one stanza of *The Lake Isle of Innisfree* to Yeats, who said wearily, 'Enough,' and she had the job, and made her first visit to America.

Once again back in London she played Perdita in Granville-Barker's production of *The Winter's Tale*. Henry Ainley tried to seduce her while his mistress was having a baby. Harold Macmillan saw her Perdita and later told her how enchanted he was. Rupert Brooke saw it several times, asked to be introduced to her, and was at a party given by Eddie Marsh, later Sir Edward and a friend of Churchill and of Maugham. So began their affair.

Brooke was not the languishing romantic that his reputation has made him. 'Oh, good God, no,' says Miss Nesbitt. 'He walked miles and taught me to walk miles.' At weekends they always took a train somewhere, then walked, and sometimes stayed overnight at an hotel. Mrs Belloc-Lowndes once saw them together in a railway carriage and felt a wave of magnetic attraction between them. Miss Nesbitt understands this. Today, in a tube or a bus, she sometimes watches people, and, if they're not conscious they're being watched, can feel what they are thinking about or hear what they are saying to themselves in their minds.

Brooke read her Donne and Shakespeare. She remembers Shakespeare's terrible sonnet beginning: 'The expense of spirit in a waste of shame/Is lust in action . . .' Brooke had written a poem called *Lust*, which the publishers retitled *Libido*. In the copy he gave her, and in all his presentation copies, he crossed out Libido and wrote Lust in his own hand above it.

They always had separate hotel rooms. 'That would seem so strange today. He would come in and talk to me, and sometimes talk away, and lay down his head and go to sleep. But he would always go back to his own room. So we were never lovers together in the modern sense of the word. I suppose in today's climate we'd be living together from the word go.' As it was, she was getting over Henry Ainley, and Brooke was recovering from an unhappy affair with a girl at Cambridge, who had lived with him, who had suffered a miscarriage, and with whom he had fallen out of love. So they were both thinking that this time they wanted to be certain.

There were long absences during their acquaintance. They met in December, 1912. The following May he went across America and to Tahiti, where she thinks he was in love with an island girl. Something in his letters told her this; she knew that he had found something warm and comforting. When he returned in May of 1914, the war was upon them, and soon he was dead.

'And then I suddenly felt, "Oh, it's so awful. He's gone, and there's no issue. And if I'd had a child by him . . ." ' They last met at Yarmouth, when he came to see her on tour. They were very close then, and she thinks that if his leave had been longer they would really have been lovers.

Did he want children? – 'Yes.'

Did Miss Nesbitt still feel she ought to have had a child by him? – 'Still, I sometimes do. Particularly when I used to go and stay with Mrs Brooke, his mother who's godmother to my son (by her later marriage). When I brought the baby there to spend weekends, I'd feel a little pang. If only I'd had more sense . . .'

After Brooke's death she went again to America, in the middle of the war. A Russian called Boris, who sold tickets for a travelling company, told her she had the face of a lioness cub and asked if it was true that she was still a virgin. She was then about twenty-nine. She thinks the Russians are amazing people. She told him she was. He was astounded, and very gently said goodbye.

Late in 1920 she accepted Charles Morgan's invitation to play Cleopatra in the Oxford University Dramatic Society's production of *Antony and Cleopatra*. Her Antony was Capt. C. B. Ramage, president of the Union, who proposed to her and was accepted at the dance the night after the play. 'I'd only met him in the time we rehearsed. He was very good-looking. He'd a beautiful voice . . . I suppose playing Antony and Cleopatra together we got closer than if we'd known each other as just people who met in the street.'

Ramage became a Liberal MP in 1923, and then, says Miss Nesbitt, there was an election and something called the Zinoviev Letter, and he lost his seat. He never won another. They had a son and a daughter. They separated in the late 1940s.

Throughout the 1920s and thirties, and throughout the war, Miss Nesbitt's career went well. In 1949 it flowered when she played in *The Cocktail Party* in Edinburgh, London, and then in America. She settled in New York, going out to Los Angeles every now and again to do a film or some television. It was only in 1969 that she returned to live in England again. She can't remember how many films she has been in. She would have said seven or eight, including *So Long at the Fair, Three Coins in the Fountain,* and *Separate Tables.* But the other day an American told her she had appeared in thirty-seven. 'Pictures I'd completely forgotten. One with Maurice Chevalier. Films with – what was that girl's name? – Margaret Lockwood.'

In all that time she got on with nearly everyone, which is a miracle for an actress. Marlon Brando (with whom she played in *Desiree*) was a darling with charming manners. 'And there's an actor called Nicol Williamson, always known as a wild man. I played with him in New York and found him enchanting. He's very talented. He played Uncle Vanya terribly well, and afterwards he sang to a steel band . . . Nothing he can't do.'

She and Bryan Forbes were talking one day, and saying what nice people actors and actresses were, on the whole. She said she could think of only one she had actively disliked, and he said so could he. They both wrote the name on bits of paper, and it turned out to be the same name, that of the late Nancy Price. 'And I must say,' said Miss Nesbitt, 'she was the worst bitch.' In 1938 Miss Price was producing and also acting the mother-in-law in *Thérèse Raquin*. The posters said: 'Nancy Price in *Thérèse Raquin*,' and the names of the other actors, including Miss Nesbitt, came below. One day Miss Nesbitt arrived at the theatre to discover that all the bills had been changed, and the name of the play altered to *Thou Shalt Not Kill*.

Why? – 'She thought it made me too important, since I was playing the part of Thérèse, that the play should be called *Thérèse Raquin* . . . Must have cost her the earth to change all those bills.'

Miss Nesbitt still goes to Los Angeles whenever she is asked. In her flat she has an Emmy, a television Oscar, which is in two bits because she dropped it. It was for a Hollywood version of *The Aspern Papers*, an absurd nonsense, she says. They changed the name to *The Masque of Love* and set it in Los Angeles, and she made herself up to look like Clara Bow and doesn't think they noticed. There could not, she says, have been much competition, because it won an Emmy.

And now she is ninety. She says everyone seems to think that ninety is very important. 'In Bertrand Russell's phrase, at least I have the gift of survival. When he was in his early seventies people thought he was a silly old gentleman, but when he lived into his nineties, veneration crept in. And so it is, one finds. People in the theatre, which is a great democracy of age and everything else, do rather bow down and open doors for me, and things which they never did before.'

But one's friends all died. 'I was talking to Rebecca West today, and we were both saying how many of them had died. I mean – Gladys Cooper, Edith Evans, Sybil Thorndike. And then you suddenly think back, and all the people you knew when you were young, they've all gone.'

But did she feel the loss of friends with the same passion as she had when she was young? – 'I personally find I can take things, both good things and bad things, with less passion really. Because I remember I was surprised. A very good friend, Zena Dare, I met her in the King's Road one day and we made a date to get together the following week, and two nights after I was listening to the six o'clock news and they said Zena Dare had died. And if that had happened thirty or forty years ago, I think it would have taken weeks before I got over it, but as it is, it gave me a shock, and I thought: "Oh God, we were going to see each other," but . . .'

25 November 1978 **Terry Coleman**

Stopes go

The Marie Stopes family planning clinic has decided to make contraception fun. This Christmas, the clinic in London will be decked out with balloons bearing the most appalling verse which goes as follows:

Heyho, heyho, it's off to Stopes we go/Just you and me/For an IUD/Or Vasectomy/Laparoscopy/Or a pack of three/and a partridge in a pear tree.

If I were in the habit of having Christmas competitions (which I'm not), I think I would ask readers to come up with a more dreadful and groan-making verse. The Stopes hymn was written by the staff, which also produced a slogan to be used on some future occasion: Close Encounters of a Safe Kind. I don't know why they don't borrow the famous one from the Egg Marketing Board – Go to work on an egg.

1 November 1978 **Peter Hillmore**

Shirley in Wonderland

There is a look of misty might-have-been that comes over remarkable numbers of distinguished middle-aged men when they remember Mrs Shirley Williams at Oxford. No one actually leaped off Magdalen Bridge on her account, but everyone of note appears to have been in love with her and quite a few of them subsequently went into some form of politics – which must have made the House of Commons an unusually friendly place when she arrived there in 1964.

As an undergraduate she was beautiful, she was brainy and her Cordelia to Peter Parker's Lear in the OUDS production that toured America has passed into legend like Harold Acton's parties and the King and Country debate. Her admirers, even though she spurned them all for Bernard Williams, still admire. Only one, rather left wing, fellow now denies his membership of the swarm that buzzed around her. Too late; his contemporaries had ratted on him. Her court embraced all shades of Labour Party opinion.

These True Romances are important because they brought out in her a quality which has stamped many of her friendships and has a serious bearing on her political career. 'Even then she had this genius for making people do things for her – a sort of sophisticated equivalent of carrying her books home from school,' said one former suitor. 'If you loved Shirley, you were somehow put to work. Little things, mostly, and all done by kindness; she took it for granted that you would comply and you did.'

Another contemporary, also a willing victim, defined it as 'something close to an aristocrat's inbred expectation that if he dropped something someone would pick it up. It was much more nicely done than that, but a form of egocentricity all the same, an instinctive feeling that by being an exceptional person she rated an equivalent return from the world. I think she was quite right, but it was an unusual feature in a girl of her age.'

Shirley Williams was born to the political Left in much the same sense as an infant Hon. is born to the hereditary peerage.

Her birthright, as the daughter of Vera Brittain and George Catlin, was not silver spoons (though it was a comfortable middle-class family). It was knowing the intellectual establishment of the Left as friends round the tea table; it was sitting on Pandit Nehru's knee; it was being taken to Transport House when she was fifteen to join in the victory celebrations after the 1945 election.

She never had to beat her way into politics through the ranks of a trade union. She never had to find her political bearings out of anger, struggle or oppression. She was born and raised to them and that piece of good fortune may explain, partly at least, the absence of visible scar tissue, the grace with which she appears to take her politics.

Not that she had it easy in her personal life or in her career and not that she traded on her antecedents. She stuck firmly to being Shirley Catlin, for instance, while her brother signalled his relationship to their rather more famous mother by calling himself Brittain-Catlin and Shirley Summerskill dropped her father's name altogether.

She worked hard to get into Parliament, serving one election as a political agent and three as an unsuccessful candidate before becoming MP for Hitchin. She was a high flyer in her own right; her upbringing never got her a safe seat – just perhaps fewer psychological calluses before she got to sit in it.

Within two years she was Parliamentary Secretary at the Ministry of Labour. She and her husband represented 'the New Left at its most able, most generous and sometimes most eccentric' wrote Godfrey Smith in the *Sunday Times*. Her reputation as a talented woman, straight, strong and capable of tackling any job, grew steadily until, when Roy Jenkins laid down the leadership of the party's right wing, she was seen as a natural successor.

She did nothing whatever about it. It was a time of personal unhappiness – her marriage ended in 1972 and despite her Catholic scruples she consented to a divorce two years later. She was pouring resources of energy and love into bringing up her daughter. She is still prevented by her religious commitment from marrying again though she would like to. Whatever the reason, she didn't lift a finger to stake her claim and the 'Shirley is a busted flush' theory has been in currency ever since.

There was no need to speculate about the misery she went through when, possibly for the first time, her life went badly wrong. It was written all over her face. She looked dreadful and was clearly in no mood to disguise her state of mind by putting on a front as many other public figures would have done.

Such an inability to dissemble was characteristic and probably even enhanced public affection for her. But for a woman politician it was a dangerous display of vulnerability. Male MPs can go through divorces (large numbers of them do) without casting serious doubts on their professional resilience. It is still assumed that a woman in domestic turmoil will go to pieces in every other aspect of her life.

It happened to Shirley Williams at a crucial point in her career and she had to struggle harder than a man would have had to to re-establish her credibility under stress. She is clearly a much happier woman now but she has never quite recaptured the early momentum.

'These days she's simply washed out with exhaustion from going to all those education conferences,' said one MP. 'She's got herself trapped in that bloody Department of Education, all headaches and technical arguments about capitation allowances and core curricula: no real power to do anything,' said another. When she made a rather good speech at this year's party conference it was greeted as a resurrection.

She has been known to fret at being given 'women's' portfolios both at her DES and at Prices, but when friends urged her recently to get out from under in the interests of her own career it was she who insisted on sticking it out. She has suffered from lack of exposure to a mainstream economic job; she has also suffered the backwash from Mrs Thatcher's rise to the leadership of the Tories. Too many women at the very top is thought to be upsetting for the electorate.

So at forty-eight, what does she do next? Is she being wasted where she is or has she already missed her best opportunity?

She has one golden asset, recognized by even the crabbiest of her critics: she makes people believe that she is sincere, honest and caring. So far as it is possible to tell, she is indeed what she seems. You can't fake it that well with the exposure top politicians get these days, however good an actress you are. She is a pretty, smiling woman, with nice blue eyes and a way of listening with her head bent intently to one side which is deeply flattering to whoever is speaking to her.

But that is not enough. Her personality pours out to meet you, where Margaret Thatcher, for instance, seems to be holding her breath for fear some fragment of her real self might escape with the words. In an age of cynicism about politicians and all their works it is a priceless commodity. No doubt it will be used for all it is worth in the next election campaign and it will earn her the right to a substantial reward should Labour win.

Most people like Shirley Williams. A straight bat, they say. You get a fair hearing. Never mean. She can be larky too – a nosey civil servant, forever wanting to know who she was having dinner with, saw 'Evening at Covent Garden. Royal Box,' in the diary. It was none of his business, it was a private invitation from the Bonham Carters, but he insisted. 'Just put "Charles" and let him dream,' she instructed her political adviser.

Mr Callaghan, who is good at horses for courses, uses her as a conciliator when colleagues squabble. When industrial democracy was a bone of contention between the Departments of Trade and Employment she was given the job of sorting it out. 'Her mind goes as fast as a lizard, straight to the point; she is decisive and skilled at seeing the compromise that will bring a solution,' said a senior trade union official.

She has enormous energy and works extremely hard. Other Ministers may skimp on the background reading and hope that a good civil servant and some skilful waffle will make it all right on the night. Not Shirley. She is clear and forthright on big issues like Marxism (anti) and Europe (pro), impressive in the House of Commons, dazzling on television.

Good. But is it good enough to beat off the tough, professional operators who are challenging for the available space at the top and whose experience in government has given them a better chance to shine? For there are doubts.

Years ago Margaret Thatcher is said to have remarked that she would always beat Shirley in the end because she was better organized. It wouldn't be difficult. Throughout her career, there has been a disorder about her appearance, her behaviour, even – as a perceptive friend pointed out – about her use of language, that is so overwhelming that it cannot be explained away as mere scattiness or reluctance to cut short a conversation for the sake of her schedule.

People do not arrive consistently late for everything including Cabinet meetings, skid to an eternal series of breathless halts, look, act and sound that tousled without there being something profoundly tousled about their state of mind as well. Her friends insist she is a reformed character and it must be said that when I saw her recently she apologized for keeping me waiting $3\frac{1}{2}$ minutes and her office, her person and her thoughts were all in perfect order.

It is also said against her that she flaps under certain kinds of pressure. Her threat to resign if the Cabinet voted against the Common Market is sometimes cited as an example of her ability to do disastrous things on the spur of the moment. Ever since her first stint at the DES there have been damaging criticisms (emanating from the Civil Service) of her abilities as an administrator.

'Everyone loved her but she had the place in chaos and dithered badly over day-to-day decisions,' one then middle-ranking bureaucrat put it. A member of one of the two Cabinet committees she currently chairs describes the proceedings as a shambles. 'She is endlessly stimulating, quite often right but just a catastrophic organizer of an agenda.'

The obverse of her skill at mastering a brief is her tendency for knocking herself out with detail instead of identifying priorities. 'One of the oldest tricks in the Civil Service book is to tangle up their Ministers with piles of bumpf. I'm afraid that with Shirley they succeed, though she has so much stamina that she can sit up till two in the morning reading files and arrive raring for work next day. Still, it is a waste of her energy which she ought to control,' said a colleague who claims to have learnt his lesson the hard way.

There is one school of thought which says that Shirley Williams is a tough lady. It is based on her performance in internal party affairs. She is labelled as by far the most right wing member of the Cabinet and her politics come with more than a dash of moral principle which adds a certain rigour to her point of view.

'Watch her on the National Executive Committee,' said a trade unionist intending nothing but the warmest admiration. 'She is no jolly schoolgirl; she's an operator of the best. Jim trusts her to watch his back there when he has to leave early and that's a serious job.'

But surely Messrs Bill Rodgers and Roy Hattersley provide all the muscle that wing of the party requires to keep its interests served. 'They get labelled as hatchet men, but Shirley is just cleverer than they are. She doesn't get involved in loopy conspiracies, saves her guns for the winnable battles. What's more she reads the damn stuff first which gives her a considerable advantage in argument,' said a voice from the Tribune Group.

Remarkable if true. How can she be so disorganized and yet so effective, such a bruiser and yet smell so sweetly of roses? A friend outside politics had an explanation which chimed curiously with the Oxford stories. 'Shirley gets away with a lot of things because she can get people to do things without seeming to push. I mean she somehow managed to be a journalist without being able to type; she somehow travelled about the place without being able to drive until about six or seven years ago. She does it by getting people to love her and she does *that* by very hard work, genuine niceness and an enviable ability to forbear from making the quick, malicious crack that raises a laugh but makes enemies.

'The being loved thing is quite important to her. I know she'd jump at a job like the Exchequer if it was handed to her, but I also think she hasn't the stomach for a fight if that was what it would take. You can't spend all those years getting people to like you and then throw it all away. Incidentally, she is only disorganized about some things; she remembers birthdays, for instance.'

The bottom line, however, is not the NEC or her skill at dealing with paper. It is her Ministerial performance, specifically at Secretary of State level at Prices and now at Education. There is praise for her 'change of style', at both, but what has she actually done? Prices, during her tenure from 1974-6, went up

109

faster than at any other stage in post-war history. Possibly no power on earth could have stopped them doing so after the oil crisis and the last Barber Budget.

But where was she when Denis Healey put up the price of a whole range of essentials from electric light to train fares when he upturned the pricing policy for nationalized industries in his March 1977 Budget? Thinking of the national interest, say her friends. Losing a crucial battle in Cabinet, say her critics.

There was also the embarrassing business of the Red Triangle price check scheme. Unfair, say the friends. It was never intended to be trumpeted forth as an answer to inflation. It was an idiotic press office that did that and Shirley got the blame. It is a credible version of events; cheap gimmicks are not, on the whole, her style. But it still does her image no good.

Education is a job which is by general agreement poison to a political career. Contrary to appearances it has almost no power, controls almost no funds, and is at the mercy of a bunch of local authorities who may be Conservative, may be incompetent, and who certainly care more about pleasing their ratepayers than conforming to the wishes of the Secretary of State.

Shirley Williams sits there at a time of public spending squeezes and great demoralization in the teaching profession – which means that the NUT is even more awkward to deal with than usual. Even the Prime Minister's personal involvement in the Great Debate did not bring her any more money. On the contrary, it just stirred the whole pot of problems up a bit.

What she has done is to give the Inspectorate a new lease of life by encouraging them to speak up loudly, frankly and subjectively about what was wrong with the schools and what ought to be done to put it right. She convinced them they were safe to do so with her steadfast backing and as a result a series of good, important, and topical reports have come out instead of everyone hanging back until some ten-year study could establish an intuitive observation beyond fear of contradiction.

She has also set up the means by which the teaching force can be weeded, stimulated and where necessary retrained. Most of her plans will remain plans – or at best small pilot projects – until some more money arrives from somewhere, but at least the work is done.

And she has grasped the nettle of the controlled handling of falling school rolls which is technical, likely to prove unpopular with hundreds of teachers and parents but urgently had to be done. It urgently had to be done by more than one of her predecessors as Secretary of State, but none of them would touch it with a barge pole.

As a bringer back of the goods from Cabinet she is not rated as high as Margaret Thatcher by the education world. But as a conscientious goer to teachers' conferences and patient winner of consent she is infinitely superior. By comparison to her immediate predecessor, Fred Mulley, she positively glitters. 'It was quite clear when he went to his first NUT conference that he knew nothing whatever about the subject. The trouble was when he came back a year later he still knew nothing. Shirley knows her stuff.'

What will she do if Labour loses the election? There are three authoritative versions. She will not do another stint in opposition but will be off to head some American college. She will hang on whatever happens. Or she will stay until Jim's successor is chosen: if it's Healey she'll hang on but if it's Benn she'll leave on the spot. Shortest odds are probably on the last.

And if next time she gets the Treasury, the Home Office, or the Foreign Secretaryship, will it be the lizard mind decisive and darting straight to the point or will it be a case of the Peter Principle, promotion just above her maximum potential?

It was one of her most devoted supporters who suggested that the best thing the Labour Party could do with Shirley Williams would be to make her Home Secretary – 'but, and this is an absolutely essential corollary, with extremely good junior Ministers under her.'

To carry her books, perhaps?

4 November 1978   **Liz Forgan**

An MP hangs up her sword

Leaving the House of Commons is rather like arranging one's own funeral. There are effects to be disposed of. A stern letter from the Serjeant at Arms informs that, after dissolution, rooms will be locked and there will be no access to the Precincts. A friendlier letter from the invaluable library asks courteously for the return of books on loan and expresses the hope that, 'we have been able to help you over the years.' Of course they have – beyond accounting. Sadly I had to return two unfinished books – a volume of Keats's letters, and the most recent life of Andrew Marvell. I am fascinated by Marvell – an MP under both Cromwell and Charles II and, like me, a one-time servant of Her Majesty's Government in our embassy in Moscow.

I hasten to add that I shall not follow Marvell's action of publishing correspondence with his constituents – 400 letters between 1660 and 1678. They couldn't have minded, because they sent him ale and salmon and, as Members were not paid in those days, they agreed to collect for his wages six shillings and eight pence a day during the session.

The problem is that, the more I read the letters, the more hesitant I am to throw anything away. Should I not keep to hand on to my successor the twenty years of correspondence about Mrs Smith's still uncured damp flat? Bells ring from long ago – letters about the hunger-striking Price sisters; about the emptiness of the still vacant Centre Point – that monument in my constituency representing false values and undeserved money-making.

What has happened about research at University College Hospital into thalassaemia among children from the Middle East? Will the Elizabeth Garrett Anderson Hospital and the Royal Homoeopathic Hospital be kept open at the end of the day? Will sad Cyprus ever be free, united, and independent?

And after a parliamentary delegation to Belize one had to ask why the Americans were selling arms and training Gautemala to threaten Belize. Did the Seychelles hospital ever get a new lift to replace the crank-handed levitation I saw there? These questions hang like bats on the wall of a cave and I cannot ask them again.

There is a peg in the Members' cloakroom with pink ribbons for each MP, to tie up a sword. It's easier to tie up your sword than find somewhere to work your typewriter. So you leave the souvenir pink ribbon behind and trundle the typewriter home.

So many ties bind a Member both to national and local issues, fixing one tight as Andromeda to her rock. And no Perseus ever comes. It's easy enough to send formal letters saying that, 'as I am no longer your MP there is no action I can take to help you . . .' As you wonder about throwing the letters away you cannot immediately renounce concern.

The sudden acceptance of impotence is one of the most difficult aspects – how to tell the woman in the baker's that you can't help get her senile mother into a home, or bring her little boy from Allahabad; tell the anxious man at the bus-stop that you can do nothing about his son in prison, and absolutely nothing about his housing application, or the noisy dog upstairs. You slough off the layers of responsible skin slowly.

On all sides it is said that politicians are losing public prestige (an impression encouraged by broadcasting Parliament – and may there never be television further to distort and devalue). I sometimes envied John Stuart Mill, who stood for Parliament in 1865, only on condition that he would not canvass, nor pay agents to canvass, nor attend to the local business of the constituency. He spoke, under pressure, at only one meeting. He lasted only three years as a Member of Parliament but his influence was worth a hundred years of other Members. Not least because he moved an amendment to Disraeli's Reform Bill to omit the word 'man' and insert 'person'.

But I must say that when anybody wants anything done, they enhance their Member of Parliament with total omnipotence. The man in the pub last week who was saying that politicians are a useless lot of parasites, was on one's doorstep yesterday saying that as you are an MP you should get his electricity bill cut, reduce his rates, get more legal aid for his errant brother, improve the 53 bus service, and castrate all cats.

The continuing problem in an MP's life is working from

concentric circles. You start with responsibility to the local party which selected you. You accept that there are changing patterns within that comparatively small group, and that a resolution passed last year might be defeated next year as personnel alters, especially in volatile Central London constituencies.

Then you have to try to assess the opinions of constituents who may not be attending, voting members, or supporters of the local party. And here an MP cannot win by being all things to all men and women. Constituents want more shops open on Sunday, or all shops closed on Sunday; they want more abortion or no abortion, hanging or no hanging. This is where you cannot be arithmetically answerable to your constituency.

I have received a majority of letters in favour of capital punishment, of keeping the blacks out and against abortion, all accompanied by threats of vote withholding. But, democracy or not, I believe, without any mandarin pretensions, that the House of Commons often has to give a lead to public opinion and not always follow it, sometimes in spite of lobbies and demos.

Certainly it would have been easier to count the letters and take Vicar of Bray instructions in the hope of majority votes. But that is not right. Back to Burke: 'Your representative owes you, not his industry only, but his judgement; and he betrays instead of serving you if he sacrifices it to your opinion.'

Then there is the discipline of party policy, which is not always the same as Government policy. The Labour Party is a broad church and there is much more tolerance and respect for deviance than when I first arrived and the Chief Whip (William Whitely) seemed to spend most of his time seeking for MPs to expel.

Much has been made of the tensions between the National Executive and the Government. But this is nothing new. I found in my compost heap of files an extract from a Party Political Broadcast by Dick Crossman on 11 October 1960: 'Now the conference is, of course, the final authority and we, the members of the National Executive, are elected to carry out its decisions. It goes without saying that we shall do so. But it has always been recognized that the Parliamentary Labour Party is in a very special position. On no account can it be instructed or ordered about from outside. Having said this, however, I must repeat the warning which Morgan Phillips gave last August. A Parliamentary Labour Party, he wrote, could not for long remain at loggerheads with the conference without disrupting the Party. I believe every Labour MP should bear this in mind during the coming weeks.'

So you fill an old carrier bag with your coat-hanger, a spotty little mirror, the spare shoes for lobby-tramping, a half-empty bottle of face cleanser which tried to take the midnight grit out of the wrinkles. This is all the luggage left to take across the Styx. And you drive off, knowing that now you must take the House of Commons label off your windscreen and buy some plain writing paper with no crest upon it. And a lot of stamps. For you have finished with OHMS – and she with you.

24 April 1979   **Lena Jeger**

Heavenly bodies in the Lords

The Earl of Clancarty launched a full-scale debate in the House of Lords last night to call attention to the 'increasing number of sightings and landings on a world-wide scale of UFOs'.

'Suppose,' said the Earl in a chamber which was suddenly thronged with peers who had been absent for such mundane matters as the committee stage of the Arbitration Bill, there was 'a mass landing' of UFOs in Britain. He thought that there might well be panic because the people were not prepared.

Despite centuries of prior warnings and thousands of sightings, with fleets of flying saucers sighted as early as in ancient Egypt BC, we were still suspicious, he said. In World War II the British and German pilots alike kept on seeing 'strange circular lights' outside their fighting craft, and thought them secret weapons. Since then the world over thousands of people have had the encounters.

His Lordship conceded that there might be the odd crank or 'hoaxer' among them but the majority were sincere people – policemen, radar operators, pilots and, of course, Lord Clancarty himself. He has a picture of one in his study.

His Lordship had the courage not to conceal from the House and the packed gallery the unacceptable faces of flying saucers – their lights were often so powerful that witnesses' faces and hands were burned. They stopped cars, tractors, and aeroplanes. They lurked in the vicinity of power lines in America and seemed to cause blackouts, they even loitered close to arsenals where nuclear weapons were stored.

This was no reason for fear. Lord Clancarty reminded the House that in spite of all this we had not been invaded from outer space. It was we 'earthlings' who had tended to be 'hard' on the saucers. Was it not time, the Earl appeared to be saying, that we gave saucers their due and prepared ourselves, and reversed the attitudes of international governments operating a cover-up? The House of Lords should set up a study group, he suggested.

19 January 1979   **Nicholas de Jongh**

Dancing on the grave in Amin's dead city

Tanzanian soldiers danced wildly with one another with AK47s on their shoulders last night in the disco at the International Hotel in Kampala. Outside it is a ghost city with the streets deserted and huge piles of rubbish blowing across the pavements. Every building is completely vandalized and looted.

The International Hotel is an oasis of working normality in this dead city where most of the people on the streets in the city centre are Tanzanian soldiers. In the night club only the band and the good-time girls are Ugandans. The Tanzanian soldiers with bottles of beer and whisky on their knees are like schoolboys on an outing. One soldier had an RPG (rocket propelled grenade) on his shoulder which could have blown us all out of the hotel if he had slipped and fallen as he danced.

In the restaurant Tanzanian soldiers and journalists are fed on rice and beans or spaghetti. Journalists flying in from Nairobi bring bottles of wine, but there are no openers and waiters take turns to press in the corks with their thumbs.

The same makeshift air still hangs around what were the

edifices of power less than two weeks ago. The State Research Bureau headquarters, Amin's house, Makindye police barracks are unguarded and still littered with the torn papers and photographs which the looters have not carted away. But these places are so seared into the memory of Ugandans that after the initial wave of destruction by out-of-control mobs no individual Ugandans want to look inside. 'Tell me about it, I know I could not go in,' said one professor at Makerere University.

The only university staff still driving their cars are those who say they had been storing jerry cans of fuel for months thinking of a possible flight by road to Kenya.

In the grounds of the university red-gowned groups of students are going round trying to find some of the property which was looted, but found to be too heavy to carry away or useless to its new owner. Typewriters, desks and bits of machinery dumped by the roadside are being carried back into the university.

At a celebratory lunch at Makerere one professor said: 'It is so extraordinary to be able openly to invite a foreigner home – I had begun to feel it would never happen again.' People who had taken the risk of speaking over the telephone from Kampala to Nairobi in recent weeks about what was going on have been transformed. Big open smiles and words gushing out replace the strained faces and sparse phrases of their visits to Nairobi.

At the Mulago hospital there are few patients as everyone ran away last week when the shelling began. But the patients are beginning to come back and the new Minister of Health (an exiled dentist in Mombasa for years) arrived for an emergency meeting with doctors in the afternoon to see what the hospital's immediate needs are.

In Government ministries the switchboard girls are back at work and the civil servants are returning to their desks though with the inevitable feeling of not knowing where to begin with the immediate needs of reconstructing the devastated city. Tanzanian shelling caused minimal destruction; Kampala's own citizens destroyed what had become to them 'Amin's City'.

But the huge sense of relief among every kind of Ugandan you speak to is beginning to be dulled by the fear of what is happening in Northern Uganda. A priest with contacts in Lira said that the State Research Bureau had moved into the town and surrounding villages with a final death list for Acholi and Langi and had swept through killing everyone on it and warning that anyone who touched the bodies would die too. One doctor at Mulago who sent his children for safety to Tororo when the shelling of Kampala began said he feared it would be at least another week before he would know whether they were alive. The Tanzanian army and the exiles are still walking east and north of Kampala in two columns. At their present speed, even with virtually no resistance on the roads, it must take a month to liberate the north.

More than a week after the fall of Kampala the young soldiers' exhilaration at their achievement is still the most positive thing in this broken city. One soldier neatly summed up the problem of the liberation of the northern half of Uganda when he said, 'Getting to Kampala was enough – I have been walking for two months now.'

Getting to Kampala for anyone else now means a charter flight from Nairobi. All the small planes available with pilots willing to land with no clearance at a guarded military airport are booked days ahead by the television companies and an occasional rich refugee returning. One of these flew in from Nairobi yesterday with a six-seater plane completely filled with sheets, clothes, radios and all the paraphernalia of a comfortable middle-class life in East Africa's most European city – the poverty of their relations here has stunned them.

The television companies' planes are weighed down with their more immediate needs – crates of tonic water, trays of eggs, French bread, steak in a picnic freezer, and, most important, cans of petrol for a car.

There is no transport at Entebbe. The few cars working in Kampala apart from official vehicles are hired by journalists at eighty dollars a day. Some soldiers get around on bicycles and three drove up to the hotel yesterday on a tractor. Buying petrol is a long job requiring connections in the army and it costs fifty shillings a litre.

We were lucky to land at Entebbe at the same time as a Tanzanian military transport plane bringing in some civilian aides from Dar es Salaam. A bus was waiting to take them first to Entebbe State House – where President Lule yesterday met the

British representative, Mr Richard Posnett, on the manicured lawns with their gardenia trees – and then in to Kampala.

In the vacuum of power the Ugandan police are reluctant to make any decisions or authorize anything such as journalists getting into a Government bus, but the Tanzanian officers are efficient, unbureaucratic and not only allowed us on the bus, but ordered the police escort to drive us to the hotel.

Tanzanian socialism in action is impressive. Both officers and men still involved with the tail end of a war are overwhelmingly friendly, casual, and having efficiently checked your papers, only too happy to talk quite openly.

'You mustn't write that this is a coup,' one of them explained. 'We have rooted out a whole system and it is going to be completely rebuilt however long it may take, there are no short cuts.'

21 April 1979   **Victoria Brittain**

A country diary: Derbyshire

Various things are said to concentrate the mind wonderfully – one such is to have influenza far from home, marooned (if comfortably) in a small sky-facing room which looks down a gully of red-brick Victorian houses, roofed with wet, purple Welsh slates, to the Derbyshire hills. These are low hills, not even the outlines of the Peak, but seen at a distance they have a remote, mysterious quality no doubt totally different from what they would have on close acquaintance. They have been hidden lately in mist, rain and snow, but when light falls on them they give a promise of open country beyond. What will the Cumbrian fells look like now – very wintry no doubt? When I left my garden there the witchhazel was ready to burst into its first sweet yellow flowers and the green snowdrop spikes, white-tipped, were coming up under the hart's tongue ferns. Here I can only see the bare spikes of pear trees and the top of a thin beech which still has a few sad, brown flags of autumn's leaves – but the starlings come both to sing and to murmur together, seeing out the daylight. One clear noon-day lately a few plovers went low over the roofs and, above them, a big flock of fieldfares whose wind voices seemed unbelonging to this place – all went purposefully South and West. They belong to open country, but after all it is not so long – maybe a hundred years – since this was open country, too, and maybe there were cottages by the pear trees. If you dig deeply in this garden you come on dark soil and many pieces of broken clay pipes and you must dig carefully under the compost box in spring – toads winter there and I am told that an especially fine one is comfortably asleep under a stone's lip below my window.

8 January 1979   **Enid J. Wilson**

Why 40 gallons of frogspawn hit the road

Risking one of the most disgusting car crashes in history, Mr Eric Slote triumphantly drove across Britain yesterday with forty gallons of frogspawn. The perilous journey was the start of a pioneering venture to return the common frog, *Rana temperaria*, to the pesticide-sprayed fens of Huntingdonshire.

The frog is now so scarce in the county that local children under five are unlikely ever to have seen one. Naturalists estimate that the survivors of chemical spraying, which took its worst toll about ten years ago, probably number fewer than 1500.

On the other hand, on the hills of Snowdonia, Mrs Esme Kirby has been used to estimating her local frog population in millions. She reckons that every ditch on her 3000-acre farm near Capel Curig contains more frogs than the whole of Huntingdonshire.

So when Mrs Kirby met Mr Slote at a meeting of the Snowdonia National Park Society, there was only one possible outcome. The talk turned to frogs, the two discovered their respective surplus and shortage, and the great spawn transfer was the result.

This month, the female frogs of Capel Curig started to release their annual spawn of roughly 3000 globules each. When the first signs of jelly appeared in the dykes and ponds, Mrs Kirby got on to Mr Slote at his farm in Ramsey St Mary near Peterborough, and Mr Slote got into his Land-Rover.

Together they searched the ponds and eventually filled six oil drums with spawn. Mr Slote then set off on the 200-mile transfer and arrived back in Huntingdonshire yesterday.

The frogs face a gruelling battle to survive. The odds against a tadpole reaching adulthood are many hundreds to one. Apart from its natural enemies, which include everything from hedgehogs to small humans, the tadpole's first instinct on birth is to eat its brothers and sisters.

Mr Slote is confident, though, that Ramsey St Mary will never be frogless again. The Nature Conservancy Council and local farmers are interested in repeating the experiment, as the common frog is a useful destroyer of crop-eating insects, especially ones which attack East Anglia's vast fields of sugar beet.

The episode is a further credit to Wales, which has an honourable record of kindness to *Rana temperaria*. Two years ago a £750,000 land reclamation scheme at Blaenau Ffestiniog was deferred to allow scores of volunteers to move a settlement of common frogs from a site earmarked for hundreds of tons of slate waste.

23 April 1979   **Martin Wainwright**

Hot dog days at the Nursery End

Woolmer pushed Old's fourth ball through mid-wicket. Gower gave gentle chase, slung a leisurely parabola back to Bairstow – and the first two runs of the summer were on the board.

The fielders warmed their hands in the armpits, except Brearley, the captain, who defiantly kept his in either side or back pockets, as if to underline his outburst of the night before that the dying MCC diehards 'traditionally reckoned an unconventionally or sloppily turned out side must lack discipline and had been convincingly squashed again by success'. Not to say hands in pockets . . .

At 10.50 the man in the ice-cream van at the Nursery End was quickly changing his signs to 'Lovely hot dogs'. The man on the gate, the chap in the book shop caravan, and the old fogey in the Museum each had no change for a fiver.

There was not a cup of coffee to be had in the press box bar. The general welcome at Lord's was a disgrace. Sure, there were not many of us there – but there were little thanks for the faithful ants who had travelled many miles with their sandwiches to be in on Old's opening over.

Within an hour, wouldn't you know, the drizzle drizzled. By which time, having said hello, we were on the way to Twickenham to say farewell. At least the English rugby season ended with more spirit and verve and enthusiasm than the old place has been used to of late. The once white hope, Cooper, looked now as grey and 'wise-owlish' as Brearley; it was good to see what the fuss has been about in terms of Gifford and Cusforth and Hare and, of course, the yeoman Cowling. Laird can die happy after his try. So, I suppose, can Kenney. It was the best try, the best game and the best crowd in this final's short history, but, in spite of such resolute effort from the Midlands, it was hard not to think that Britain's truly competitive season ends with the revels next week at Cardiff. Bridgend v. Pontypridd – JPR v. Tom David on Saturday must be The Match.

By the time we had returned to Lord's at least the whole place was warned by Knott's little knock. Apparently frozen fingers clapped him in and out. Packer's perky little Mr Punch had played like he used to. Certainly he had scored more runs this day than he had managed in the whole winter of the so-called World Series.

It was hard to believe that Knott and Underwood had not trod the HQ grass for fully twenty-three months. On those green hills far away, at the Jubilee Test of 1977, Knott scored a measly next to nothing in both innings and Underwood got Walters off, I seem to remember, a leg-side skier. Mr Packer had just sniffed his substantial snout into things and they were gone. Things were never to be the same again. Or so we thought. Now Pax with Packer seems to be imminent. Thank the Lord for that.

But in those two years, you know, things have really changed. In the early evening at Lord's yesterday a chap screwed up his fountain pen and tucked his scorecard into his wallet, announcing that, sorry, he had to get home to watch the snooker. 'If you know last night's result – then don't tell me,' he insisted. Snooker's suddenly got a real grip.

And soon the most unlikely folk were oohing and aahing at the news that Lucinda Prior-Palmer had done it again at Badminton. That pleased me more than I can say. A stupendous effort by a stupendous girl. Not forgetting the nag.

I looked up a quote of last week: 'Brains and foresight, planning and calculation alone are not enough to jump you round Badminton – notwithstanding a word with your Maker. Do not ever forget you have to get out there and ride. Treat every fence as if it were your last and kick on.' Apparently she did just that.

Hail and farewell to the old traditional seasons of cricket and rugby! Indeed? If we are seriously keeping a diary, this weekend was memorable because of the victory by Lucinda and the defeat of Reardon. That old order we loved is changing, I can tell you.

23 April 1979   **Frank Keating**

Horses, courses and gels

There was a classic picture in the *Daily Express* this week showing the Duke of Edinburgh, hands behind his back and wearing his haughtiest face, watching the nags go by – his shiny shoes in the middle of a steaming, newly minted load of horse dung. 'Standing on his dignity while the horses are losing theirs,' went the caption.

There was a lot of it about on top of the hill in Gloucestershire yesterday – a lot of dignity that is, and a lot of horse dung, a lot of hyphens with haughty faces, horsey accents, Range-Rovers, plus-fours, twin sets, gold tie-pins, silver hip flasks passed round by tweedy chaps in tweedy caps. Rosettes on the windscreen and a nice drop of rosé in the boot. Men with military moustaches marched about in brogues. Gels with long legs stepped out of *Vogue*.

And after the plebs and the debs came the proles in their shoals. Thousands of us in our woollies, wellies, and St Michael anoraks, with Instamatics on our wrists. The first Badminton, thirty years ago to the week, was attended by 6000. Tomorrow, for the cross-country alone, they expect more than 200,000, not forgetting a few million television viewers.

Everyone was craning for a gawp at Princess Anne. Or Mark Phillips, who is vying with everybody's darling, named Lucinda, to become the first rider to win the event four times. The Captain is riding his mother-in-law's Columbus, whom he took over the Grand National fences for the BBC three weeks ago. Someone said that the Queen was now the most successful owner and breeder of three-day event horses in the world.

The title is typically British and eccentric, for it is a four-day event. Two days of dressage, the cross-country, and Sunday's show jumping. Compared to Harvey Smith's sport, it's a whole new ball game, the equestrian version of a modern pentathlon.

The jamboree was dreamed up by the present Duke of Beaufort, who is coming up to eighty but has been called simply 'Master' in these parts since he was a toddler. He is the tenth Duke to have lived in the sensational Palladian manor house between mellow Malmesbury and Chipping Sodbury. In 1948 he walked the Olympic Games equine cross-country course at Sandhurst. He picnicked on a rug with Colonel Trevor Horn, a leading light in the horsey world.

'Another grape, Horn?'

'Not for me, Master. Perhaps a slug o' port, what?'

'I say, Horn, why don't we set up one of these shows at Badders next year? Splendid wheeze, what?'

'Absolutely spiffing, Master.'

'Right, Horn, begin work tomorrow.'

'Top hole, Master.'

Horn's first 'office' was the piano top in the music-room. Later he was given a cottage on the estate. The owner of the village shop typed the entry forms for the first competitors. The colonel spent the summer and winter riding over ploughed fields with a milometer on his bicycle. In a year he had set up an institution.

Travel the world, and anyone with straw in their hair or bow legs in the jodhpurs will mist over all soppylike at the mention of Badminton. In thirty years it has become as much a proper noun in sport than the game of the name, which was 'invented' one wet afternoon of the 1860s by two great aunts of the present Duke in the entrance hall of Badminton House.

I went to that very first Badminton. In the Easter holidays of

1949 my Uncle John and I cycled up the long hill from Nails-worth. I remember it because we were charged ten shillings to leave our old bone-shakers against the railings. And that was nearly half a year's pocket money! His Lordship is still coining it in. Deservedly so in a way, for now the event is outstandingly organized.

Last year's winner, Jane Holderness-Roddam (see, the whole thing's fired by double barrels), has to gallop through extra unfair acres of emotion if she's to do it again. For those patriots who aren't waving Union Jacks for Mr and Mrs Phillips – locals now, for their new estate is only a handful of miles away – all seemed to be rooting for Lucinda Prior-Palmer to break the record.

I don't blame them. I have met her only a handful of times. I never fail to be enchanted, a real laugher. As bright as polished buttons and as brave as a VC. And when, like yesterday, she's crisply dolled up in her dressage rig well . . . drool, drool . . . I can't take it for long, and have to head for the beer tent to cash in my Luncheon Vouchers.

I telephoned her last week to arrange an interview at her home near Andover. 'Has your style improved since that last bit of rubbish you wrote about me?' she asked. 'Yes,' I drooled. 'I don't believe you,' she said. 'Please,' I mooned, 'I'll just stand quietly in a hedge and won't interrupt the horses at all.' 'It's not that,' she said. 'It's just that you're so sarky – all that pathetic stuff about peaches and cream complexion and Jaeger scarves . . .' 'Please,' I pleaded. 'OK, I'll think about it if you send me some of your recent bits of twaddle so I can see if you have actually improved. I can't believe you have, you sarky old bee.'

It was the nicest brush-off I remember. Of course, I didn't dare send any cuttings.

In six Badmintons, Lucinda has been first three times, second once, and tenth in her single aberration in 1974. She first entered in 1972 when she was just out of her Wantage schoolgirl's gym-slip. When she walked the course that first time she came back to her parents with uncontrollable nose-bleed. Total fear. She came a staggering fifth.

The following year was the most infamous Badminton of all. The course was the most testing and dangerous in its history. *The Horse and Rider Year Book* of 1974 recalls: 'Nobody, competitor or spectator, will forget it. The severity brought dire results.' One leading official wanted to abandon the meeting. 'It is suicide. We have put the thing outside the realm of sport. What are we trying to prove?'

Half the field pulled up or pulled out. There were some rotten injuries. Lucinda won it by a mile. It was a sensational performance for a nineteen-year-old. The whole world doffed its reinforced velvet cap.

The 1975 meeting was cancelled. Lucinda won again in 1976 and 1977. She was second last year. 'Do you think she can do it again?' I asked a fierce old shire horse who was walking the course yesterday with her tweed suited husband. 'Well, the gel keeps finding the horses, doesn't she? Or is she so good that they keep finding her, if you see what I mean? She treats every fence as if it's her last – and then kicks on to the next. Kicking on regardless, that's the infallible secret in this game, chummie.'

And, just to make the point, the old girl nearly took my cartilage out with a swipe of her shooting stick. I walked gingerly back through the horse dung. It was still steaming. So were the *Harrod's* kettles at the picnic tables – just in time for tea.

20 April 1979   **Frank Keating**

Flying tonight

The Dryfly trout fishing season is just coming to an end. And a highly eccentric one it has been, as even the enterprising Japanese gentleman (who rarely smiled anyway) discovered.

In the North of England, the salmon have been so thick in so little water that it has been possible, as some fishermen expressed it, to walk across them without being Jesus Christ. On the other hand, in the South of England, there has been heavy rain which has dragged mud down into the chalk streams, obscuring the fisherman's view, while high winds have driven off the natural flies which the trout come up from the depths to grab. This has meant the elusive devils haven't grabbed at the fishermen's bait – the artificial fly - either. Expecting to hear the wailings of lamentation almost as soon as I left London behind me, I went down to the Itchen and the Test near Winchester, to see Izaac Walton's fishing grounds where, in spite of everything, an increasingly diverse number of people have been making the pilgrimage and have caught more fish than the weather promised.

There was, for instance, that Japanese. He was a telephone engineer, not of enormous personal means, who saved up to go fishing in France, Yugoslavia, and Britain. He arrived at Winchester with the very finest equipment (British), conversing in what other fishermen called 'cocktail English', and armed with 1000 flies he had tied himself, meticulously laid out in trays. Inscrutable-faced, he cast into the Test and got a fish almost at once, much to the envy of the natives fishing nearby.

Only one slight snag. He protested that it was against Japanese religion and custom to kill a fish. Every time he caught a fish, therefore, he had to appeal to someone nearby to come and hit it over the head.

Hard-pressed American tycoons can be even harder on themselves when they are fishing than when they are at their desks. A group of six wanted to fish the Test, starting at six in the morning every day. They told Lieut-Col Eric Hay, who runs a Winchester fishing shop, the Rod Box, and a complete fishing booking service with his son, that they would like someone to bring them their breakfast. So the Colonel, an easy-going man with a roaring laugh, who became something of a psychologist in his personnel selection days in the Army, brought the tycoons their breakfast personally.

American senators can be even more hard-pressed and unpredictable. One arranged a week of fishing, with extras, for £700 all-in, paying in advance. Then he had to cancel because of some important vote in the Senate. His wife wrote a charming letter apologizing; but such was the pressure on the available rivers that the Colonel was able to cancel most of the arrangements and send the senator a cheque back for most of the money he had paid. Result: the senator immediately booked for next year. Fishermen certainly know how to bait the hook.

Lieut-Col Hay pooh-poohed any suggestion that trout fishing in Walton's waters is only something for the well-heeled. A day's fishing can cost under £10 per rod or it can cost over £40, depending on the exact location and the extras. Most local landowners in the area now allow fishing in their waters, subject to supervision, and their hospitality is rarely abused.

There are exceptions. The Colonel can remember only one contretemps in the decade he has been arranging fishing, at the rate of about one thousand fishermen a year. 'This chap was banned because he was caught in a ghastly situation. He was caught fishing downstream,' said the Colonel.

What harm did it do? 'It is not a question of *harm*,' said the Colonel, drumming his fingers and looking as if he had caught me cheating at cards. 'If you go to a wedding where everyone else is in morning coat and turn up in what I am wearing now' – green fishing jacket and green trousers – 'it is the *wrong thing to do*. It is simply not tolerated.'

The offender was a director of several companies. He was politely asked to leave. He shrugged, said, 'Yes I was fishing downstream because I couldn't catch any fish upstream,' and left, apparently still secure in his private logic. The Colonel said he supposed he would greet the chap civilly if he saw him again; but of course there was no question that he personally would ever arrange any more fishing for him.

2 October 1978   **Dennis Barker**

Professional standards

What makes a good doctor? How should we choose which candidates will make the best doctors at the end of their long training – a £40,000 investment by the state?

I sat in on a day of interviews with prospective doctors at one of the top teaching hospitals. The Dean of the medical school, a physician, conducted the interviews, together with a colleague who was a consultant surgeon.

The Dean's attitude is solidly old-fashioned, surprisingly undeterred by some of the doubts and anxieties that other university admissions tutors suffer from. He placed the social backgrounds of applicants in an unashamedly important position (twenty-five per cent of the successful candidates are the children of doctors). He is a man with a strong character, plenty of idiosyncracies, boldly outspoken and more obviously confident than most people in his own perceptions of the world.

'There has been an enormous change in our intake in the last twenty years,' the Dean said. 'We get much higher attainers than we used to, and they are on average much younger. Young people who were good with their hands used to want to be surgeons. Sometimes their headmasters would send in samples of their woodwork.

'Now they have to be much more academic. The intellectual, scientific side is much more important. It isn't a matter of just learning diagnoses and cures. The diseases we see now may not exist in twenty years. They have to understand principles which they can adapt to new developments.'

That day, three girls and four boys were being interviewed. Girls make up about a third of the intake. Fewer girls apply and a slightly higher proportion of them are successful. 'There has been no change in the social class of our intake, or in the types of schools they come from,' the Dean said. 'I'm afraid we take as few working class and as few from bad schools as we did twenty years ago. We get many more applications from foreign students. We could fill the school with candidates with four A-levels if we took all the little chinki-chonks who flood the public schools. They get wonderful academic results but they don't make very good doctors. In any case they tend to go abroad and set up lucrative private practices.'

Before each candidate came into the room the Dean read out their particulars, first their name, then their father's occupation, then their school, and their exam results, followed by their interests and a résumé of their teacher's report on them.

The first girl had bad A-levels which she was in the process of trying to improve. She said she wanted to be a hospital doctor. 'I'd like to be part of a team, working with nurses and physiotherapists,' she said. What branch of medicine, they asked?

'I'm interested in surgery,' she said. 'I like working with my hands.' The surgeon said, 'Well, there are very few openings for women surgeons. In fact I think there are none for women general surgeons, and it is very unlikely that there will be any. There are some openings in obstetrics, gynaecology, and eyes.' She nodded. 'What do you think about women in medicine?' he pursued. She answered quickly. 'I very much want a career, and I think you can combine having children with medicine, if you take a part-time job while they are young.' 'Did you know the fall-out rate for women is three times greater than for men and the training costs the state £40,000?' he said. She paused and lowered her eyes and said, 'Well, perhaps from your point of view, I wouldn't choose so many women.'

The Dean leant back in his armchair and turned to the surgeon. 'Well, what do you think, old boy?' he asked. 'She'd really be rather useful in the hospital service, working in a team, probably doing something pretty practical.' They decided to set her two Be as a condition of acceptance.

The Dean tended to ask the girls more about their personalities and their emotions. One girl revealed that her mother was Italian. He asked, 'Does that mean you are a very volatile person? Do you fly into passions, great rages? Do you have great ups and downs, and throw your hands about?' She said she didn't.

Another candidate was a boy from a grammar school in Manchester. He was the only candidate that day with a strong regional accent. Although his father's occupation was read out as accountant, the interviewers unhesitatingly decided he was working class. He was a small dapper boy but quite grown-up in appearance. He had a glowing school report which said his B and two Cs at A-level had been most disappointing. He had travelled and hitch-hiked, and had taken jobs as a bookie and an industrial cleaner. He said he loved the idea of coming to live in London, and had wanted to be a doctor since he was thirteen. He had great ebullience and fluency, and at the end of the session when the Dean asked him if there was anything he would like to know, he was the only one who dared put some questions about the school's outlook on medicine.

After he had left the room the Dean smiled, and so did the surgeon. 'He's extraordinarily young in so many ways. He's had plenty of real life, with his jobs, but has he got the intellectual polish? How well would he fit in here? That's what I wonder. It mightn't be fair on the poor little old chap. The social strain could be too great.' I pointed out that of all the candidates this one had been the most relaxed. The Dean said: 'That was because he was so naive that he didn't really realize what he was up against. He has no experience of the world of professional medicine. He doesn't understand about the social differences, though he might manage well enough as a doctor. I don't think he would feel all right here unless he had very good A-levels and was absolutely sure that he was at least entirely equal to the others academically.' They set him an A and two Bs which was the highest requirement they fixed that day.

The next candidate was quite different. He came from a public school, was the son of an old student of the Dean's, was keen on rugby and rowing. He had a B and two Cs at A-level which he wasn't intending to retake. He was the only one with a distinctly sour school report.

He was a big shambling clumsy-looking young man. When asked, he said he had already been guaranteed an unconditional place at his father's hospital. 'Well, they could hardly turn you down, could they?' said the Dean drily. He had applied for Sydney Sussex College at Cambridge, and said that was because he'd heard it was the easiest to get into. He wanted to go to Katmandu in a van in his time before university. He was the second one to say that.

Picking up his report, which indicated laziness, the Dean asked, 'If you could lead a life of ease, if your father left you a fortune, would you choose to work at all?' He said he wouldn't. What would he do with his time? 'I'd buy a big house and go sailing and shooting all day.' Did he really want to be a doctor? 'Yes, I'm dead serious.' What sort of doctor? 'A country GP, working on my own. I couldn't stick the routine of hospital life.'

The surgeon said, 'You sound a bit anti-establishment?' He said he wasn't. 'Did you engage in societies at school?' 'Well, I was captain of sailing.' 'What do you really take seriously in life? What matters?' He answered, 'To do something useful and to enjoy myself.'

As he got up to go the Dean smiled at him and said, 'Give my best to your father. You're very like he used to be. Tell him that if I take you I will do my best to improve you just as I improved him.' The boy smiled and shambled out of the room.

'What do you think?' the Dean asked the surgeon. 'I knew his father, and he was just the same, but he's a very good doctor now.' The surgeon laughed. 'I would say that under no circumstances whatever would I admit him, if it wasn't that you knew his father and you say he was the same.'

The Dean said, 'Well, I'm happy to have him.' I was surprised at the decision. The Dean said: 'He's already been accepted at another school, so you see we aren't deciding whether or not he should be a doctor, but only what sort of a doctor, and I think if we take him we can make him a better one.'

The last candidate of the day was also the son of a doctor. The Dean knew his father too. 'His father is a bright chap, but completely incomprehensible,' he said. The boy was intense and serious but with a speech impediment. He spoke a great deal about the need for doctors to 'co-co-communicate' with their patients, which afterwards made the Dean smile.

He spoke enthusiastically about the role of doctor as counsellor, pointing out that recent research indicated that GPs had to deal with people's psychological ailments as much as their physical well-being. The Dean said a medical social worker could do that as well, without the highly specialized training of a doctor, and the boy had no reply to that. The Dean is wary of people who want to do good of a socio-psychological kind. Analysis of the school's drop-outs showed that desire to do social work and a wish to bring about change in society to help the roots of patients' problems was one of the main reasons for students failing to stay the course. This boy was turned down outright.

How can you tell which of these candidates might or might not make good doctors? Perhaps a single interview with people at A-level age could never reveal very much. It seems even odder that at some universities students embark on their long courses without any interview at all. As the investment involved in training people to be doctors is so great, and the character of a doctor is of such importance, it might be a better idea to run summer courses for likely candidates, or to make them work in hospitals for a while before the final mighty decision is taken.

18 December 1978   **Polly Toynbee**

Some of my best friends

If Batman's so intelligent, I asked this pretty social worker in an Indian restaurant in Bristol, how come he puts his underpants on over his trousers? It was no use: she was waving her Tandoori chicken leg, scolding the rich, explaining the new anti-Thrush campaign, and generally improving society. Every other person in Bristol, it seemed to me, is a social worker: the alternative society are the ones wearing suits.

I could have pointed out some of my doubts about social work: that we're paying for the bureaucracy rather than the field work; that it's difficult to know if social workers are effective, and which of them are no good (the jargon they talk in the notation with which they write, is strictly non-falsifiable); that perhaps prostitutes, or barmaids, do more and better social work.

I didn't tell the young woman that clients I know act differently when they do the rounds of the social services social security probation offices. They've read the play, and learned their part. Others, who really need help, don't get it because they cannot beat the system, get hold of a script.

I tried her with a Knock Knock. 'Who's there,' she said, to give her her due, 'Avon, and yer bell's knackered,' but she didn't smile, and I don't blame her. When you're altering society, there's no time for jokes, or washing up the dishes for old people. Bring me your poor and your lonely and I will remember what I was taught of Freud, and draw my salary.

I was on my way to Cahirciveen, in south-west Ireland. It's a town of some one thousand six hundred people, who smile at you, say hello when you pass them in the street. The largest building in the place is a church. I enquired whether they had any social workers: they do, but they call them priests. They have social services departments but they call them bars and street corners, and the clients talk to each other in a beautiful Irish accent with neery a mention of Freud.

Sailing towards the Skelligs, two massive rocks jutting out of the Atlantic, I saw what I thought was snow on one of them. Then, as we approached, 20,000 white birds, gannets, flew into the sky, above our heads. On Skellig Michael, I climbed the steps to the bee-hive huts of the monks, 500 feet above the sea. 'Impressive,' a German woman said to me (those Germans are everywhere). 'No social workers,' I said. Don't spread that in Bristol. They'll be here in a flash with a community scheme.

In The Anchor, that night, in Cahirciveen, Sean O'Shea tells me it's rained a lot in Kerry this year. 'We're thinking of roofing the country,' he says. Pauline McGuire (who wrote plays for the Abbey Theatre and served Brendan Behan his breakfast of a raw egg and a bottle of Tio Pepe on his non-drinking days) is serving up the Guinness. It's strange. These people are happy. They are lovely, kindly Irish people touched by the hand of God and given the sense of the crack. And they've done it all without the help of social workers or, indeed, the British.

Next morning, we go fishing, off Valentia Island and out to St Finian's Bay. I'm no fisherman (I'm really on the side of the fish) but I catch a 30 lb fish, with the help of a grey-haired old man called Covey, aged sixty-seven. Covey is a skipper; he knows the sea. The conger eels give a little scream before they die, but Covey kills them. They have to die, that's how it is, but I don't see why, not by my hand. Then at the end of the day, Covey fishes no more but goes into the cabin and looks across at the Blaskets. You will die one day, Covey, and I will be very sad.

In the Fishing Festival, Martin catches an Irish Record fish, and Harold catches a specimen, and I drink the Guinness. Everyone is happy, Covey too: they give him jobs to do in the bar, look after him. It's not his boat, but he's skipper; it's not his bar, but he moves in and out of the living-room. They seem to have time for Covey, and they don't even get a salary for caring or the title of social worker.

'Sean,' I say, complaining, 'people round here talk a lot. I can't get a word in edgewise. How long does it take you to get down the street?' He tells me about GBS getting a card saying Mr and Mrs Smithers will be At Home next Tuesday at 6.30 p.m. and GBS writes back saying so will I and then he answers my question. 'Two days,' he says. A lie. I was there two weeks and he'd only made it to the third corner.

Next day, the children smile at me in the streets, and the adults and the old. Why does everyone around here look so happy? Surely to God someone must have Thrush, an oedipus complex or something? That night, Paddy gives Hal a silver cup to borrow and Hal takes it home, carrying it carefully to drink the whisky. It's for the best shark. They're very generous with their cups around here. The fish Hal caught was a pouting.

I've never been to Ireland before. The Irish are great, especially that lot in The Anchor. We leave Cahirciveen with heavy heart, over the Irish Sea to Bristol, where we go our separate ways. Before we do we get it again: the plight of dogs and cats, the mentally handicapped, the spread of non-specific urethritis.

I dig into my curry. I could point out that social workers seem to be into the strike ethic (i.e. money); that, to help other people to be happy, it's just as well to make sure you're not miserable yourself; that do-goodery can often be a displacement activity for not accepting oneself.

I say nowt. Many of my friends are social workers. They are nice people, idealists. I believe that they want to work for a more compassionate society, that they really believe in what they are doing. They care; maybe it's because they're paid to care that I'm a bit sceptical.

The pretty S.W. tells us about an old man she sees who is alone, his wife has died, and he's very sad and depressed. She sees him once a fortnight. But do you tell him, I ask myself, that you can't bring his wife back, cure his sadness? Do you tell him that, in the evenings, when you've counselled him and others, that you go home to watch the mugs' lantern, or sit in here with your Tandoori chicken, and your denim-clad friends and pour scorn on our materialistic society?

What's the use? There are many social workers I respect: women and men, heroines and heroes, and the dupes, of our pathetically anti-social society. I could tell you a story where they took out an old man's gas stove and gave him a brand new electric one. He didn't use it: he was used to gas. I could tell you about the good social workers, too, who, in their own time, and with their own money, take deprived children to camp, because they believe society, and people, can be better.

'We have this scheme for painting old people's houses,' she

says, ordering coffee. One or two houses in Cahirciveen could do with a lick of paint; the people don't have the time; they're too busy living their lives.

I can't take any more. I leave the Rezzy. There's something sad about social work, about Bristol, about us. You'd know what I mean, Covey, if you could read this, but you don't need fancy words to tell you that it hurts to live and it hurts to die.

4 October 1978   **Tom Crabtree**

The Great Commons Gold Rush of 1979

'Order, order! The question is, comrades, do we accept the management's generous offer of two hundred and fifty quid a week, or do we not?' Cries of 'For shame', 'Too much' and 'Think of the nation, do'. Hon. Member then proposes 9 per cent plus comparability study, with £1 on account. Carried by acclamation . . .

At this point your correspondent woke up. It was horrible. Not even years of reporting mass meetings at Dagenham or riots on the Stock Exchange could prepare one for the explosive return of free collective bargaining to Westminster after years of restraint. MPs were tearing themselves apart. And for what? Gold! It was Klondyke, or Lord Barber's Budget, all over again.

Human tragedy lay all around. Helpless, we watched as Labour MPs threw themselves into a frenzy of old negotiators' dodges (linkage, up-dating and the differential abstention) to justify their demands. Heartbroken we witnessed Tory Nicholas Winterton thoughtlessly jeopardize an untainted career of blind partisanship by urging the management spokesman, Mr Norman St John-Stevas, to reconsider 'the very moderate and responsible' suggestion from Mr Callaghan.

Readers who get this far expecting a firm moral denunciation of all this should turn to one of the cheaper newspapers. Are not MPs creatures of the age, too? Have not, as Labour's gold-fevered Joe Ashton pointed out yesterday, average wages gone up by 60 per cent since 1975 (when MPs got their last decent rise),

136

while theirs have only gone up by 17 per cent? Are they not entitled to be as overpaid now as they were then?

No, what tore the heart was the masochistic ineptitude of the protracted saga, the combination of principled piety and cowardice, managing to get the worst of all worlds. Other groups who fix their own pay – company directors, plumbers – don't have this trouble. What couldn't Clive Jenkins do for these lads! True, the threat to withdraw labour would not be appropriate for all MPs and productivity bargaining had best be kept back until the Scotland Act has been repealed a little longer. But the unsocial hours, the stress, the flexible working!

Productivity-wise, the House was touchingly full for yesterday's announcement of how £12,000 a year was to be staged. And though ugly cries of 'disgusting', 'resign' and 'cowardice' punctuated Mr St John-Stevas's noble efforts to walk the tightrope not all MPs were militant – though most were.

It was hard to pinpoint the minority groupings. Obviously some Tories are stinking rich and have no objection in principle to a little more money. It can be added to the private collection of bank notes which many of them already have. The stinking poor on the other hand, those Labour MPs who believe that their pay should be tied to the average of the Bolsover tram driver, were unexpectedly cowed. Mr Michael Foot, spiritually one of their number, had to make the case for the militant majority, which he did with such reticence that Jim took over. This was only fair, since on his own admission the mess was largely his fault.

It fell to the Ulster Unionist, Jim Molyneaux, to achieve the distinction of being the only MP to suggest that the public would think better of the House if it did not vote itself 'a vast increase'. Apart from Jack Ashley, who wanted the House at least to debate the poor first, this was a minority view. With the confidence of men who face no election for five years most MPs were adamant that the public would understand.

In the middle stood Mr St John-Stevas, advancing the Government compromise hand in hand with an appeal to higher things like public respect and duty. 'Spare us!' they cried. Norman, as befits a gentleman, seemed a bit vague about the nuances of wage bargaining and insisted that the three-year deal was a two-year one. If you subtract 1978 from 1981 what do you get, asked Labour's Jack Straw patiently. Norman hedged. 'You should have gone to a comprehensive school,' cried Russ Kerr.

22 June 1979   **Michael White**

Striking attitudes

There was I, clinging to the radiator grille of a Ford Transit van, being dragged off by a police constable young enough to be my son, and at the same time taking care not to actually damage the vehicle.

Very undignified, this picketing business. Very schizoid, too, fighting the paper I have been helping to improve for nearly twenty years.

But it had to come to this. As our pay has fallen behind year after year, union activists have gained in influence. Our bourgeois values have been displaced and now we're quickly learning the tactics and attitudes of the organized working classes.

We're standing on the lines outside the *Oxford Mail and Times* building, home of a local evening and a weekly series. It's a strange picket at Oxford. The police who are clearing the way for the vans can seldom have seen the like, certainly not in an industrial context.

The abuse hurled at the boys in blue after a scuffle doesn't come from the gutter (except physically) but from the play-grounds of private schools. 'That was *quite* unnecessary,' protests little Jean, five foot nothing of fury, after a particularly vigorous shove from the arms of the law. She lets rip a haymaker at an enormous PC, missing his elbow with a tiny fist. He is incredul-ous, angry, amused. He decides to do nothing about it, and rejoins his mates.

The police and pickets form their own groups in the lull awaiting the next van. They make their own small talk. 'We'll have to arrest that one,' says an Inspector, nodding towards one of our firebrands, speaking quietly. But he means to be over-heard. When they do arrest they pounce without warning.

'That one over there's an utter *bastard*,' grits Anne, who can't be more than seven-and-a-half stone. 'My arms are an absolute *mass* of bruises.'

Around a third of the pickets are girls. We chaps as a rule are pretty sedentary and there's a sprinkling of grey hairs and bald heads among us. There's roughly one policeman for every three pickets although stone for stone it's probably more like two to one. And there's another vanload of bobbies round the corner.

The police are much better drilled than we, but we learn. Two picket members holding on to each other are worth four separate. But no violence, mind you.

There's a tarmaced area between the actual gate of the works and the public pavement. The area was provided by the company's thoughtful architect when he tastefully contoured the walls. Although it is company property it provides a sort of no man's land where the ritual of let and hindrance may be carried out.

Of course we do more than picket. Our fund-raising cake-stall at the open-air market on Saturday was a worthy rival to anything the WI could put on.

And we are producing an *Oxford Mail Strike Special* at one of the little printers hereabouts. It is shot through with indignation and dark humour and its lack of typographical elegance is compensated for by its scurrility. We sell it for 10p and salt away the takings for the weeks ahead without strike pay.

If the editors of the local papers could galvanize our energies the way the union has they would have a prize-winning edition every day.

The anger of the journalists is deep and wide. Sober-sided and formerly management-minded Institute of Journalists members, many of them middle-aged executives, who have continued working, are not working very hard in Oxford and the hilarious travesty of a paper that comes out of the works disgracefully late every day does much to raise our spirits.

The provincial editors, appalled at the consequences of their historical acquiescence to management's budgetary demands, are wringing their hands on the sidelines, pleading with the government to consider us a special case under the pay code.

Even management say we deserve more, but their hands are tied. We suspect their fingers are crossed, too.

But it *is* serious. The country needs competent and dedicated newspaper journalists, and provincial journalism is at once the nursery and the bedrock of the profession.

This is more than a strike about pay. It's a howl of protest from a profession that has been sat on too long. It must not be suffocated through lack of cash.

20 December 1978 **Jon Hartridge**

'If you're going to take the morning off for a union meeting, I had better write you a note to give to the children.'

A marked man

Lord Denning has been a judge for nearly thirty-five years,
which he believes to be longer than any other man has ever been
a judge in the whole history of English law. He will be remembered. Some judges leave no more than a few footnotes, but he
has left his mark on the law. He is almost universally remembered
as the judge who last year told the Attorney-General of England,
and told him in the rich Hampshire accent which he still retains,
'Be you never so high, the law is above you.'

Well, the Attorney-General won on appeal to the House of
Lords. And, as it seemed to me, a close reading of Denning's
judgement showed that it was not the Attorney-General he was
admonishing at all, but, on a strict construction of the words, the
Post Office Union, which happened to be mixed up in the case.

'Ah,' said Lord Denning, 'but it would be taken as (referring
to) the Attorney-General.'

It was so taken by almost everybody, surely? 'Quite right. I
think that's true . . . It was taken in a way out of its context. Ah
. . . but I don't mind that.'

Quite right indeed. Denning is a judge who would have been
happy denying the prerogatives of a Stuart king, and later in a
meeting he enacted an exchange between Chief Justice Coke and
James I. Lord Denning is not Lord Chief Justice. He is Master
of the Rolls. This means that he is chief judge of the civil Court
of Appeal, which, since very few cases go to the Lords, declares,
and in declaring sometimes makes, large parts of English law.

He lives in the village of Whitchurch, sixty miles from London,
where he was born. His father was the village draper and sang
fifty years in the church choir. The war memorial bears the names
of two brothers killed in the 1914 war. Inside, on the church
wall, is an illustrated table of the Ten Commandments, with one
vignette (which might be out of the Rake's Progress) depicting
both murder and adultery, the first as a result of the second.

We sat first in Lord Denning's library, I in a handsome red
wooden chair, with the Prince of Wales's feathers painted on the

back. Lord Denning said they were Lord Snowdon's chairs, designed by him for the investiture at Caernarvon. 'He designed them. He's in the news now.' He had bought his own and Lady Denning's chairs, and four others, from peers who did not want them. In his London flat he had six Coronation chairs too.

'Now,' said Lord Denning, having told me about the chairs, 'you've got a lot of questions to ask me? Because of my birthday, or what?' He is eighty on 23 January. We talked about the Ten Commandments, and then about trees. Thieves had been chopping down trees in his plantation of Norway spruce, for Christmas trees. 'Spoiled my lovely trees, ninety-six of them.' He talked about his two brothers who survived, one to become an admiral and the other a general, and then about his own early years. At Andover Grammar School, from the age of eleven, he always won the English prizes. When he went to Oxford he got a first in mathematics, and taught maths for a year at Winchester College before he decided he was not a good enough mathematician, and had not the instinct for it.

Why had he then chosen law? Because, he said, he was ambitious, and saw that as the best way to advancement. He took a first in law in eight months. One day, in hall, the President of Magdalen handed him down a note saying he'd won the Eldon Prize. 'Saying, "You're a marked man. Perhaps you'll be a Lord of Appeal some day." I wish I'd kept that note.'

Having no means of his own, he lived on the £100 a year that came with that prize, and the further £100 a year which he won later for coming top in the Bar exam. He practised law. He became one of the editors of *Smith's Leading Cases*, never being content just to report the case but always thinking what the principle ought to be ('ought to be' are his words), and putting that into the book, too. He took silk. In 1944 he became a judge, in 1948 he went to the Court of Appeal, in 1957 became a Lord of Appeal in Ordinary (in the Lords), and then in 1962 went back to the Court of Appeal as Master of the Rolls.

Next month, on the very date of his eightieth birthday, he is publishing a book called *The Discipline of Law* (Butterworths). As its epigraph he has adopted the following words from one of his own judgements: 'What is the argument on the other side? Only this, that no case has been found in which it has been done before. That argument does not appeal to me in the least. If we never do anything which has not been done before, we shall never get anywhere.'

'That was quite a good little thing to put in,' said Lord Denning, 'wasn't it?' (Laughter.) 'I thought to myself, well, that rather shows my attitude to things.'

In saying that, wasn't he saying the same as the first medieval Common Law judge who ever allowed an Action on the Case? (Where the law offered no remedy but the judge, considering the case 'similar' to an old one, which it often wasn't by any stretch of the imagination, in fact created a new remedy and a new cause of action.) 'Oh yes . . . That's been my approach. But of course, 'tisn't everybody's.'

The medieval judge would have done this to expand his jurisdiction and therefore his revenue? Lord Denning hoped the judge might also have done it to ensure justice, but yes.

Lord Denning, too, would have done what he did to expand his jurisdiction, say between the citizen and the State? He said that would be his instinct. In dealing with tribunals, he'd searched for ways to control them, and had done ever since.

In that sense he was clearly in the line of Common Law judges. But he had also praised the proceedings of the European Court of Justice at Luxembourg, which was Civil (derived from Roman) law. But some of the European judges saw the Treaty of Rome as a constitution of a federal Europe, and gave themselves the widest discretion in interpreting it? 'That's right. Same as the Supreme Court of the United States. Far more political than we are.'

He would have been happy in the United States? 'Well, I don't know I would have got the others to agree with me. Nine of them.'

Lord Denning has said he is 'a Portia man'. It has always seemed to me, considering Shylock's case, that she wasn't the brightest of counsel. Any competent advocate should immediately have taken the point that the contract was not only void but criminal. Surely he was better than a Portia man? (Laughter.) 'Well yes, in that way. But I'm a Portia man in so far as she says: "For, as thou urgest justice, be assured. Thou shalt have justice, more than thou desirest." '

To go, as Lord Denning did in 1962, from the Lords to be Master of the Rolls, seems, on the face of it, a demotion, though it gave him far more power. It is generally assumed he wanted less glory, but more power. 'I don't know what discussions were made when I became Master of the Rolls. I didn't solicit it. I perhaps murmured it once or twice. I hadn't really said anything about it. They must have been taking a chance on it, asking me to go there.'

Many more cases in the Court of Appeal? 'They (the Lords) have such a few. And they all get very upset, and I got upset, that the case you'd like to be on, you're not on.' As Master of the Rolls, he had a good say in what he did.

An absolute say? 'Well, I can't do everything. I have to leave something to the others, you see. But I do have a general super-vision of it. Some people think that's wrong. But I say, "What am I Master of the Rolls for?" '

Lord Denning's most celebrated recent case is that of Gouriet. The Post Office Union announced that it was going to stop all mail to South Africa for a week. This was unlawful. Mr Gouriet, whose standing was no more than that of any citizen, asked the Attorney-General for leave to bring an action to prevent the proposed breach of the law. This was denied. Gouriet went to the Court of Appeal, who on a Saturday morning gave him his injunction. Lord Denning told the Attorney-General he had no prerogative to tell the courts whether the law should be enforced or not. He also remarked that the Attorney-General's claim was a challenge to the rule of law, and uttered his words about being never so high.

It happens that he was reversed by the Lords, but for the moment that is neither here nor there. But wasn't Lord Denning, by denying the prerogative and virtual dispensing power of the Attorney-General, going in a straight line back to the constitu-tional disagreements of James I and Coke. 'I was perfectly conscious of that.'

Then Lord Denning, in his forthright Whitchurch accent, enacted a passage of conversation between monarch and judge.

James I (very angry): 'Am I to be under the law? 'Tis treason to utter it.'

Coke (quoting Brackton): 'The king is under no man, but

under God, and the law.'

But, I said, look what happened to Coke? 'Yes. He was sacked. I can't be.'

Lord Denning is one of the few judges still to have a freehold. Those appointed in recent years have to retire at seventy-five. He can stay as long as he lives or likes.

Lord Denning called himself a turbulent Master of the Rolls. His reference was to a previous Lord Chancellor, Becket. He agreed that no judge of his rank had ever delivered so many dissenting judgements, or had so many judgements reversed. Except, he thought, for Justice Holmes, of the US Supreme Court, but he doubted that. Then we came to religion. Lord Denning is very much a Ten Commandments man. He believes that without religion there is no morality, and without morality no law. And, to me at any rate, his most convincing demonstration of this had not been in his frequent denunciations of sin and immorality, but in his comments, made in a lecture twenty-five years ago, on the celebrated case of Donoghue v. Stevenson, 1932. This case virtually created the law of negligence. A manufacturer of ginger beer left a snail in a bottle. A woman drank it and became ill. She could not claim in contract because the manufacturer's contract was with the wholesaler, not with her. Lord Atkins (and this is how I read Lord Denning's account of, and gloss on, the case) said that a man ought to love his neighbour, that therefore he ought not to harm his neighbour, and that in law his neighbour was anyone who was so closely and directly affected by his actions that he ought to have them in mind when he acted. The woman recovered damages.

So, thence the whole of the English law of negligence? 'It can be said to have developed from that, yes.'

From the tenets of religion, and from a Commandment, Love thy Neighbour?

'Yes.'

And was that the single biggest change in the English civil law this century? 'Oh yes; altered the whole picture completely.'

Lord Denning had to go out to pay his gardener. He pointed out the stream and the island on his estate, the silk mill in the middle distance where they made the material for QCs' and judges' gowns, his plantation of poplars, and, over by the church, a yew tree 1000 years old. He spoke again of his Norway spruce. 'All over the country,' he said, 'there's this thieving of Christmas trees.'

Back in his library which is, he thinks, better than any other judge's, because the others sell their books, we talked about women. First the case of Gillian Ward, 1971.

'The Bradford one?' he asked.

It was. She was found with a man in her room at night at training college. She was expelled. She came to the Court of Appeal. On the face of it, there was not just one breach of natural justice, but several in the manner of her dismissal, the sort of breaches on which Denning might have been expected to fasten, and had fastened, in his development of the judicial control of tribunals. But he found against her. Why?

'She'd had a man in her bedroom for over three months, from outside, and was concealing him there. 1 didn't think that was at all right.'

But there were many irregularities in the manner of her dismissal? 'Perfectly true. If I thought it was a wrong decision I would probably have taken (advantage of) those to interfere.'

But ought he as a judge to allow his personal view of her conduct to overset his knowledge that the tribunal had acted improperly? 'Well, I would say so, yes. No injustice was done to her. She deserved all she got, so to speak. You're right in this sense, I was overriding the irregularities in the procedure.'

Condoning them? 'Well, yes, if you put it like that; or overlooking them, in favour of what was in the end a right decision as I regarded it.'

But what about the next case? Suppose a judge of first instance were taking the next case, where the merits might be different but the facts the same? The irregularities of a tribunal would have been condoned, and by Denning of all people, and he would have to follow the precedent. What could he do? Distinguish the case on narrow grounds? But Lord Denning would not approve of such distinguishing? 'No, but I am prepared to say, you see, that sometimes I am wrong. I may have been wrong in that case.'

Then we talked about women in general. In 1950 he addressed the Marriage Guidance Council on the equality of women, a proposition he clearly favoured. But he had referred to ancient

146

Rome, where, when woman became more free, the results were disastrous to society. He quoted Bertrand Russell as saying that women who had been virtuous slaves become free and dissolute. We should look upon this and take heed.

That was twenty-eight years ago. Women had since become more free. Had they become more dissolute? 'Ah, you are asking me to form a judgement on contemporary society now.'

No. I was asking him what he had observed. That, he said, was almost a judgement.

I insisted that mine was a fair question, and Lord Denning that he would rather not make a judgement.

But he was now showing a caution which he had rarely shown in court before? (Laughter.) 'I know you may well be reporting this. It may have more notice. Yes.'

Neither of us more than mentioned the Profumo enquiry, which Lord Denning conducted. He said it was old hat now. He felt sympathetic towards Profumo.

We talked about his family history. I said I hoped he might write it. He said he would if he had time. 'Although my father was a small draper here,' he said, 'he had a long and distinguished lineage.' This was derived in part from the Poyntz family, who had come over with the Normans. Lord Denning asked if his book was going to be a flop, which is a strange question from a man famous for the lucidity of his judgements, and who could easily have made a living, and a great reputation, as a writer had he chosen.

He talked about the longevity of judges. Coke, Mansfield, and Esher had all, he thought, been eighty-two or eighty-three.

Now, he did not need to retire. He could not be obliged to retire. But when he was eighty, in January, would he retire? 'No. The newspapers have been speculating, but I'm not going to retire.'

20 December 1978   **Terry Coleman**

Government on the line

The Government can tap your phone as much as it likes, in probable contravention of the European Convention on Human Rights, with no accountability to Parliament or public, no redress for the innocent citizen if this power is abused, and the only restraint on Ministers an out-of-date code of practice which is already broken time and again.

This is the situation as it has been left by yesterday's High Court judgement, when Sir Robert Megarry pronounced the English courts powerless to control phone-tapping. The unusual feature of the Malone case was that Mr Malone could prove his phone had been tapped: a detective had unwisely made a transcript which was accidently quoted in court. Normally, the whole business is kept a total secret.

When Ministers are questioned about abuses of phone-tapping, they have a ritual reply. They summon up the Birkett report of 1957, and announce that the recommendations of the Privy Counsellors in that report are strictly complied with. This is not true. Birkett said only two Ministers – the Home Secretary, and the Secretary of State for Scotland – had the power to authorize interception of communications – though a deputy could be appointed in case of illness. This was not true then – the Foreign Office and the Ministry of Defence were running international radio eavesdropping operations from Signals Intelligence HQ at Cheltenham. It is not true now for a second reason. The Secretary of State for Northern Ireland, currently Roy Mason, authorizes widespread phone-tapping there under direct rule, in the name of an 'emergency' which has now lasted ten years.

Birkett assured the public that the telephone of the innocent citizen was never tapped, only those of suspected major criminals and suspected major Russian spies. 'Under the safeguards we have set out, the telephone of the ordinary law-abiding citizen would be quite immune, as it always has been.' The report said confidently, on the assurance of officials concerned, that private

THE SPEAKING CLOCK

AT THE THIRD STROKE I WILL BE RECORDING EVERYTHING YOU SAY

BUZBY

1 March 1979

conversations were carefully sifted by 'carefully chosen' officials, matters not strictly relevant to criminal investigation were destroyed, and the remaining material was kept strictly secret. In police investigations, only about half a dozen officers had access to 'sifted' material. In the Security Service, only two officers did, although matters 'of security interest' were put on the records.

There is good evidence that these assurances are not true. The head of the Northern Ireland Department of Commerce information section disclosed in a drunken moment in 1977 that he had access to tapes made of a journalist he believed to be anti-Government quarrelling over the phone with a personal friend.

Birkett also said the Home Office should not refuse to introduce phone-tap evidence into court in order to keep the practice totally secret. The Home Office ignored this.

Birkett did indeed take up the contradictory position of both publishing all phone-tap statistics up to 1957, and recommending no more statistics should ever be given· successive Home Secretaries have relied on this to keep the extent of phone-tapping quiet. But on careful reading, all Birkett said, at the height of the Cold War, was that the number of Security Service phone-taps must not be disclosed in future. It would greatly aid the operation of agencies hostile to the state if they were able to estimate even approximately the extent of interceptions of communications for *security purposes.*'

There is no reason in the report why the number of interceptions by police, rather than security men, should not be given. (Since Birkett, the 'New Left' of the sixties, international terrorism and resurgence of IRA activity have led to the size of Britain's special branch rising from 200 to more than 1200 men.)

Birkett also assured the public that every application for a warrant to tap phones was given 'personal consideration' by the Home Secretary. This is unlikely to be true today, given the admitted increase in 'political' surveillance. Birkett did not cover the ability of police to get from a Post Office 'printometer' lists of numbers dialled by a subscriber, without having to bother with a Home Secretary's warrant.

Last year's judgement at Strasbourg in the Klass case made it reasonably clear the British Government would stand little chance of defending itself successfully there against a charge of breaching human rights. The European Court said governments could not tap phones as it pleased. There had to be 'adequate and effective guarantees against abuse'.

The British citizen, after yesterday's judgement, has no way of finding out if his phone has been tapped. If he should find out, he has no guarantees against abuse, either through the courts, or through Parliament. There is evidence that abuse takes place.

1 March 1979   **David Leigh**

Willie whirls in with whiffs of grapeshot

Mr William Whitelaw, the Tory deputy leader, descended like a tornado on the North-West yesterday.

Mr Whitelaw meets the electorate in the way a combine harvester meets a field of wheat, with impressive, even ruthless efficiency. 'Hello, how nice to meet you, how very nice to meet you, thank you so much, very good to meet you, thank you so very much,' he will say to a single voter. Show him a group of shoppers and he is among them, scattering greetings and hand-shakes like grapeshot. 'Very nice to meet you, very kind of you, so nice to see you!' While greeting one group he might spot another moving out of range a few yards away. But there is no escape. 'How are you? Oh good! Very nice to meet you!'

A team of Tory campaigners is sent on ahead to line up people to be introduced. Feeding the Leviathan is a full-time job and sometimes they accidentally catch journalists, Mr Whitelaw's detectives, and each other – anyone to gorge the endless appetite.

Now and again he bursts suddenly into a shop and rains greet-ings on half a dozen customers and assistants in less than five seconds. 'Marvellous to meet you! Very kind! Very good to see you!' One longed for someone to clutch his sleeve and say: 'But you don't know me, Mr Whitelaw! How can you know the real me, my hopes, my fears, my secret dreams?' But of course no one did. A few stopped to discuss politics and they all got a straight answer, even if it risked votes. 'I wouldn't vote for me on that basis, because I don't believe it,' he told one woman.

Almost everyone recognizes him and looks pleased to see him and only a handful declined to meet him. One teenager said: 'I am not into that kind of thing, man.' At full tilt he can meet the voters at the rate of thirteen a minute, more than 700 an hour, quite enough to swing a marginal seat.

In Barrow, the first of twelve engagements in the day, he attracted crowds of old ladies who wanted to kiss and cuddle him. Many were lucky. One tried to kiss him twice. 'You mustn't do that, they'll talk about us,' he said. Some were so smitten that they hung round and were introduced two or three times.

We descended on Tesco's where the pickings were sparse – no more than half a dozen people to be greeted at the dairy produce counter, but the dotty ladies were in wait at checkout. One of them gave him a playful but painful looking slap on the face. Another said slyly: 'I have already met you.'

'Lovely, marvellous, very good to meet you again!' To a woman who walked backwards waving a Liberal poster: 'Well, if you want to vote that way you will have to make up your own mind!'

Some of the old ladies were worried about law and order, but he flatly refuses any talk of hanging and flogging. 'Most important to boost police morale, mistake to change the law too quickly, thank you so much, very good to have met you.'

His ebullience disappears only when Ulster is raised, which it is surprisingly often. One old lady said: 'I hope you'll do something for Northern Ireland.' And he answered, sadly: 'Well, I did try, didn't I? I had such hopes when I was there, and I can never get quite away from my feelings about it.'

One supporter said: 'Your party leader is losing votes,' and he said: 'No, I don't think so, I really can't accept that.' Mr Whitelaw was always the ultimate loyalist, making faithful dog Tray look like Benedict Arnold.

Yesterday afternoon he spoke to Asian immigrant leaders in Preston. It was a good speech, though the policy might not be recognized by some Tory hawks. The gist was that all dependants will be allowed in as soon as possible, and that the controversial quota system will largely restrict new white immigration, since Asian entry is now as restricted as it can be. But the leaders, in spite of the exquisite politeness most Asians show, were clearly baffled and suspicious. It seems clear that in marginal seats like Preston, the immigrant vote will not be swinging the Tories' way.

24 April 1979   **Simon Hoggart**

Benn's bid

Tony Benn once wrote that 'the borderline between a crank and a prophet is not always easy to draw'. How true that is, and how true in particular of the Secretary of State for Energy. Certainly his crankiness is well-known and constantly described in the newspapers and the gossip of Commons bars: such as his obsessive concern with taping his own words (one BBC TV programme was held up for some time by mysterious electronic sounds, until it was discovered that Benn had switched his recorder on to playback instead of record). Perhaps the crankiest thing of all is his strange belief that though his father was a viscount and lived in a large country house – which he persists in calling a 'cottage' – he is somehow one of the working class.

But even the famous one-pint mug, which he takes everywhere to be filled with tea, gives the game away. After all, no real working class person would dream of going to a railway train buffet and demanding a pint mug of tea. They would settle for horrid Maxpax in a plastic cup like the rest of us.

And yet there is also a lot of the prophet in him. How grudging his fellow politicians are to credit his ideas after they have scorned or ignored them for so long. The referendum on the EEC was Benn's idea, and though it did him little good, it established the head count as a part of Britain's political life. Mrs Thatcher is now all for referendums.

It is Benn who has been demanding and predicting industrial democracy since the 1960s, an idea which is now the very essence of the centrist, Callaghan, Liberal philosophy. In 1975 Benn said that the Common Market had cost us 500,000 jobs, and was vilified by his closest colleagues for saying it. There are few Europeans who would dare to argue with that now.

The reform of Parliament, freedom of information, the right of constituencies to sack their MPs: all these schemes were attacked at the time as mere symptoms of Benn's lunacy, yet over the years they have edged their way to the centre of the whole political spectrum.

There are layers upon layers of myths about Benn. He is alleged to be a wild-eyed raving fanatic, yet in real life is the mildest and most courteous of men. He is not sour and dour but has a perky and witty sense of humour. In November last year when the power workers were on strike and the Government actually feared that it might be driven to another three-day week, Jim Callaghan was constantly on the line to the Department of Energy, desperate for the latest news. In calm contrast, Benn was jokingly telling his private secretary to get on the line to Helmut Schmidt and order up a few German riot police.

To read some newspapers, you would imagine that Benn wanted to set up a Stalinist corporate state in which everything would be controlled by the trade unions and anti-socialist dissent firmly trod upon. Yet the opposite is the truth. Life in Benn's ideal republic would be a constant and wearying round of democracy.

There would be discussions, debates and votes about almost everything. Hardly a decision would occur, at the highest level of government or on the factory shop floor, without motions, minutes and voting. Saloon bars would ring with talk about the choice of a nuclear reactor; the passengers on the Clapham omnibus would be avidly reading the latest Cabinet discussion document on control of the money supply.

As for silencing opposition, one of Benn's greatest obsessions is the need to legitimize all forms of dissent, whether in the Cabinet, in the trade union or at work. The danger from Benn is not that he wants to take away our freedom; rather that he might give us more freedom than we can cope with.

He is, according to his friends, a political loner, who is unwilling to join any fixed set. He has always refused to join the Tribune group. Yet he is a natural conspirator, perhaps without quite realizing it. Just before the Cabinet and Parliamentary decision on the European Monetary System, he joined with some Labour back-benchers and organized a campaign against our belonging to the EMS. Two back-benchers were instructed to send out papers to MPs setting out the Anti position.

It is quite extraordinary for a Cabinet Minister to organize party opposition to a Cabinet decision, secretly, before the decision has even been taken, and the operation was carried out in a sensibly clandestine manner with Benn's name never involved Yet he refused to believe that he had taken part in any conspiracy, and seemed genuinely offended when colleagues suggested he had.

The present row over the Labour manifesto for the next election is another good case. Benn is chairman of the Home Affairs Committee of the Labour Party which has passed a draft version of the manifesto. Though it is a fairly leftish document, it consists largely of ideas and promises which have been made several times before. It will be too left-wing for Jim Callaghan and most of the Cabinet, who will do their best and will probably succeed in watering it down.

Benn may well dig his heels in, and let it be known that he is totally opposed to this dilution. Callaghan may let it be known that he is thinking of sacking Benn (which he has done sometimes before). In the end Benn will argue that even though he is a member of the Cabinet, he has a perfect right to disagree with what a government might do in the future, even if he is obliged to support what it has done in the past. And he will argue too that a Cabinet Minister has as much right to disagree with anything as any other citizen.

Somehow the question of whether Benn will resign or will be sacked is always hovering over his career. One colleague said that what he was waiting for was 'a return ticket to the political wilderness', that he wouldn't mind moving into obscurity provided he knew he would get back. Certainly he has been near to departure several times. In 1975, just after the referendum on Europe, Wilson demoted him from the Department of Industry to Energy, and he consulted several people about resigning. In the end pressure from close associates such as his political adviser Mrs Frances Morrell persuaded him not to. In April 1976 he refused to vote on the party National Executive in favour of the Cabinet's decision on public spending cuts, and at one stage Number Ten was asserting that it was his last chance – next time he would go. In spite of numerous other small rebellions he is still there.

There are two views about this: some of his friends say that he should either resign or let himself be sacked. He would then take over as head of the now leaderless Left. These people say that he is trying to ride two horses, by staying in a centrist, essentially capitalist government while attempting to spread outside the gospel of radical change. They say that you cannot lead the men in the trenches if you spend your time in the converted chateau of the staff headquarters. The others, and they are in the ascendant among those closest to him, say that you cannot afford to quit the centre of power. A resignation might bring a few days' glory and the support of the Left. But it wouldn't bring the backing of the centre ground which he needs to become leader.

His qualities are formidable. He is a good administrator, an astonishingly fertile man of ideas, a persuasive talker. He must be one of the hardest working members of the Cabinet. His thoughts, set down on paper, are by no means as lunatic as many of his colleagues would have one believe. He attacks the 'huge accumulation of financial power in our society', the tyranny of the military establishments throughout the world, the ability of the media to sit upon dissent, and the powers of the Common Market. He wants to see working people have more control over their place of work, more public accountability, more free speech. He believes that the establishment which has allegedly run this country for so long has failed, and we must harness Britain – in his phrase – 'to the dynamo of the working class movement'. Whether the working class is quite as dynamic as Benn imagines is not clear, but certainly the rest of his views would – one might think – be acceptable to most Labour MPs.

Where he fails, in the words of a friend, is to recognize the sharpness of his ideas. You cannot sound off in quite the way Benn does, you cannot be so sure of yourself, so eager to push your thoughts to their illogical conclusion.

He has an ingenuous belief in the force of rational argument. Earlier this year he faced trouble in getting his bill to reorganize the electricity industry through the Commons. He suggested talks with his Tory opposite number Tom King to convince him of the virtues of the bill. What he simply didn't see was that the Tories would oppose the bill for purely political reasons, and as much as anything because Benn was behind it.

He is also more ignorant than he thinks about the working class. Take the great sandwich row when he was industry secretary. Trade union officials by the hundred came to visit him and they were offered tea and sandwiches for lunch, since Benn clearly believes that working people, like hamsters, have a staple diet. It was his working class deputy, Eric Heffer, who insisted that they should be served good hot food, such as you expect when lunching with a Secretary of State. He seems to believe too that the working classes can be harnessed like wave power or solar energy. This may be true, but it is a dangerous lesson to learn from strikes.

Does Benn wish to be leader of the Labour Party? Yes, he does, more than anything else in the world, even more than he wants to be Prime Minister. Does he think he will be? No, not unless the party changes the means by which it elects its leader. The MPs, who form the voters now, will never pick him and he knows it. The conference with its block trade union votes will never choose him. The constituencies, who put him top of the NEC elections year after year, might possibly one day do exactly that.

16 December 1978   **Simon Hoggart**

Is there mullet still for tee?

It is reported that a fish weighing 1.5lb was dropped by a seagull 300 feet on to a golfer on the fifteenth green at Melbourne, costing him a winning position in an important open championship. The fish was a mullet and the golfer was knocked out. Although sympathy is due to the golfer it should be pointed out that a mullet of that weight, dropped from that height, will inevitably cause a fairly painful blow. The mullet would have been travelling at about 140 feet per second (95.5 mph) when it struck the golfer and its kinetic energy would have been twice that of a cricket ball bowled by Trueman at his best. (Mathematically it would have been equal to half the product of the mass and the square of the velocity, which equals 14,700ft/lb.) It is not known whether the mullet was vertical or horizontal during descent, and this could have had a critical bearing on the injury caused. For if the mullet fell upright the air resistance would have been slight (fish make use of that fact in their more normal medium)

157

and the impact concentrated on a smaller area of the golfer's body. Horizontally the resistance would have been greater and the contusions more widely dissipated.

The golfer, a Mr Staatz, is particularly unfortunate in that 1.5lb is approaching the maximum weight of mullet that a seagull can reasonably carry, although fish of 3lb and more are not unknown in Australian waters. He is unfortunate again in that had the mullet been only slightly smaller the seagull would probably have been able to hang on to it and the regrettable incident would not have occurred. (Not only would it not have occurred: no one would have given any thought to the possibility of its occurrence.) Mr Staatz therefore appears to have had the worst of both worlds. It is true that his chances of being struck by a falling mullet a second time are so small as to be, for practical purposes, negligible, but that can have been of only small comfort to him at the moment of collision.

21 April 1979   **Leader**

Packing a mean hump

Ipci, the camel of the man who sells rope, and the undefeated champion of Asia Minor, was there; so were the camels of Yusuf the Cook and Khazim the Chauffeur, Black Paradise, the Rich One, the Aggressive One, Indefatigable, Happy, Fire and Fate, and the Pumpkin; altogether there were forty-eight camels fighting for the Grand Championship of Kusadasi in Western Turkey.

Camel fighting (actually dromedary fighting) is uniquely Turkish, for nowhere else do they fight professionally. It is thought that the Greeks first practised the sport several thousand years ago when owners of rival camel caravanserai wagered their finest animals.

Fighting was introduced into Western Turkey about a hundred years ago when Nasuf, son of Haci Mehmet, challenged Nazilli the Greek; and now, in the province of Aydin, contests take place every weekend during the rutting season of January and February when the snow is melting on the mountains and the days are cool.

Camels are normally used in this remote area of Turkey

as beasts of burden, transporting the olive crop down into the towns. But fighting camels, which are never used as pack animals, are haughty, vindictive, and picked for their meanness: they are naturally very aggressive. These hybrids – called Tulu – are bred from a female Arabian camel with one hump and a male Bactrian (originally from the steppes of Russia) with two. They start fighting at the age of five, are at their peak at fifteen, and live for about forty years. During the summer they are fed a special diet of wheat, barley and oats which enables them to build up their weight to a colossal 1200 kilos; a normal camel scales around 400 kilos.

At the end of November these great animals become exceedingly irritable. Their coats are thick, their hooves close up, and their tails stand erect. They eat little, nourishing themselves from the fatty tissue in the hump, and froth at the mouth. They fight for the attention of a female, who is usually placed attentively nearby, and in a survival-of-the-fittest contest will fight to the death, the winner suffocating his challenger by knocking him down and lying on top of his head.

But fights today are stopped before this happens, for a champion camel is worth at least £4000. The contests take place over two days. At Kusadasi the camels were paraded around the town, each animal saddled with a pack, gaily caparisoned with bells of varying sizes, rugs, embroidery, and blue beads to ward off the Evil Eye. Dancers and gypsy musicians – playing drums and the ancient double-reeded shawm – preceded the procession, and the cacophony of sound was so intense that it produced the required effect on the camels: they glared at each other, shifted restlessly, and belched enormous quantities of foaming white spittle.

Ten thousand people paid £1 each to watch the Sunday contest. At stake were twenty-four Turkish carpets worth £70 each, and a cash prize for the champion of £130.

The rules were somewhat incomprehensible. Five referees categorized each fight into *ayak* (foot), *orta* (middle), *basalti* (lower head), or *bas* (head); and animals were matched who were known to fight in a particular style – 'the left hander', 'the camel who hooks the hooves of his opponent', and 'the one who crushes his opponent's head under his two front hooves'.

The bouts usually lasted about fifteen minutes, the winner

being decided either when his opponent snorted in pain, was suffocated, knocked down or, as frequently happened, being chased off into the crowd, who would then hoot, whistle, and cat-call as the musicians were brought on to stir up additional excitement for the next contestants.

After seven hours' vicious excitement came the climax when the Crazy One fought the undefeated camel of the man who sells rope – Ipci. He won, of course.

21 February 1979   **Jeremy Hunter**

Secrets of the East

It is always well to keep an eye on the East and that includes the East Midlands. (Who, before Cromwell, bothered their heads about Huntingdon?) Now, with Grantham Woman mated to Selsdon Man and the prospect of a Lady Protector on the way, it is time to pay attention to a county which has so far escaped it, but which more than any other embodies the proper pride of small towns.

Lincolnshire is one of the biggest counties and probably the least known. People go through it a great deal but seldom seem to stop. Yet much of its countryside is pleasant and even beautiful, and its towns have both quality and character even if for the most part they lack drama. (That could hardly be said of Stamford, the first you come upon as you move north, and near sensational in its visual impact.)

After Stamford you cross a pocket of what was Rutland and is now Leicestershire. Both nameplates are up on the border like flags, the official one and the forbidden one. Not only does extinct Rutland refuse to die, it claims equal status. People keep saying the word out loud – much more than they did when it was alive.

It is the sort of gesture Lincolnshire ought to appreciate, particularly since it has itself lost so much territory up at the other end of the county to the new Humberside. To take away Grimsby was rather like taking Belfast from Ulster, and it seems to have been accomplished with surprisingly little fuss.

Was this quite the spirit one might have expected from

Thatcherville? Grantham at least remains staunch. With its famous spire and its blue pubs (Blue Lion, Blue Horse, Blue Pig, etc.), its old bones and its new industry, Grantham has shown its readiness to move with the times, whatever way that might seem to require.

But for all its vigour and versatility, Grantham can't hold a candle to Stamford when it comes to looks. This must be among the front runners in any contest for the handsomest, the best preserved town in Britain. Stamford looks like a displaced Cotswold town, or would if the Cotswolds still had anything as good. This is no accident; it comes from the same limestone belt and was shaped in much the same building style.

The astonishing thing is how little it is known. It makes no obvious attempt to solicit the tourists, and if they can't discover it for themselves their loss – since it still manages to project an air of quiet prosperity – is Stamford's gain. Perhaps it is all a carefully kept secret, in which case this article does the town no service.

So bright is Stamford that everything near is shadowed by it: pleasant but drabbish Bourne, sleepy Folkingham with its exaggerated square, bricky Sleaford with its powerfully agricultural air and its Gallic-looking market under the trees. No two places are alike. Those who find Lincolnshire monotonous can't have the proper use of their senses. These towns and villages differ as the contours differ, change with the changing landscape, and that is seldom the same for five miles on end.

Stamford is mainly stone, harmoniously spread over several centuries. Louth, perhaps the next most comely town, is predominantly eighteenth century and Victorian brick, and very pleasing. Such is its modesty that, despite Louth's obvious residential status, I actually saw an end-of-terrace house offered in an estate agent's window at under £3000. Can it always be as demure as it looks? Between the wars its sedate little river, called the Lud, suddenly reared up and killed twenty-three people.

This is Tennyson country but they don't brag much about that – uneasily aware, it may be, of the miserable time the poet had at Louth school. Nor is Somersby anything like the tourist draw of Grantchester, yet the appeal seems to me far greater, part of the theatre of understatement. The village church displays the Laureate's head near the sanctuary and a couple of his clay pipes in a small showcase.

The nearest Louth ever brings itself to boasting is over its superb church spire, and then its claims are immediately challenged by Grantham and Boston. If height were the last word, and it never is, the Louth spire would win with its 294 feet, against Grantham's 285 feet (though it claims to *look* higher), and Boston's (which really does look the highest of all) mere 272 feet. A local sport when headier amusements flag is to challenge strangers to guess the size of the handsome gold weathercock on Louth spire. Responding to a kind of double-bluff, the guesser almost invariably over-estimates.

Past secret Wainfleet on the coast road, through Wrangle and Old Leake, and so to Boston where life looks an eternal market day, a chaos of cars and shoppers punched by a wet wind. Every human need is met – pieces of timber or china, lengths of lace or of corrugated iron – as well as less obviously human ones like broken marine engine parts. Everything possible or impossible is being bought or sold, and rising above it all – you can see it for twenty miles – is that superb Gothic lantern tower.

The church, the whole town, has in abundance the one thing the county in general lacks – theatricality. Here is a civic drama, all right, and by nature rather than calculation. And if you want total contrast between what you might expect to be twin towns, push on round the Wash to quiet, cultivated, festival-fostering King's Lynn. But that is in another county, and another world.

One hesitates to disturb Lincolnshire's privacy, but it could be that there are things to learn from it. Among the county's more distinguished graffiti is the name of Isaac Newton self-carved in a window-ledge of the King's School. Young Margaret was presumably too well-disciplined to leave her own mark on the girls' high school. But she will know that Oliver Cromwell won a key Lincolnshire victory in the Civil War. She will know that he had his horse shot under him, but still won. The Lady Protector Designate won't be forgetting things like that.

2 September 1978   **Norman Shrapnel**

Wanderers go West

On a draining night of emotion down in the West, Exeter City deservedly beat Bolton Wanderers 2–1 last night at St James's Park. So yet another First Division side go out of the League Cup. Exeter have never before got past the third round.

Delve put them ahead early on, and after Gowling had equalized soon after half time, Delve won the penalty for Kellow to wrap it up. Then the songs started. Delve's beautifully struck early score set the quaint little ground on a roar which, with Bolton continuing to strain, grew in volume as the pattern of the evening took shape. Around the quarter hour Bowker lobbed a twenty-five-yard speculative bobbler from deep in midfield, and with the Bolton defence standing rooted as trees Delve put his ears back, hared past them, and waited for the bounce before walloping it home in full stride from the eighteen yard line.

Bolton went in looking very sorry for themselves. But within five minutes of the second half they were level. The ground was stunned when Exeter hesitated as Walsh's free kick sailed in from the left and Gowling lashed in the loose ball.

Things were hotting up, and at once Hatch took the ball to the other end and struck a fine left-footer against the bar.

Delve's contribution to his night of nights was doubled when he was rudely flattened by Burke when trying to repeat his first trick. Kellow planted the penalty joyfully past Poole, whose baptism was turning out to be neither memorable nor serene. But it continued to be very, very noisy – especially when Bolton lost Whatmore and, it seemed, all hope, with about twenty minutes remaining. He was sent off after a retaliatory foul and then a barney with Mr Stevens.

5 October 1978   **Frank Keating**

Twickenham's apartheid

The present vendetta being prosecuted by the Rugby Football Union against the British Amateur Rugby League Association is both embarrassing and distressing to those like myself who love both games. We were born into rugby. My own particular cradle was South West Lancashire, in a cluster of mining towns clinging to the coal seam before it dips deep and unreachable beneath the pastures of Cheshire. Babes don't toddle there; they sidestep. Queueing women talk of 'nipping round the blind side'. The game provides our cultural adrenalin. It's a physical manifestation of our rules of life, comradeship, honest endeavour and a staunch, often ponderous allegiance to fair play.

In my day we still suffered the eleven-plus. Apart from dividing us educationally and socially, it split our rugby. Those of us who passed went Union; kids who failed played League. At eleven we were already learning to correlate Rugby Union with our social superiority. League, along with soccer, was the council school game, the dinner-time pursuit of men in overalls grunting and cursing on the works waste ground.

Nowadays comprehensives are killing this stone dead. Union and League are available to all. The choice is the schools'. Many choose both codes – even three. No longer are the rules by which he kicks a football a reflection on a child's social or professional aspirations. Boys are allowed to be boys – to play, for the fun of it, any game they fancy. Marvellous, until they reach eighteen.

Then the Rugby Union authorities drive a brutal wedge between the games, retreat behind a laager of paranoia, defending the purity of their tribe with all the subtlety and finesse of the old-time voortrekkers. In the history of sport only apartheid has been prosecuted with such vindictiveness and downright pettiness as the campaign of prejudice now being waged against those young men, particularly in the universities, who have shown a desire to play rugby under the rules of the Amateur Rugby League. Life bans, club expulsions, denial of facilities, even,

I am told, veiled threats against future academic careers, all these have been levelled against those who in a sane society would be regarded as fellow exponents of the game of amateur rugby football.

Although Twickenham has been operating these Ku Klux Klan techniques for eighty years now, ever since the original Northern Union was formed, the divisory system of education which operated until recently ensured that those playing either code had little social intercourse. Undergraduates invariably came from public or grammar schools, steeped in Union tradition, and so those Union citadels, the universities, remained inviolate. The army might have been a problem but, with the Rugby Union authorities anticipating and fearing the formation of an Army Rugby League, they conveniently bent their own hitherto unbendable rules to allow Rugby League rookies to share a scrum temporarily with their betters.

Now the whole complexion has changed. A new generation of students is flooding into the universities from all-in schools. To them games are games. They have a natural and healthy hunger, for all sporting adventures. If they did not play Rugby League at school they have watched it on the box. Why not give it a go? Why *not*, indeed?

The British Amateur Rugby League Association fully understands the Rugby Union's totally defensive attitude towards professionalism. They themselves are as stringent, if not more so, in their determination to retain their amateur philosophy and structure. Players on their tour of Australasia in 1978 deposited £200 a man on their selection as a contribution towards travel. They were obliged to buy their own blazers, badges and so on. And they received not a penny in day-to-day expenses. They were given one gift, a tie. Could a British Lion put his hand on his heart and say the same? Incidentally the tour included matches in Papua New Guinea. It was the first visit by any organized sporting touring side in history.

It is impossible for a layman, given these facts, to understand the present neurotic attitude of the Twickenham powers-that-be. It is embarrassingly difficult for rank-and-file Rugby Union club members like myself. And that embarrassment turns to indignation and disgust when one hears details of some of the particular acts of vindictiveness that have taken place up and down the country.

Bob Mahuter's name has gone down in the annals of BARLA as their first martyr. An Oxford University post-graduate and a happy-go-lucky Maori, he had played Rugby Union in New Zealand all his life. Recently, at the age of thirty-eight, he trotted out with the University Amateur Rugby League Club for one game. The Rugby Football Union immediately banned him for life. Bob still smiles and shakes his head in disbelief.

Oxford again. West Bowling, an amateur Rugby League side from Yorkshire, journeyed to play the university side in the first round of the National Cup. They arrived to find that no pitch was available although many lay empty. The two teams had to go forty miles to Heathrow Airport to complete their fixture.

Last Sunday Swansea University had arranged a match with Normanton. It was to be a great day out. Two coaches had been hired. Wives, kids and girlfriends were invited to travel. A wonderful social occasion was in prospect. Then Dr Phil Melling, a lecturer at the university and founder of the Rugby League club, phoned to say that, due to banning threats by the university's Rugby Union authorities, he was finding it difficult to raise a team. The match was cancelled and no doubt the Union buffs were buying pints of victory. But students being students, thank God, the news got about and a defiant side was quickly raised. Hull University stepped quickly into the breach, hastened down to Wales, and a smashing time was had by all both on and off the pitch.

Such tales are so numerous as to be humiliating to all of us who love the handling game. What warped priorities promote such juvenile behaviour from grown and otherwise intelligent men? I absolve from this criticism most junior Rugby Union clubs in the North, especially where Rugby League is part of life. I know from experience the sensible and often defiant attitude adopted by junior sides when faced with amateur Rugby League recruits. They play them – and to hell with HQ.

John Burke, a young professional with Workington, broke his neck playing against Wigan recently. He is now paralysed from the neck down and has a wife and baby. Local Rugby

Union sides have had no hesitation in promising events to help provide for his future.

I myself, when a player with the Newton-le-Willows Rugby Union club, qualified as a Rugby League schools coach. It's sane, it's sensible, it's adult. Why cannot the Rugby Union authorities see it as such?

The secretary of BARLA makes this appeal: 'All we ask is to be afforded the same rights and dignity as any other amateur sportsman.' On behalf of the ever-increasing army of defiant Rugby League amateurs up and down the country, in schools, factories, colleges and universities, I say to Bob Weighill and company – how about it?

2 March 1979   **Colin Welland**

Behind the pixie smile

Deng Xiaoping chose a boy's head for his public relations masterstroke. As the National Children's Choir stood politely to one side of Washington's Kennedy Center stage, after the gala performance in his honour, the Chinese Vice-Premier approached a small boy in the front row.

He did not hurl him into the air and hug him, as your run-of-the-mill Hubert Humphrey might have done. He did not shake hands with the mock familiarity of a Jimmy Carter. Deng bent slightly, made his fingers into a V in front of his chest and touched his lips to the boy's hair. He did the same thing to the next child in the line.

It was perfect – part a benediction and part a gesture of humility and innocence – as child-like and appealing as the little targets of his attention. Many of the audience in the Kennedy Center felt a tear well up.

It needed only one touch to spring open the expectant well of naive excitement and enthusiasm here over what *Time* magazine called China's great leap forward. By the second day of Deng's visit to Washington, the news agency wire services were already telling us that the American people had taken the 'diminutive' (that was the word it had to be) Deng Xiaoping into their hearts.

The media said he was just like an American politician: 'pragmatic and blunt'. He was opening China 'to democracy, individualism, profit and the spirit of "get up and go"'. This was not another stuffy patronizing European statesman. This was earthiness itself come to town.

The Associated Press confided that Deng had a sense of fun like an American, 'quick, intelligent and appreciative of incongruity', as when he shook hands with a seven-foot-tall member of the Harlem Globetrotters – all the things they used to say about Nikita Khrushchev until he took off his shoe at the United Nations.

A White House official put it, only half cynically: 'We invited the Yellow Peril and we got a cute little Teddy bear.' At the State Department another official marvelled at the gullibility of his compatriots: 'We are astonished at the dramatic shifts in Chinese attitudes to the West, but overlook the swings in our own attitudes to China.'

For twenty-five years the dominant American feeling was a mixture of racism and violent anti-Communism. Now, there's a return to the pre-1949 sense of a special mystic bond between America and China – a bond which other people do not share and cannot understand and one which goes back to the early condescending missionary penetration of China.

With his hooded eyes and pixie smile Deng Xiaoping has played on that feeling – pleading for American money and military help against the horrid bully to the north-west. Fear and contempt for Russia are cheap instruments in the political arsenal and Deng requires no great skill to use them. The subtlety comes in acting as the kind of polite and meek beggar whom no one minds, while retaining your dignity which everyone respects.

In an interview with *Time*, Deng said: 'China is quite poor and you have made a poor friend.' The questioner was puzzled. 'You don't mean a bad friend?' Deng replied: 'No, not a bad friend, but economically poor. In Chinese, the word poor has no bad connotations. Of course, that does not mean China is no use. We do not look upon ourselves as inconsequential.' Then he added, pulling at an imaginary forelock, one presumes: 'We must obtain capital from the developed countries and learn from their experience, especially in the field of management.'

168

After remarks like that, it is hardly surprising that American executives are queueing up to hand Deng a dime – especially as they see prospects of reaping a dollar in the 800-million population Chinese market. The other day, I was flying back to Washington sharing a row of seats with two American businessmen. As we circled the city, one said to the other: 'Look at all those potential consumers down there.' Just imagine their excitement if we had been landing in Peking.

As Deng travels around America, the tinkling of mental cash registers will become almost deafening; nothing must be allowed to disrupt the pursuit of business happiness and good PR. It is hard to know whether the greed or the naivety is the worst aspect of Deng's reception.

The one hopeful sign is that at least within the State Department a few reticent souls realize that Deng is out to destroy the still fragile basis for détente between the super powers. They wonder whether the risk of bringing nuclear war one inch nearer is worth the price of Deng's kiss on the head.

Not for nothing has he often been compared to that great survivor in American politics, many times purged, and as many times brought back again. Like Richard Nixon's, Deng's whole career does not suggest that he is a person from whom you should buy a used chop stick.

7 February 1979   **Jonathan Steele**

Sunset strip

A golden age in American pop culture dies today.

Li'l Abner, the hillbilly Candide of Dogpatch USA, will make his last appearance as a weekday cartoon strip after forty-three years of taking the mickey out of the nation's most sacred institutions: money, marriage, and motherhood. In his prime Li'l Abner, who looks like Arnold Schwarzenegger but has the naive morality of an altar boy, was in 900 newspapers with almost one hundred million readers from Maine to California.

Much of Li'l Abner has been absorbed into American folklore – Sadie Hawkins Day, when sexual roles are reversed and girls chase and catch their men, Kickapoo Joy Juice with its amazing restorative powers, and the Schmoo, a small lovable animal which threatens the very existence of capitalism because it has the gift of dying happily to fulfil any human need. John Steinbeck once suggested Abner's creator, Al Capp, for a Nobel Prize. And erudite critics have compared Capp to Mark Twain, Daumier and even Voltaire.

Such assessments are more pretentious than the strip ever was. Li'l Abner was broad slapstick with its roots as much in Minsky's burlesque theatre as in the tall tales of Davy Crockett. At a time when the population was shifting away from farms and small towns to the big cities, Capp's vision of rural America – a mixture of send-up and nostalgia – struck a deep chord. But its real significance is that it was the first humorous strip to attempt serious political satire – and get away with it.

Before Li'l Abner came shyly scufflin' up the road, the American 'funnies', as daily cartoon strips have been called ever since they began in the 1890s, were in a feeble state. Originally full of coarse, vulgar, ethnic humour aimed at an audience of semi-literate natives and first-generation immigrants, they were a kind of pre-electronic television.

Around the turn of the century, before anyone had time to make ground rules or taboos, strips like Bringing Up Father (puncturing the social climbing of Maggie and Jiggs, a nouveau-riche Irish couple) and Krazy Kat (a surrealistic strip, with Joycean dialogue, about a cat in love with an anarchistic mouse who constantly hurls bricks at it) could be both socially subversive and magnificently drawn. But, like the early movies whose techniques they both borrowed and influenced, once cartoons were taken over by the big money salesmen, the wacky eccentrics had to tone down their satire or quit.

Comic strips as we know them really are an American invention. Addicts and cartoon snobs like to claim as artistic ancestors Goya, Hogarth and Gillray, even the Bayeux Tapestries and Lascaux cave drawings. But the plain fact is that William Randolph Hearst, the evil genius of American journalism, was the spiritual godfather of the comic strip.

In the fierce battle between Hearst and Joseph Pulitzer for newspaper supremacy of New York City, it soon developed that the strongest circulation-builders were the Sunday colour comic supplements. The two Victorian press barons brawled like stevedores over the rights to a particular favourite dubbed The Yellow Kid, a saucy slum urchin who wore a yellow nightshirt on which were emblazoned irreverent messages.

Hearst bribed the artist R. F. Outcault away from Pulitzer, who bought him back: Hearst upped the ante and stole Outcault back but without legal title to the cartoon character. Pulitzer hired another artist to continue the Kid, and for a while – amidst raids, counter-raids, injunctions and lawsuits – two rival Yellow Kids appeared in Hearst's *Journal* and Pulitzer's *World*. A new phrase was born to describe the unscrupulous practices of the sensational press: 'yellow journalism'.

An interesting postscript casts light on the hunger for respectability the early cartoonists had in common with their readers. Outcault, the Yellow Kid's artist, grew ashamed of his creation's rude status. So he contrived a second strip, Buster Brown, a little middle-class boy in a velvet suit who played savagely ingenious pranks but in the last panel always promised piously never to do it again.

Soon overtaking the Yellow Kid's popularity, Buster Brown became enormously influential as a kind of ideal child.

The public's huge appetite for more comic strips largely created the instrument by which they got standardized and denatured: the distribution syndicate. In a small way syndicates had been around, mainly to supply pre-written features and ads to rural papers, since the 1840s. The United States never has had a national press, so provincial newspapers occasionally found it convenient to buy 'boiler plate copy' – fiction, big name interviews etc. – as filler. But when the syndicates began buying up the comic strips and selling them nationwide, the funnies became in effect the first genuinely mass medium.

So, early in this century, a pattern was set which has not basically changed. A few giant syndicates, sometimes owned by competing newspaper chains, quickly gained artistic control of the strips. Cartoonists were bought and sold like baseball players. Again and again, strips were watered down to meet a national norm which, until the comics came along, had not existed. And, until quite recently, the creators of even very successful strips, because they did not legally own their own material, could end up broke. Jerry Siegel, who with artist Joe Shuster thought up Superman, sold the idea to a syndicate for $130 and today is destitute.

After the First World War 'normalcy' was the watchword in American life and in the strips. Little Orphan Annie, a curly-headed blank-eyed paragon of free enterprise with a millionaire guardian called Daddy Warbucks who ranted against labour unions and socialism, become the new Buster Brown.

The knockabout misanthropy of the early strips now could be detected only in their oblique mirroring of the sex war. Male cartoonists – I know of only one woman artist in this period, and she was doing a doggy strip – particularly resented the galling supremacy of a materialistic matriarchy personified by Jiggs's brutally snobbish wife Maggie, Dagwood's Blondie and all the other flighty, money-mad ballbreakers whose contempt for their henpecked husbands was barely concealed.

This feminization of the strip, like so many other American institutions, broke down as a result of the great Depression. The cartoon syndicates' response to the stock market crash was to supply anodyne in the form of the first true adventure series: Tarzan (superbly drawn by Burne Hogarth) and Buck Rogers In The 25th Century. Both appeared in 1929.

Li'l Abner burst upon this purely escapist scene in the same crisis-ridden year, 1934, that ushered in Flash Gordon, Jungle Jim, Secret Agent X-9 (written by Dashiell Hammett, no less), Mandrake the Magician and Terry and the Pirates. Capp's six-foot-three yokel with bulging biceps and a heart of mush was an instant success.

At a time when most cartoonists were patriotically rallying round the flag and mother's blueberry pie, Al Capp took careful aim along the barr'l of Abner's fav'rite shootin' iron and blew them all to hell with the stinging buckshot of pure, malicious ridicule. Cherished American values were not only questioned but demolished.

Southern politicians (Senator Jack S. Phogbound), captains of industry (J. Roaringham Fatback), statesmen (Henry Cabbage Sod), militarists (General Bullmoose) and even the work of brother cartoonists have all been mocked within the strip.

172

Next to Li'l Abner himself, perhaps Capp's most popular hero was Fearless Fosdick, a cruelly hilarious take-off on Dick Tracy, a square-jawed eagle-nosed detective who stood in the hearts of conformist Americans second only to J. Edgar Hoover of the FBI. In the 1950s one of the few places one could see Senator Joe McCarthy lampooned was in Li'l Abner.

Yet Capp prospered where safer strips fell victim to the cartoon industry's notoriously high mortality rate. At his peak Capp earned 500,000 dollars a year from the strip and its profitable spinoffs, including a Broadway musical and a Disneyland-like amusement park in Kentucky called Dogpatch USA. How did he get away with it?

Basically, I think, because Capp sincerely believed in the system whose foibles he was attacking. He is not unlike Frank Capra, whose movies in some ways resemble Li'l Abner. Both Longfellow Deeds, the tuba-playing country boy Gary Cooper portrayed in *Mr Deeds Goes to Town*, and Jimmy Stewart as the aw-shucks hero of *Mr Smith Goes to Washington*, might easily be mistaken for Li'l Abner in their ability to defeat city slickers with simpleminded rural virtue.

'Goodness is stronger than evil because it is nicer,' insists Abner's invincible, pipe smoking Mammy Yokum, the undisputed ruler of Dogpatch.

Pushing aside her useless little husband Pappy, Mammy doubles up her fists and, radiating militant goodness, triumphs over threats to her clan posed by a succession of grotesque villains: Evil Eye Fleegle whose 'triple whammy' reduces strong men to tapioca pudding, and especially lecherous sirens like Stupefyin' Jones and Moonbeam McSwine who lust for her son's chaste body. Mammy Yokum may be a parody of an overprotective American mom but one feels that Al Capp likes and respects her all the same.

That probably is true as well of Capp's attitude to Li'l Abner himself. A perpetual nineteen, Abner is utterly unneurotic; he may be built like Superman but he's too dumb, too nice, to have any of Clark Kent's identity problems. With his slightly idiotic facial expression and strong-chinned fear of nothing except gettin' 'hitched up' to loyal, bosomy Daisy Mae, he is both an affirmation and a conscious caricature of American masculinity.

When, in response to readers' demands, Capp reluctantly let Marryin' Sam, the pompous preacher, 'splice' Abner and Daisy Mae in 1952, it was practically a national holiday. The wedding made *Life*'s cover. Americans take their funnies seriously.

Although Al Capp, at sixty-eight, insists he is hanging up his pen because of ill-health, there's more than a hint of the biter being bitten in the retirement of America's most popular satirist.

Li'l Abner, who survived a depression, three major wars and several social 'revolutions', was finally poleaxed by his creator's irascible refusal to truckle to anyone, even to the idealistic young.

In the 1960s Capp, perhaps tired of being identified as a mere cartoonist, branched out into television and newspaper punditry. To the surprise of his admirers, who had always taken for granted that Capp was vaguely Left, he began lashing out at long-haired hippies and radical students.

College kids objected to his panels caricaturing radical singer Joanie Phoanie (Joan Baez) and the hairy rent-a-mobs from SWINE – Students Wildly Indignant About Nearly Everything. They deserted him for more congenial strips like Pogo (a political possum), a counter-culture Oblomov named Doonesbury, and Peanuts. Li'l Abner now is enjoyed by a dwindling, ageing readership – though it's still in 400 newspapers.

Al Capp denies he has switched sides. By insisting that his views have remained steadfast but it's the world that has changed, he probably is honestly speaking for a whole New Deal generation of liberal humanists who feel betrayed by the direction America's young have taken.

Like them, Capp is a child of disillusionment – with the flag-waving ideals of the First World War, the hypocrisies of the Prohibition era, the Panglossian blindness of three mediocre presidents in a row (Harding, Coolidge and Herbert Hoover) who all seemed to be impersonating W. C. Fields in the White House. But Capp has always kept his protest within limits.

Blacks who set fire to their own homes . . . homosexuals who call themselves gay and are proud of it . . . students who burn the Stars and Stripes while high on lurid substances previously associated only with the Tong wars in Terry and the Pirates . . . and women who insist on being addressed as Ms, practise karate and feel insulted if you open a door for them. Gulp, one can almost hear Al Capp gasp along with Li'l Abner.

Equally, Li'l Abner's allegorical adventures look increasingly puerile to young American rebels weaned on affluent notions of unchecked acting out as the norm of healthy behaviour, mind-bending trips of self-exploration – and on *Mad* magazine.

Mad, which first came out (crawled from under a rock, some irate parents might say) in the same year that Abner and Daisy Mae wed, revolutionized the comic field. It was a comic book, not a newspaper strip. In fact, *Mad* freely plagiarized the best-loved characters from the daily strips to crucify them.

With tremendous visual flair and outrageously amoral wit, it slyly lumped together television commercials, Senator McCarthy, team sports – and Li'l Abner (among other cartoon heroes) – as examples of authoritarian stupidity all gutsy kids ought to fight against. The age of satire had arrived, and Dogpatch USA, which Al Capp had invented to pillory a whole system of clichés, had now itself become a cliché.

One day social scientists may discover the roots of the 'permissive culture' not in rock music or the Vietnam war but in the weirdly iconoclastic comic books that climbed so successfully on *Mad*'s bandwagon. While Mommy and Daddy were contentedly still chuckling over Blondie and Li'l Abner in their local newspaper, Junior was locked in the lavatory greedily devouring copies of *The Fantastic Four* (a plastic man, an invisible woman, a human torch and The Thing), *The Amazing Spider-Man*, *The Incredible Hulk* and a series of semi-satiric horror comics like *Tales From the Crypt*.

A growing underground of bright, bored kids delighted in the new 'put on' comics, with their erotic satire, their blurring of the boundaries of good and evil, and their ambiguous moral atmosphere. (Was Captain America laughing at the CIA when he cracked so many Commie skulls with his bullet-proof body or was he playing it straight?)

The way was clear for the first real 'underground comix' – *Zap* and *Slow Death Funnies* and *Big Ass*, Robert Crumb's *Fritz the Cat* and other authentic creations of the 1960s dope-and-protest movement. Sure, only a minority of the type of people Al Capp now despised read these comics. But it was, and is, a prophetic minority. Al Capp's days as an idol smasher were over.

Wisely, he has decided not to keep Li'l Abner artificially alive by letting lesser hands 'ghost' the strip, a common practice. Indeed, way back in the early thirties, Capp got his big break as a full-time assistant to Ham Fisher, creator of a prize-fighting strip, Joe Palooka.

When Capp left the strip, taking with him a prototype hill-billy character named Big Leviticus, his former employer became so bitter he later had Capp dragged into court on charges of criminal obscenity, the evidence for which Fisher supplied as clumsily forged Li'l Abner cartoons. Easily exposed, Fisher was expelled from the US cartoonists' guild and committed suicide.

The funnies aren't so funny behind the scenes.

5 November 1978   **Clancy Sigal**

Spellbinders

What do you want tonight, kids – the story about the dotty ventriloquist who gets taken over by his dummy, or the one about the mad killer who escapes from the asylum and terrorizes a small town on Halloween? Never mind that both *Magic* (Odeon, Haymarket) and *Halloween* (Odeon, Kensington) are both X films. We'll get you in somehow.

Magic was directed in America by our own Sir Richard Attenborough and I ought to tell you straight away that this little film, a positive minnow beside *Young Winston* and *A Bridge Too Far*, has taken the States by storm. In fact, it's doing so well that a *Time* review which opined that it was one of the worst for some time is being made to look as nutty as the ventriloquist. Anthony Hopkins plays him and is very good indeed if you excuse a variable American accent. And there's Ken Russell's own Ann-Margret as the girl he gets mixed up with. She's good too, thriving best when playing against a really stylish English actor.

But those can't be the reasons for the huge box-office takings, though it will be interesting to see where Hopkins, now much more bankable, gets on from this point in his career. Perhaps it is simply that William Goldman wrote the screenplay from his own book and people remember that gratefully enough to go along.

It is all rather like a latterday remake of *Dead of Night*, or that part which had Michael Redgrave impelling his dummy towards murder. Sir Richard directs studiously, even meticulously – almost as if it were a period piece that might break apart in his hands at the slightest untoward touch. We can see what's coming rather a long way off but no matter. Jerry Goldsmith's music is good, so are the ventriloquist scenes and Goldman's quite acid script, full of f's and b's, allows the piece a certain spontaneity lacking in other departments.

Altogether I enjoyed it while never being quite able to persuade myself that it was good enough to muster the clout it has on the market. I don't think Attenborough would claim it as his best film but if it goes on like this it will certainly be his most successful. *Halloween* is by John Carpenter, who is as much a cult director as Sir Richard is not and may just have been overrated on the strength of *Dark Star* and *Assault on Precinct 13*, which made far less headway on the all-important American market than the British production.

I still think, however, that he is unquestionably talented since he extends *Halloween*'s wisp of a storyline over the full length of a feature without ever attempting the calculating pyrotechnics that split Brian De Palma's *Fury* at the seams. His summation of small-town life in Illinois as seen through the eyes of a posse of teenagers is quite masterly, and the camera-work is impeccably all of a piece. Time and again when the film ought to collapse, it doesn't – not even when poor Donald Pleasance, now remorselessly cast as something like the parody mad psychiatrist, says: 'Death has come to your little town, Sheriff . . .' To which the estimable arm of the law replies: 'More fancy talk!'

Carpenter wrote the script, by the way, with the producer, Debra Hill. And he also composed the effective staccato music. Nice performances from Jamie Lee Curtis, Nancy Loomis and P. J. Soles as the teenage baby-sitters (who seem to be virtually the only inhabitants of Haddonfield on the night in question) add to a sense of atmosphere very skilfully orchestrated to suggest that there's a bogeyman in front of all of us just waiting to be seen. *Halloween* may not be as original as *Dark Star* or as full of panache as *Assault*. But it works. And in many another pair of hands it certainly wouldn't.

25 January 1979   **Derek Malcolm**

The Revolution's image maker

The scene is the state advertising works in Moscow. The date, some time between 1923 and 1925. The leading Soviet poet, Mayakovsky, and one of the greatest revolutionary artists, Rodchenko, are delivering the daily batch of poster designs produced to boost the economy.

Mayakovsky writes the slogans (example: All that we have left from the old world are the cigarettes, Ira). Rodchenko does the designs. They work on them every night, and deliver every morning. This morning they run into disapproval of a tea ad. Rodchenko writing in 1940, after the imposition of social realism, tells the story: Someone said, 'Why doesn't the Chinaman have a plait?' On the poster the Chinaman was drawn full face walking with raised arms and in his hands tea-chests in an arc in the air from one hand to another. The Chinaman looks up at them as if he were juggling. Mayakovsky answered: 'There is a plait but it is at the back. If you turned his back the plait would be visible.' Another man asked: 'Why do the chests stay in the air like that? It's unreal.' Mayakovsky: 'The Chinese are famous as jugglers.' Laughter. The poster was accepted.

Rodchenko's account of his partnership with Mayakovsky was first printed in Moscow in 1973. It is just one of many documents that throw a warm and human light on the period of Russian revolutionary art that we have come to interpret as heroic. Such documents are among the accounts by artists and students of the time included in the splendid book that accompanies the first ever retrospective of Alexander Rodchenko (1891–1956) at the Oxford Museum of Modern Art which will later travel to Eindhoven in Holland and Montreal.

For Rodchenko the design of advertisement posters, humble

though it might seem to us, was a natural part of the extension of the new art into every nook and cranny of the new society. The exhibition in Oxford even includes his designs for sweet wrappers: brands beloved by the people keeping the familiar flavours but wrapped with revolutionary fervour. When everything is in a state of change, every object becomes significant.

Rodchenko's work covers every visual field that could convey a message. This was the Productivist ethic: to bring new forms fitting to the new society. Rodchenko more than any other of the great artists of the time like Tatlin, who shared the Productivist ethic, or Malevich who did not, changed, developed and adapted throughout the years from pre-revolutionary days to the 40s. The fact that this is the first retrospective of his work ever staged speaks for the slowness of the world in recognizing that posters and photomontage, sweet wrappers and designs for workers' clothing can, in a revolutionary society, be as much of a challenge to the artist as painting and sculpture.

It was with painting that Rodchenko started, after training as an engineer. Early works share the pre-revolutionary inclination for the medieval fairy tale atmosphere loved by Kandinsky. The engineer and the artist met when Rodchenko cleared his palette and his mind to develop his version of the revolutionary language of abstraction free from the ties and associations of the old order. This was the nonobjective world of colour and shape: 'dramas known to us all', lovingly executed in watercolours and rough scumbles of paint, modest in scale and more anecdotal than the severity of Malevich's spiritual quest for purity.

Rodchenko experimented with sculptural form too. In Oxford you can see reconstructions made by John Milner in Newcastle University of Rodchenko's basic wooden explorations of form. Newcastle has quite a tradition for reconstructing the sculpture of the Russian revolution – these Rodchenkos follow the big red Tatlin Tower now in situ outside the Polytechnic of Central London. They are some of the objects that have long tantalized the imagination through the grainy old photographs of the 1921 *Obmokhu* (Society of Young Artists) exhibition in Moscow. They illustrate another important characteristic of the revolutionary art: the search for material. That could mean material in the Marxist sense, for these works differ from pre-revolutionary art in being exactly what they seem: material unadorned and without mystification.

But in 1921 Rodchenko abandoned painting and sculpture for design. Leading theoreticians of the day had greeted his monochrome red, yellow and blue canvases as the Last Paintings (the last picture has been painted). How wrong they were, but how right where Rodchenko was concerned. From this he went on to further attack the preciousness of traditional fine art by giving away original drawings in the little catalogues that make the exhibition of Russian Revolutionary Books still showing at the British Museum such a treat. But his greatest works, in posters, photomontage and stage sets, were still to come. This was the time of collectives, of work with others including his wife Stepanova in the Free Studios and Vkhutema's school, where Constructivism and Productivism flourished.

It was as a poster designer that Rodchenko produced some of the most inspiring images of those idealistic days. His film posters for Eisenstein's *Potemkin*, for Vertov's *Kino Eye*, for Mayakovsky's *Bed Bug*, for the new bookshops and industries, are rare examples of dynamic propaganda fused with superb and revolutionary design quality. Recognizable elements from the everyday Russian world, like the battleship, an eye, or the face of a woman, are combined with abstract line and colour with a clarity and directness never seen before. Rodchenko's liveliness in photomontage has never been rivalled, and when he took to straight photography in the later twenties, the objects of every day were also brought alive through the new vision learnt from painting.

Unrivalled too is the sincerity of his designs, so fresh in their fervour that they still retain an air of almost enviable naivety born of great hopes. In Oxford you can sit in a reconstruction of his 1925 workers' reading room. You will find the chairs upright and to the point, the kind that no worker had ever sat in before, or since, although we will perhaps never know now how the workers reacted. A student of Rodchenko said that he was 'the man who taught us to understand the contemporary situation in a creative and concrete way'. Public projects show how he tried to spread this understanding in the brief years when such things still seemed possible.

Half a century later we can see why such designs were revolutionary. We can also understand why the directness of Rodchenko's visions made him less of a victim to Stalinist drudgery than his fellow artists and poets. He could, to some extent, adapt to orders for 'a true historically concrete depiction of reality', the edicts of social realism.

16 February 1979 **Caroline Tisdall**

Mystic materialist

In mid-August I called on Hugh MacDiarmid, for the last time. Although dying, he was still alert, sharing a noggin of malt, signing a book with a clear but shaky hand. His eighty-sixth birthday had gone unnoticed in *The Times*, but he was used to such slights. He did not even seem afraid of death, although he hoped to see his *Complete Poems*.*

And here they are, two months, alas, after his death, but ensuring that 1978 will be a landmark in both Scots and English literary history. For there is no denying the massive achievement here, on several levels. *Sangschaw* (1925) and *Penny Wheep* (1926) were the finest lyrics in Scots since Burns. And for added richness, *A Drunk Man Looks at the Thistle* (1926) was the finest long poem since Dunbar. In a few years, MacDiarmid had revived and revolutionized Scottish literature.

But he was never one to rest comfortably on his laurels. During his middle years, MacDiarmid wrestled with a vision which would make him not only a local but an international thistle. *To Circumjack Cencrastus* (1930) is a failure, compared to *A Drunk Man*, but the scope is enormous, an invocation of the snake on the Cosmic Tree, with its double nature, creative and destructive. And moving between the swarming horror of the Glasgow slums and the remoteness of the Scottish moors and islands, collections like *Stony Limits* (1934) are both frightening and magnificent.

For those who are uneasy with greatness there are always the marvellous lyrics; 'At My Father's Grave' in *First Hymn to Lenin* (1931), 'Of John Davidson' in *Scots Unbound* (1932), 'The Skeleton of the Future' or 'In the Foggy Twilight' in *Stony*

Limits (1934). But longer poems, like 'Water of Life', 'Depth and the Chthonian Image' and above all, 'On a Raised Beach' have the energy of great poetry, hymns to that mystic materialism which is the centre of his Communism.

> *These stones have the silence*
> *of supreme creative power,*
> *The direct and undisturbed*
> *way of working*
> *Which alone leads to*
> *greatness.*

In such poems he is the nearest equivalent in English to Pablo Neruda (who was also, both personally and poetically, obsessed by stones, like the French Communist poet, Guillevic). It may be galling to some but on the strength of these volumes it is MacDiarmid, and not the modish Auden, who is the major poet of the thirties, the only really Socialist voice. Invalided from one war, a factory hand in the second, the postman's son from Langholm was well equipped to speak for the working class. Even if, fed on popular newspapers and football results, they were unlikely to hear him.

> *This Scotland is not Scotland*
> *But an outsize football pitch . . .*

And the literary middle class, in Edinburgh as well as London, did not wish to come to terms with such a prickly presence: he is still excluded, even from such sympathetic surveys as Robin Skelton's *Poetry of the Thirties*. It was this lack of understanding, as well as personal problems, which seems to have driven MacDiarmid back upon himself, in a skirl of defiance. The third, or didactic MacDiarmid, the logomaniac who paints his own magnificently immodest portrait in *Lucky Poet* (1943), is the most difficult to judge. Especially as many of the best passages are quotations, not always acknowledged.

> *This rag-bag, this Loch Ness monster,*
> *this impact*
> *Of the whole range of*
> *Weltliteratur on one man's brain*

is how he describes *In Memoriam James Joyce* (1955) which, with *The Kind of Poetry I Want* (1957), best represents this attitude. Both are sustained by a fierce loneliness, the boy who ransacked a village library still present in the isolated poet, determined that the world which had not recognized him should flood into his work. I can testify that the Irish and French at least are reasonably correct, and who else would couple Sequoyah, and his Cherokee alphabet, with Johannes Scotus Eriugena?

Pound might, because he was also an admirer of the Irish philosopher, and their approaches have much in common, although MacDiarmid's reliance on the prose line makes for a heavier music. Having succeeded in two major areas, it would be churlish to emphasize his partial failure to invent a new mode of world poetry, to which English society and literature were inimical. Where then do these amazing volumes place him in English literary history?

A possible answer. Not since Wordsworth has there been a poet who so combined the brilliant and the banal, the poetic and the prosaic. The parallels are many: the flowing waters of childhood's landscape, the stern lack of intimacy in the middle years, the didacticism of the later. Both achieved an early masterpiece but had to abandon more grandiose projects. And more than any poet since, MacDiarmid has tried 'to follow the steps of the man of Science', as prescribed in the 1805 'Preface'. But we must remember that they were both Borderers, aliens to literary London; from Langholm to the Lake District is but a day's ride!

* *Hugh MacDiarmid*: Complete Poems 1920–76, vols 1 and 2, *edited by Michael Grieve and W. R. Aitken* (*Martin, Brian and O'Keeffe*).

30 November 1978   **John Montague**

Sade and prejudice

One may as well begin with Angela Carter's cats, with the Marquis de Sade waiting to erupt, like the devil in the old morality.

The cats were crashed in her pad – she is to be identified, she says, by geriatric hippy speech patterns – in Clapham, to which in thirty-eight years she has made a physical progress from her native, neighbouring quarter of Balham. Via Japan.

Plus the cats, catalytic and catastatic, and their catlings, she lives with a guy, gracile and grave, whose head and features are almost entirely immersed in hair, and who makes pulpits. It is an occupation, he says, which he has given up trying to explain. Had he been less hirsute, I could be more sure of observing that he smiled in saying this.

His only other verbal incursion was to demand a book from her to read on the way to Cardiff, where he has a commission to make another pulpit. She denied the request, on the grounds that she must review it. Very well, he said stoically, he would twiddle his thumbs. Though she was plainly wrung by this image of pathos, it was not strong enough to earn him victory, and he went to Cardiff twiddling.

All women like herself, says Angela Carter, have an affinity with cats. She has expressed this in a text for Martin Leman's *Comic and Curious Cats*, loving each cat, whether edacious and epicurean or ugly and ungrateful; right the way through from A to Z in an alliterative style that reminded me of a counting book. Perhaps, she says, but she specialized in medieval literature, so alliteration comes easy.

The catbook industry is not merely buoyant, it swims across oceans. Ah yes, she says, and it's also across class and across sex. Reviewers reserve small corners of irrationality for cats.

But Leman's monolithic cats seem to be aiming for the wombat market too, even if they have cats' faces. Well, she wouldn't mind a wombat. She saw a stuffed wombat in the Natural History Museum and thought what an exceptionally pleasant chap it looked.

The truth is that most mammals, made of very similar stuff as ourselves, seem to her pleasant chaps, rather better than humans. When she writes about Beauty and the Beast, which she does very often in her dazzling fictions, the true dignity lies in the beastliness.

Of course she and her pulpit maker do not love their cats with any particular letter. Indeed they try not to love them at all, but to have an equal relationship. The relationship of the cats, however, is at present disturbed. The female is a mother, which causes her mate to sit in the garden looking as though a fellow's occupation's gone. Seeing him like this makes Angela Carter think that the whole of human culture is devised to give men something to do while women reproduce the species.

The tom in the garden, *désoeuvré*, has human parallels in her memory. Speaking, later, of the working class patterns of her youth in the coalfields of south Yorkshire and of being brought up with a very, very strong sense of her natural superiority as a woman – an embarrassing cultural heritage to take into the middle class – she recalls the Saturday night pub scenes. The stately ladies, deep in conference, elaborately coiffured, drinking shorts, toasting the pregnancies, in charge of the pay packets, indulgently watching the men over there playing darts. They seem to be saying, 'Play, little things.' They're really fond of them; they just don't take them seriously. This, she thinks, is one of the very hardest things for the women's liberation movement.

Like any high-octane intellectual, she would not put forward a partial view as if it were total. To widen the analogy, she has been fascinated by matriarchies anywhere. In Italy she sees the mama's position as one of absolute power with absolute lack of responsibility, wreaking a horrible vengeance on the sons. Again, the libertarian row is difficult to plough.

In Japan, where she spent three years, she experienced the concealed matriarchy. A prostitute society, the wives' response to their situation is one of delighted parasitism. Her married Japanese friends were sorry for her without a man to pay the rent for her twelve by six paper house, but encouraged her to think there was always hope of latching on to somebody. Again, they concentrate a massive input to their sons, and neglect the daughters.

185

Considering Africa, she says that the tribes have matriarchies actually run by women past the menopause. Which of any of these structures would want to give up so much power? She has a theory: whoever can discern the fertility rates and the nature of the intercourse taboos, can immediately divine whether the society is matrifocal or patrifocal. If the intercourse times coincide with the dates of easiest conception, you are looking at a matrifocal society.

Her own mother was a cashier at Selfridges, her father a journalist. Theirs was a period romance begun not at the cash desk but on the tennis courts of respectable Clapham, with a cross-cultural shock, when her father discovered the girl to whom he had presented his card came from disreputable Battersea. Angela Stalker was conceived at a high period of national fertility, but probably eccentrically so, in as much as her mother discovered she was carrying on the day war was declared. Her brother is twelve years older, so in effect she is an only child.

It was a pre-TV childhood, of omnivorous random reading. The house sported all Dickens, in the funny edition Harmsworth gave away, saturating lower middle class homes. The circulation builders, in squashy covers. Thus GBS squeaked in, a feast of prefaces. Her mother was addicted to Victorian aristo memoirs, like the *Diaries of Daisy, Duchess of Pless*. There were notable gaps, like *Moby Dick*.

Angela had an adolescent fever for anarchism. In her maturity she still thinks them right, and righter all the time: none of that fussing with transcendence. You can't build an elaborate metaphysical structure as you can with Marxism, but the idea of humanity is better, better than being strung out between abstract concepts of good and evil. Beneath the shit, the gold. Well, some decency anyway. The trouble is, she reflects ruefully, when two anarchists meet, there's straight away a split.

She tells an anecdote of communist Bologna, a demo of millions of cops and about thirty anarchists, old men with a record of aeons in gaol, and kids. Oh, it was a proud moment for her when she first saw the red and gold unfurled! But what a shock when she located the point of the demo: a protest against English brutality in Northern Ireland. Now this is a thing that gars her greet. Every French intellectual went into print over Algeria, but do the British in a like situation? They're stones.

She took a degree in English at Bristol University, because she was the only person who couldn't get a job on the *Bristol Evening Post*. Her then husband had a job in Bristol, but this move aggrieved her father, who had charted a rung-by-rung course for her to Fleet Street. She was a medievalist because she wanted only to read Joyce and Pound, and thought it rude to have opinions about them. About the Middle Ages it is not possible to have opinions, only to do wonderful cultural slotting. She still doesn't like to have opinions, but works from prejudices, lively and exploratory, giving rise to fresh, dynamic prejudices.

Handicapped by anorexia, with its hideously volatile blood-sugar levels, and the daily threat of a sudden lurch into suicide, she nevertheless began a stream of novels. Suddenly, between *The Infernal Desire Machines of Dr Hoffman* and her recent tour-de-force *The Passion of New Eve*, the flow dried up. Why was that?

She says that her novel *Love* had been a small book, mildly commercially unviable. *Hoffman*, a big book, was magnificently commercially unviable. So she had to scrape around to make a living which is contraproductive. Then she says she was having a nice time and adds that no, she wasn't having a nice time. Then she says that she couldn't think of anything to write about. Then she says that she is forced to confess that the psychic compulsion evaporated when she left her husband.

The psychic compulsion is back. Apart from *New Eve* and the cats, a play of hers is about to go out on Radio 3. This week, *The Sadeian Woman* is published by Virago. In May a collection of fables, richly upholstered stories of vampires and werewolves and recondite passions in castles, enquiries into the metamorphoses of beasts and beauties, called *The Bloody Chamber*, comes out from Gollancz.

In all her work she has a number of persistent images, chiefly that of the old dark house, usually semi-ruinous, though it can be quite spick, and even Gothically glamorous with an umbilical causeway connecting the castle of the beast to the mainland. It has many associations for her. It's the medieval conceit, the glass palace where the grail was kept; the Castle of Perseverance; at the back of it all Plato's Cave. And sometimes, in its dilapidated form, it means Britain, the crumbling house packed in its secret crannies with the relics of an Empire we can't cope with. Any child of the fifties, she says, is bound to be affected by the image of *Bleak House*.

The Somerset Maugham Award, which obliges the winner to travel, took her to Japan. It changed her, yes. She thinks the old chap would have smiled at her as she worked in a bar, brooded in cafés, walked at night about Tokyo in an aimless existential fashion. It was hard for a woman and you get pinched in the tube, but Japan is the mirror image of Britain and, after the paranoia of America, she felt immediately at home with the old familiar class struggle.

To be metaphysical, she says, she wanted to live in a non-Judaeo-Christian society, and another ex-Imperialist power. A prostitute society maybe, but they have no sense of sin and guilt, and a view of suicide which is pure rationality. A great shock for a European. Like the Frenchman who left a suicide note saying that nothing distinguishes man from the animals except his capacity for boredom? Exactly, she says, very Japanese, and they savour the flavours of boredom first.

And now in the foreground, considering the nature of the beast, since the fall of Adam and Eve, primates surely, is Sade, Marquis into Citizen, and also poor sod, the title he would wear most proudly. And the two icons of womanhood he built with the insights of his own pathology – the holy virgin of the brothel whose descendants twirl their pretty tricks like drum majorettes their batons, and the sister who joined the enemy and specializes in realpolitik, with a dildo in her scabbard. On the one hand the myths of the cosmos, on the other the Cosmo girl.

There Sade is, says Angela Carter, with his awful books, an extraordinarily interesting cultural fact. Few people could have had a worse beginning, because privilege is the worst thing you can give to people. Most people born to it never realize that. But in his glimmering, fumbling way, he did realize. And at that particular hinge of history, he caused one of the great irreversible changes in people's perceptions of themselves.

30 March 1979   **Alex Hamilton**

Günter Grass's cookbook

The folk-tale from which Günter Grass derives the title of his new novel, *The Flounder**, is the parable about the insatiable fisherman's wife, Ilsebill, and the wishing fish. She asked the fish for all the patriarchal, authoritarian roles – Let me be king, then Pope, finally God. At that, the fish cried: too much! Now, it seems, the fish may relent.

As the spirit of patriarchy, the flounder first appears to Grass's hero-narrator in the Stone Age. His whispered advice frees the Grass proto-man from the emotionally satisfying but intellectually stifling rule of Mother Right. But in the 1970s, the flounder has only one thing to say to the contemporary incarnation of the hero-narrator: 'Nothing can be expected of you daddies anymore.'

The flounder, therefore, allows himself to be caught again, this time by a satirically depicted bunch of Women's Libbers, and throughout the course of the novel, he remains on trial by a Women's Tribunal. They throw him back into the sea at last. The closing pages take place on a beach, as in Apuleius's *The Golden Ass*. But in contrast to that antique and noble apologia to womankind, there is no true reconciliation with nature, or human nature.

The flounder rises once again from the amniotic Baltic, the unacknowledged legislator of a new, female-dominated history. The fish has merely changed sides; the notion of sexual equality does not obtrude on Grass's mythology. We leave the narrator pursuing the image of the Eternal Feminine along this existential beach. The romantic notion of an essential dichotomy between the sexes is implicit in *The Flounder*.

Between first and last appearance of the fish lies the history of the Vistula estuary, as microcosm of Western Europe, from the Stone Age to the Polish food-price strikes of 1970. Interlinked with the trial of the flounder is a narrative of parturition, both literal and metaphorical: a foetus recapitulates the history of evolution as it grows, the narrator recalls the history of Man. It must be said that the various narratives fuse seamlessly, defying easy résumé. It is the novel of a man at the height of remarkable powers; and also, perhaps, at the limit of his understanding.

But to begin where Grass begins. The narrator's wife, also called Ilsebill, embarks on a planned pregnancy after the couple have consumed a large meal they have prepared together. The deliberate pregnancy and the shared kitchen chores are both germane to the entire plot, for until the present bankruptcy of patriarchy, women have had no choice but to bear children and cook for men. Eating is as atavistic an activity as procreation. To eat is to copulate, says Lévi-Strauss, and in one sense the novel is a celebration of the eroticism of food.

The narrator refers to his wife throughout as 'my Ilsebill', although she is the representative of the Modern Woman, insatiable as her prehistoric avatar, but with a corrupt insatiability, a desire for automatic dishwashers and boy children. There is a suggestion that this may be the price she has paid for abandoning her mythic and historic role as guardian of the cooking pots.

For cookery, as Lévi-Strauss also maintains, is the underpinning of culture itself, and it is women, the bearers of culture, who boil the stomach walls of the elk in Grass's primeval forest, stew lamb's offal during the Reformation, and dish out bluegreen lentils in Stutthof concentration camp. As eater, copulator, priest, poet, painter, soldier, begetter of daughters, the narrator passes through history as through a gigantic bowel. But he is the maker of both the culture and the history which the women only carry, as they carry his girl-children.

Grass does not allow any of his types of the Eternal Feminine to participate on a single barricade as comrades. Which may be poetically satisying in the grand scheme of sexual dichotomy, but is historically false. Grass's imaginative vision of history is, in fact, a romantic distortion. It demands that the daddies alone made a pig's ear out of history.

He concedes, however, that though the women may not move, they may exert a moving force. The predicament of India, which inspires the narrator to a fine pitch of liberal anguish, is the result of male imperialism in itself determined by the insatiable demand of fifteenth-century cooks for more pepper.

Grass is having his anti-patriarchal cake and eating it. If he seems sometimes to be groping for a necessary dialectic between the sexes, as when Ilsebill is delivered of the narrator's ultimate daughter, he fudges it. The narrator has thwarted her desire to produce a male being from her female body. Grass will thrust Mother Right on us even if we think it reactionary, or plain undemocratic.

The Flounder has plainly been constructed to defy proudly all response except dazed awe or vulgar abuse. It is thematically complex in the extreme, exhaustingly inventive, and as full of internal contradictions as capitalism itself. Yet it is curious to find a man of the Left propounding Mother Right as the only humanly satisfactory alternative to the alleged bankruptcy of ideology. It would seem that some men prefer to lose power altogether rather than to share it; but isn't that a typical characteristic of the ruling class? Certainly, *The Flounder* is wilfully offensive to what Grass has called, in another context, 'masculine feminists'. The narrator shows us just what it is *they* really want by coupling with each one of *The Flounder*'s Women's Tribunal.

He reserves an especially bitter mockery for lesbians. An account of a lesbian picnic terminated by gang-rape is executed with such sadistic viciousness as to appear crazed, not so much in the violence of the action as in the virulence with which the women and their relationships are described. This sequence is nigger-baiting, pure and simple.

The reality of women has always presented Grass with major artistic problems. In *The Tin Drum* and *Dog Years*, his expressionist method, emblematic action and huge themes – the Third Reich, war, survival, the self pared to the bone – have conspired to hide a central ambivalence towards women which *The Flounder* reveals in full measure. For he has no means of extending a non-naturalistic technique to encompass women as they really are. He presents us instead with a spirited play of stereotypes.

This is certainly not the fault of the technique. It is not so much an aesthetic flaw as a moral one, a failure of elementary humanism, for which this excavation of the concealed matriarchal structure of Western Europe over the last three thousand years may well be intended to compensate. It fails to do that, because

The Flounder bears, not an imaginative but a fantasy relation to truth.

* THE FLOUNDER, *by Günter Grass, Secker and Warburg.*

13 October 1978   **Angela Carter**

The real Franz Kafka

'My future is not rosy, and 1 will surely – this much I can foresee – die like a dog,' writes Franz Kafka at twenty-three to his friend Max Brod in one of the letters that form the largest part of this big collection* only lately translated into English. But meanwhile, 'a terrible day at the office . . . I suppose one must earn one's grave.'

His jokes make it no less terrible to know so much about Kafka, to be obliged to accept that the flayed soul transfigured in the stories and novels actually inhabited a human frame, walked the streets of Prague and the woods of Bohemia, ate, loved, slept little, and in the mornings after writing from the darkest frontiers of the spirit also wrote careful reports at his desk at the Workers' Accident Insurance Institute ('In my four districts people fall off ladders as if they were drunk').

Apart from Max Brod's biography and first-hand accounts by other members of the Prague circle, we now have the *Diaries* from 1910 to 1923, the autobiographical apologia contained in the long *Letter to His Father*, two other important collections of letters and a fourth collection (to his favourite sister Ottla) still to be translated.

This volume lacks the dramatic cohesion of the *Letters to Milena* and the *Letters to Felice Bauer*, the latter tracing not only the peculiar agonies of a Kafka love affair but also reflecting the flares of the major period of creativity that the affair engendered. What it does, however, read in conjunction with Brod and the *Diaries*, is to make inescapably clear the daily humanity of this eight-stone Atlas who took squarely on his thin shoulders more of the burden of modern consciousness than any other writer of our century.

192

What is new in the way of biographical events is disclosed in a long letter (unearthed in its entirety by Klaus Wagenbach) which describes yet another engagement, to Julie Wohryzek, daughter of the caretaker of a Prague synagogue ('If one wanted to classify her racially one would have to say that she belonged to the race of shopgirls'): an engagement which seems to have come remarkably close to marriage, but which foundered on rocks familiar to readers over the shoulder of poor Felice Bauer.

But it is less the large life-events than the small signs, the gestures and epiphanic scenes recorded in these twenty years of letters that demonstrate the unnerving near-identity of the life and the art that grew from it. One reads a letter from a twenty-year-old boy and realizes with a kind of fear that he is enacting in his own person one of those subhuman postures whose images recur in his later writing like archetypes recalled from the half-light of the cave. Out for a walk on a day in August, 1904, his dog chases a mole, then strikes it with its paw, and the mole 'cried out: *Ks, ks*, it cried'. Later that day 'my head started to droop so badly that in the evening I noticed with astonishment that my chin had grown into my chest'.

There are dozens of these sudden brief metamorphoses into the animal, often something feral, sometimes sympathetic, sometimes antagonistic to the self, and expressive of the extraordinarily divided soul he ruled with such subtlety and brave terror. He calls his cough 'the animal', tells Brod 'I cannot write ... My whole body warns me against every word; every word, before it lets me write it down, first looks round in all directions'; says later, if a writer 'wants to keep madness at bay he must never go far from his desk, he must hold on to it with his teeth'.

There are letters here on the nature of writing and art as proud and painful as any of those to Felice, offering both the 'damnation' and the 'salvation' versions. Wrestling with the shadows of *The Castle* in 1922, he thinks writing is 'a sweet and wonderful reward . . . for serving the devil. This descent to the dark powers, this unshackling of spirits bound by nature, these dubious embraces and whatever else takes place in the nether parts which the higher parts no longer know, when one writes one's stories in the sunshine . . . the diabolic element seems very clear to me.' But later, in a less Dionysian mood, he sees the necessity of art as a kind of strategy for 'making possible the exchange of truthful words from person to person'.

His own paramount, desperate need of art, however, he expresses in a third way, which sums up with a perfect childlike simplicity his struggle with all the contending terrors – as a guilty son, a sick man, a Jew in the *Abendland*, a thinking European in the last days of mankind: 'I am away from home and must always write home, even if any home of mine has long since floated away into eternity. All this writing is nothing but Robinson Crusoe's flag hoisted at the highest point of the island.'

He is near the end now, going home after all, for there is something almost like peacefulness in the late letters from Berlin, where a premature ghost flits through the tree-lined avenues of Steglitz ('anyone who isn't looking squarely at it can't notice it'), enjoying the lectures at Leo Baeck's Academy for Jewish Studies when he can get to them, and sensing a wasting sickness that matched his own fevers in that city also marked for death.

Then the final move, to the sanatorium in Austria – very expensive, but his last story, about Josephine the singing mouse, will help to 'earn one's grave' – and the collection ends with the terrible 'conversation slips' which should be read by anyone who has tired of Kafka's 'hypochondria'. These were scraps of paper on which he wrote the sentences he could no longer speak as tuberculosis of the larynx tightened its grip. 'Every limb as tired as a person,' says one of the last; and another (raising the ghost of a terrified smile): 'Tremendous amount of sputum, easily, and still pain in the morning. In my daze it went through my head that for such quantities and the ease somehow the Nobel Prize.'

* FRANZ KAFKA: Letters to friends, family and editors, *trans. Richard and Clara Winston (John Calder).*

10 September 1978   **W. L. Webb**

Navigator only: a story

They came first on a Tuesday, and I am sure of this because on that day the shops close early, and I was so put out by Their visit that I forgot to buy bread and milk in the morning, so that we didn't have enough left for breakfast on Wednesday.

They wanted to know whether I would be prepared to earn a million pounds by pressing a button here, which would kill an old, sick mandarin in China. All, They assured me, in the strictest confidence, and without complications or tax deductions. I asked if I could think about it. Of course, They said, take your time.

When I need to think I always go down to the shore. I walked along the beach, hopping over tar patches, seeing the water melon sprouts left over from the summer bathers, and looking for ugly, flat ray fish in the shallows. The goosenecked barnacles were waving about on a waterlogged piece of wood (what sort of an existence is that, I ask you?) and I picked up a wooden sign on which was written 'Navigator Only' in red, peeling paint. Underneath was some Chinese script which presumably meant the same thing, though it might, of course, have been Japanese.

Signs and portents, I thought, and trudged along through the beautiful, regular, newly made tank tracks. I turned back only when the piles of shale at the water's edge became too painful for bare feet.

Back at home I turned to other occupations which keep my hands busy and my mind free. I scrubbed out the bathtub, and cleaned all the kitchen cupboards, first rootling around in the children's rooms till I found drawing pins to secure the clean blue paper with which I like to line the shelves.

All the time I was trying to imagine a million pounds. I worked out that at our current rate of expenditure, it would take us the better part of forty years to spend it. As one gets older and the children leave home, I think one tends to spend less, rather than more, even allowing for increases in the cost of living. Anyway, try as I would, for the life of me I could form no clear picture of 'a million'. I kept remembering stories about Germany after the First World War, when people lugged around suitcases of paper money to buy themselves half a salami, or five eggs, or, worse, a pack of cigarettes.

On the other hand, I was concerned about the poor old mandarin. He might really be sick, in great pain. If he was as old as They implied, he was probably half blind, impotent, incontinent, and possibly not senile enough to be oblivious of it all. In short, he probably wasn't having much of a life.

I went into the garden to watch things beginning to grow, and I filled the old casserole with the broken handle, so that the birds could have a bath. For some years now they have been staying here all seasons, and they enjoy using up my stale bread. So I broke up the old crusts for them, put out the crumbs and the bathwater.

When They came back, I asked for more particulars about the mandarin. They were annoyed, apparently, for They replied that They had none to offer, no time for that sort of rubbish, and that there were plenty of others who would be only too glad of the chance. Take it or leave it, They said.

Now I know that ultimately all the buttons do get pushed. But I reckoned that if I left him alive, perhaps he'd have time to enjoy warming his cold old bones on a mild and sunny day before somebody else finished thinking it over. So I declined with thanks, and They went away. I forgot all about it – insofar as one can dismiss such a thing from one's mind. I do have quite a lot to occupy me, after all.

Some time later – it must have been at least two months – I received a letter which had come all the way from China, by overseas mail.

It was, of course, from the mandarin. He had heard, he said, of my consideration, and was writing to thank me personally for my sympathetic attitude. He hoped there were more people in the world with my forbearance. Sometimes, he said, They made rather bad errors, which could be difficult to rectify. In his case, for instance, They had been very wide of the mark.

He wrote that, far from being old and ill, he was only in his middle fifties, and very hale and hearty, taking at least a one-hour constitutional before breakfast every day, and looking forward each winter to seeing the plum trees blossoming in the spring.

He has a wife, a mistress, several aged relatives dependent upon him, and four children, of whom, unfortunately, only one is male; and two of his daughters have already borne him grandsons. He is co-director of a small company which makes the paper items indispensable for daily living in China. This is how he supports all these souls.

He even enclosed a snap-shot, which is quite disappointing. He wears a kimono, but it is open, and underneath are shorts and an open shirt. He is a tubby little bald man, with protruding teeth. No skull cap, long finger nails, drooping moustaches, or heavy brocades. No look of ancient wisdom at all.

I didn't want to start a regular correspondence, so I sent back a short note, thanking him, and saying that I was glad it had all been sorted out in time, and that I hoped he would live happily for many years to come. Many months afterwards I received a small package containing a paper fan. It had a picture on it, of cranes flying over flowering cherries, and a waterfall. In the corner was written 'Made in the People's Republic of China'. The accompanying note said that this is a sample of what his company makes, and that in China fans are always given as tokens of goodwill – symbols of blossoming and flowering.

I tacked the fan up on the kitchen wall. Sometimes when I am setting the table I look at it and think: Let that be a lesson to you.

My husband is a professional man, a geologist, who loves to travel. Anywhere in the world there is, so to speak, grist for his mill. He is kindly, and rather abstracted. Though he protests when I find excuses for not travelling with him, I know that he really enjoys himself far better alone, and one, of course, can always travel further than two on a limited budget.

We are very dissimilar. He, for instance, loves to impart information – nudging one to point out sights (usually things I've noticed several minutes earlier), while I hug what I see jealously to myself, tending to become quite peeved if he happens to notice them too.

Once, on a very hot day, we drove on a throughway in a great city, and I saw on an odd green patch by the highway a very large Negro matron, bare to the waist, with a sari wrapped round her hips, dancing barefoot to music which only she could hear, stamping her feet, and waving a cloth round her head. She looked wonderfully relaxed and light on her feet, as so many big women are, and she gleamed in the heat. My husband didn't notice her at all, though she shone in my mind's eye for weeks afterwards. I never mentioned her to him. She was my private joy, a small consolation for some very unpleasant weather. If he had seen her he'd have told me, told all our friends, virtually put an announcement in the paper.

In the course of time he was invited to a conference in China. He had wanted to go there for so long, and jumped at the chance. There was no question of my joining him this time – too far, too costly, too complicated. I was glad he had his chance.

When his first letter arrived – a very long time after he had left – I was potting basil seedlings. My thumbs are as green as most, and greener than some, but I cannot cope with basil at all. The man down the street who runs the Italian restaurant has it flourishing all over the place – in plastic buckets, old zinc tubs, anywhere you like. I get frustrated thinking of it. No sooner does some of mine sprout than it wilts and fades away.

Later, after cleaning up, I sat down with his letter and a fresh cup of coffee, and prepared myself to be bored by the interesting things about which he writes. I waded dutifully through descriptions of meals on planes, rail tickets, customs duties, scenery. He missed us, he was well cared for, raw fish in Japan is delicious, everything was superb, magnificent, fascinating. For him nobody in India dies of hunger; defecation by the roadside is funny; olfactory organs are in abeyance. How nice to be able to keep your eyes above the level of your nose.

'I never knew,' he wrote, 'you had any Chinese friends. Why have you never told me?'

I don't have any Chinese friends.

He wrote: 'These people, apparently descendants of a very ancient Chinese family, seem to know so much about you.' They had asked him all sorts of questions – how well I was, the ages of the children, especially the youngest, whether I still possessed a fan they had once sent me. (It had been on the wall for about two years before he noticed it.) They said they would be writing to me, and took our address, as they had mislaid it.

Of course I realized who they were, but their concern was very puzzling. They had obviously not mentioned Them – but then, nor had I – and it was already so far in the past. I wasn't quite happy about something, but dismissed it as annoyance at one of my silly secrets coming out of the bag like that.

I told the children about the letter, and we made a map of his route, with coloured pins to mark stops.

They were so nice to me, all the time he was away. The weather was good, the beach enticing, and though I could no longer, in all decency, wear a couple of little bits of cloth to cover myself, I felt I was not doing too badly in the scantiest whole suit I could find. We relaxed, I cooked less, the house stayed tidier - we too were having a holiday. His letters arrived frequently after the initial wait.

Finally, inevitably, a letter arrived from China, written by the mandarin's daughter. The English was very odd, but I grasped the gist of the contents.

All, she said, were very well, the father still working hard, and the family larger than ever due to the addition of several more grandchildren; one of the granddaughters had also married, and already borne a child. They were no longer a family, but a clan.

Life was not easy: so many mouths to feed, so much labour to produce the wherewithal, not enough land or jobs for everyone. To forge ahead one really needed contacts. They hoped all went well with me, that the children were grown and beginning to be independent. They would write again.

I didn't reply. There was nothing to say.

He came home. We watched his films and listened to his traveller's tales, interminably, it seemed. The older children began to do their own travelling. I kept, I keep, busy. There is still enough for me to do, and more than enough to keep me interested and occupied – and thoughtful, especially since the arrival of the latest communication, more than a month ago now.

Again written by the daughter, who has married a Mr Li, it is brief and comprehensible. Life is harder than ever. The same suggestion has been made to her husband as They made to me. This time, of course, I am to be at the other end of the button. In view of the fact that my children no longer need me, they have decided to accept Their offer. They will give me time to put my affairs in order, but not too long, every day makes a difference to them. They promise that it will be painless. They wish me well.

The basil flourishes splendidly these days. You could imagine the head of my beloved nourishing its roots. I don't blame Mr Li. I have done my best to sort things out. There is too much of the world left for my husband to see for him to miss me very much, and the children have nearly all gone. I have never believed in my indispensability.

But They are not really to be trusted, I think – and I cannot see Them forking out a million – would it be Yen? – just to get Their own back. I fear the clan will be very little better off after the event, especially when tax on unearned income has been deducted, or whatever.

I am sorry, and I am afraid. It is hard to concentrate on the book I am reading. I know the kitchen needs painting, but hate the thought that perhaps it will be only half finished. The sea tells me, insistently, that this is a fortunate way to die. I tell myself that at least I shall not . . .

26 May 1979   **N. N. Joseph**

The double crossing of an eye

It was the kind of day when you know by nightfall the rain will be slanting down like a dirty glass bead curtain. The Soho air felt like a lot of people had loaned it already. David Galloway was pumping it full of smoke from a cigarette in a short black holder with a fat gold band. It matched the thin gold chain round his neck and the gold rim round his glasses. He had been monkeying with Raymond Chandler and I needed to know why.

He'd written a book about a private eye called Lamaar Ransom, who's blonde and lesbian and rents an office in the same block as Philip Marlowe. She talks like Marlowe, a couple of octaves up. She sees him in the lobby, adjusting his bandage as he leaves the men's room. The big thing about being a female PI is people don't hit you so often.

Ransom's sidekick lives in a charcoal skin and powder blue suit. His idea of fun is a night at the movies with a nice young soldier. I guessed some Chandler fans would count Galloway's book the kind you light fires with.

Galloway is an American professor with a couple of novels to his name – the critics liked his last one, *A Family Album*. He spent a year setting up Iran's Museum of Modern Art in Tehran before the Shah blew. He reckons the collection may be worth ten million dollars, and not all the art is the kind devout people like to have in the same room with the Koran. He hopes they won't burn the pictures or flush them down the john like all that Iranian embassy booze.

I'd stocked up on the kind of questions professors like to be asked. I fed him the one about the PI being the urban cowboy, and he loved it. He was nuzzling his second cigarette in that cute holder.

'In *The Big Sleep*, Marlowe has been compared to a knight.' I figured you didn't need to be a genius to get that far. *Big Sleep*, page one, paragraph two – the stained glass panel at the Sternwood place has a knight in dark armour rescuing a lady who was tied to a tree and didn't have any clothes on but some very long and convenient hair. The Sternwood girl's hair was shorter, but that was the only difference.

Galloway followed through like a pro. He said the Western was a kind of Arthurian legend – in the last reel someone comes in and slugs the guy on the black horse. 'As America became urbanized, these figures got an urban reincarnation, but they were always slightly outside the law, either because they literally take the law into their own hands, or because they are on the run.'

I thought I might have to do both. I was running out of clever questions. But a friend of Galloway's called Christian Sabisch was between me and the door. He was taller than me, and not quite as tall as the door. I stayed where I was and fed Galloway another dry crust: gunslinging cowboy reincarnates as private eye reincarnates as crusading TV lawyer? It went down like an oyster.

'I think it has a lot to do with the American cult of the individual, which is very important in the development of America; a reliance on the individual to redress grievance and restore order, especially in the West, where often there was not much law around, except vigilante law.'

Fine for the frontier. 'What's potentially dangerous is the idea that you don't have to worry about problems over much, because some crusader will come along and do it for you.'

Like the Sheriff's posse or Jimmy Carter. Then Galloway hit me with mythology. No Western ever showed you the thousands who went west on foot pushing barrows. They show you the Connestoga waggons, a nose-down model built so a man could just about handle it if all his waggon team died, only the Connestogas were the Cadillacs of their time. Most of the trailers had to make do with sore feet. But the myth said you had to have waggons.

He told me about the book he's researching this summer, about a real-life bunch of rich go-Westers who got stuck in snow in the Sierra Nevada and wound up eating each other for breakfast. He said all the accounts till now have fixed on the men and the cannibalism. He wants to write it as seen by a woman. Maybe he should. The women did the cooking.

He also told me about this international anthology of homosexual literature. That was where Sabisch would have come in if he hadn't been there already. They are editing the anthology together. Sabisch hadn't twitched an eyelash or said a word. Now he shuffled his feet.

I asked Galloway why they were putting together this fairy collection. He batted his left eyelid. Maybe both, but the left eye was the only one I could see.

The answer was because it didn't exist. There were a few collections, and some sexploitation stuff. Nothing serious or scholarly.

So what was so special about homosexual writing? '. . . Part of the problem of the twentieth century in general, the problem of identity and self-image which exists in all kinds of minority literature – Jewish American writing, black writing, and in the women's movement . . . The problem of identity and self-image is certainly not limited to people of any particular sexual preference.'

I was glad. Identity was no worry, I just checked my driver's licence once a day. But my self-image needed a drink.

I thanked him for his time. He'd talked all through in a firm, even voice he'd built in a lecture theatre. Suddenly it trilled like

Benny Goodman loosening up on the high notes: 'Thank you for asking such nice questions.' I guessed he'd been waiting for one question he'd expected, but that hadn't come. I let him have that one. I didn't need to ask, and I didn't want to know.

9 June 1979 **Hugh Hebert**

Vacating England

When I've had it up to here with people telling me Jimmy Saville is Albert Schweitzer and what *The Times* needs is a good comparability study and that, in flood, south Dorset is no worse than Chittagong, and the petrol price is finally bottoming-out, and the Common Market isn't as boring as Canada, and that all you need to appear on television is a speech impediment, and that the aristocrat who disembowelled that schoolgirl (his plea: 'But she had the body of a nine-year-old!') ought to have his Red Rover pass endorsed, and wittering on about some gloomy comedian's coronary, and shop assistants replying, 'If you don't see it, we don't have it' to every question, including the way to the toilet, and that licensing hours have nothing to do with the fact that most publicans are drunk by 2.30, and that the Royal Family are overworked and underpaid, and that Park Lane is like the Gaza Strip, and dogturds are preferable to cyclists in public parks, and beginning every sentence with, 'You Yanks – ', and – oh, that funny old England is changeless, just as Eric 'Orwell' said; then I figure it's high time I took myself away on a good vacation.

The point is (and it is the greatest misapprehension in this maddening country) that England is not changeless, and I sometimes think it is no place for children. Though I suppose if children grow up among the geriatric, the frantic and the scheming they will end up knowing a thing or two about survival, even if they do sing the wrong words to 'My Country 'Tis of Thee'.

Most people go away for a vacation; I go home. And I consider myself lucky that I don't have to live at home, that I am for most of the year on this narrow island. England has the strictness and estranging quality of school. It is an old-fashioned place in which unpredictable suffering is part of the process of enlightenment. It keeps me hard at work because I find there is absolutely nothing else to do here. But the summer is different. Ever since I was an ashen-faced tot, I have regarded the summer as a three-month period during which one swam, fished, read comic books, ate junk food and harmlessly misbehaved. In Massachusetts the sun comes out at the end of May and keeps shining until the first week in September. No one talks about the weather. There is no talk of weather in places that have a reliable climate. Once I recall staying in London in August. I spent nearly the whole month in Clapham on a roadside with a dozen crones in over-coats, waiting for a 49 bus.

Since a vacation is a period of unambitious reflection in easeful surroundings, not requiring energy or the willingness to take risks (in all senses a vacation to me is the opposite of travel: I would never take a vacation in Upper Volta, for example), my funk-hole, to which I retire every year, is my own house in East Sandwich, on the Massachusetts coast. There is no bore like a vacation bore, but I think it is worth mentioning why I happen to like this handle-shaped piece of geography, swinging from the crankcase of the Bay State. It is largely a return to childhood, to a setting I understand and one which I associate with optimism. Americans still believe that all problems have solutions and that one deserves to live happily and uncrowded; they believe in the sanctity of space and are surprisingly generous and unsuspicious. This is very soothing, and strangest of all even I am different there: in the States I own a dishwashing machine and an electric can-opener, but I have no such things here. Why is this so?

After the grimy sparrows and incontinent pigeons of London, the blue jays, the cardinals and finches of Cape Cod seem of almost tropical brilliance; the sumacs are like jungle ferns, and the sand dunes like those that people snap pictures of in Wadi Halfa. In London I am denied the pleasures I enjoy at small expense during the East Sandwich summer: swordfish, lobster, cigars, champagne (probably from Buffalo, but so what?), kosher pastrami, pizzas, and childhood treats called Devil Dogs and Twinkies which, when wolfed down, summon remembrances of things past. There are conventional recreations, nearly always a thrilling Peter Nichols or Michael Frayn play, produced among the lightning bugs and within earshot of pounding surf; and Hyannis boasts a killer whale that does impressions of Jimmy Carter. On the domestic front, we have my brother Alex who organizes games of charades (acting out book titles such as the *Principia Mathematica*) or Murder (twenty players required), or ones undreamt-of at English house parties, such as the competition in which players must give the exact phonetic spelling of certain common sounds (Q: 'The hammering of a fist on a wooden door?' A: 'Dumpf-dumpf'). And there is the mud-lark of clam-digging, which ends with *spaghetti alla vongole* or a bushel of bivalves steaming on the stove, and costs nothing but the $3 ('for the season') clam-digging licence.

An average day begins early. I don't shave. The children disappear into the woods to practise defoliation. My brother-in-law cuts the grass. My wife and I retire to our separate studies. Just before noon we assemble and carry mast, sails, rudder and life-jackets and a picnic lunch to the beach, a five-minute walk. The rest of the day we spend sailing and swimming in an empty blue bay. At six the wind shifts with the cooling of the twilit shoreline, and we head home. After a shower, we read and drink, and the soberest one makes dinner. Then Alex and ten other relatives, and games or talk.

It was how I spent my childhood summers. I didn't have a job then; I don't have one now. The beaches are wide and uncluttered, the roads are deserted (and petrol – even now – is less than 50p a gallon), the countryside is leafy; acres of poison ivy lie between me and my neighbours. The town has been a town for 350 years; and a plaque outside the local church states that it was designed – somehow – by Christopher Wren. I value the privacy, the mild climate, the tomatoes that ripen in July, even the skunk which emerges from the woods at sundown; and, when they're needed, supermarkets, American promptness and efficiency (the phone installed at twenty-four hours' notice). It is, for two months, a resting place for the imagination, a release from the confinement I feel in London, and a way of verifying that the excitement I felt during childhood summers was not illusion. My children will have the same fond memories.

In the first week of September, there is a faint chill in the air, the foretaste of what is always a bitter winter of paralysing snow; the surf is higher and whiter, and the hermit crabs swarm more boldly from the jetty. Yellow school buses appear on roads where there were only dune buggies. We hose down the sailboat and put it in mothballs. Then the flight to London, to the clammy airport where, one September, I heard a nasty porter snarl 'You're not in America now, mate' to a mildly complaining tourist. I am reminded again that I am a refugee for the winter.

20 August 1979   **Paul Theroux**

Solo lexicographer

Eric Partridge was an intensely private man, so private indeed that one wondered if he had *any* life except that of his books, his carefully guarded seat – always the same one – in the British Museum, and his regular eating places. As early as 1961, after I first met him at the Savile Club, he wrote to me and said, 'I go about, in these days, very little.' I last met him just before he moved to Devon and we lunched together at Rinaldo's, a simple little restaurant near the British Museum. He was plainly dressed and the food was plain. I had arrived slightly early and the staff told me that the elderly gentleman I was looking for always sat at the same table. I felt at the time that he would have made an excellent peasant – industrious, quiet, decent, living within his means.

And lack of means was what governed his life – impecuniousness, the bane of lexicographers since Doctor Johnson and Doctor Murray, and the consequent need to earn a living from his pen. He often spoke ruefully of the absence of security in his life: 'You OUP lexicographers have guaranteed salaries, many colleagues and experts, but I must work by myself.' Well, he did not exactly work by himself because as soon as his *Dictionary of Slang and Unconventional English* appeared in 1937 he began to receive postcards and letters from every part of the world – a proletarian army of other peasants helping the great word peasant himself.

Moving the image a little he often seemed to me to be like a fairman at a fair, perhaps on a village green: the world of graft, conmen, bright lights, dodgem cars, coconut shies, and the colourful language of gipsies. These things fascinated him. So did the language of soldiers and men and women in the other services, and the catchy phrases of the music hall, of pantomimes, and so on. He relentlessly sought and printed the strangest of words from the most repugnant areas, some by direct contact with the people that used them, but most of them from dusty old recondite collections of slang and cant words from the seventeenth century onwards. He shunned publicity and would accept no honours.

But to the end, and he wrote his familiar infectiously industrious postcards to his friends until the end, he remained dignified, unruffled, a somewhat Beckettian figure, cheerful, resolute. His books were on many subjects, shaggy-dog stories, clichés, usage and abusage, comic alphabets, catchphrases, and etymology – the last-named full of non-existent forms in the exotic languages he did not know but that he accepted from word-lords of Sanskrit, Urdu, Japanese, and so on, but also treating related words like *dear*, *dearth*, and *darling* all together and not spaced out in alphabetical sequence as in other dictionaries. I wrote a piece about him in 1967 when his *Supplement* to the *Dictionary of Slang and Unconventional English* was first published. The subeditor entitled it Absoballylutely. It was just the word. Eric Partridge knew all the other slang words that one could fit between *Abso* and *lutely* in *absolutely*, but this quiet reticent New Zealander would doubtless have chosen *bally*, no more no less, in his own speech.

7 June 1979   **Robert Burchfield**

Caught in the middle

It came as something of a shock to cricketers of my generation to read that Wood, a promising young Australian batsman, had been dropped from the side because of his erratic and dangerous running between the wickets. So well schooled have they been in this department that, as player or spectator, I cannot ever remember an Aussie being run out. I can, however, recall a Christmas party in Adelaide being enlivened by Vic Richardson, teller of many a superbly outré tale, relating and acting out an historic scuffle of long ago.

Australia won the last Test in 1930 by an innings after which we all had a nice cuppa, and the victors set off in high spirits to Bristol, there to despatch Gloucestershire. Perhaps their spirits were a bit too high for, with only 118 to make on the last innings to accomplish this, they found they had lost nine wickets with the scores no more than level. The last pair were Perce Hornibrook and Charlie Walker who sweated and struggled through three maiden overs of Parker and Goddard by which time nerves were twanging like piano wires. At that point one of them made a firm hit towards cover and the pair set out with glad cries to collect the winning run.

But cover made a good interception and brought the heroes to an abrupt halt. However, the striker seeing that the ball had not been gathered set off again, bawling at his retreating partner to grasp this gleam of hope. The partner was by this time practically at his own doorstep but he gallantly put about once more, just as the striker had lost heart and turned for home. There the striker, seeing the fielder still fumbling, made another desperate foray, but the roles were now reversed, his partner in mid-wicket having made a simultaneous about turn.

At the apex of this bizarre triangle was the fielder, not much helped, poor man, by the bellows of 'this end' which reached him from both. With staring eyes trying to judge the intentions of the runners (obviously an impossibility) he scrabbled furiously around his ankles picking up successive handfuls of air and discharging them madly in all directions, whilst the ball nestled cosily between his feet. This dictated the tempo of the runners' *pas de deux* for, at each discharge, they reacted frantically but without co-ordination so that each covered a considerable distance on a regular beat eight yards from his crease and eight yards back again. Since they were always going in the same direction they might have been Perce East and Charlie West for ne'er did they meet, let alone cross.

But all good things must come to an end and cover, at length, grasping solid leather for once, thrashed it in but to the arrival end of the shuttle service so that both escaped. And what did their agonies achieve? Scarcely had the dust and din settled when Perce was lbw to Tom Goddard and the match a tie.

The English endurance record for muddle between the wickets must still belong to 'Crusoe' Robertson-Glasgow and Tom Raikes. Playing for Oxford against Surrey at the Oval in 1922 they met in mid pitch and, after a moment's hesitation, together made for the same end, whence they immediately left again in company abreast. It was calculated that, as though attached to each other by some spectral harness, they traversed the pitch four times at the end of which all the stumps had been flattened by repeated attacks and most of the fielders by hysteria. When they paused for a moment to draw breath and consider future policy one of the opposition had the presence of mind to erect one stump and, ball in hand, to uproot it as laid down in the book. This was not quite the end of the drama for neither the umpires, nor the runners, nor anyone else present could decide who was out. The problem was resolved by tossing and 'Crusoe' won.

My old club Middlesex have had some spectacular runners over the years. Tom Enthoven headed the list with the proud record of having, as captain of Cambridge, run out his entire side in the course of the short University season. Pat Hendren had his unpredictable moments of danger and Denis Compton provided almost as much excitement and entertainment between the creases as he did in occupying them. Walter Robins was a superb runner, very fast on the straight and like lightning on the turn. The trouble here was that, in his enthusiasm, he occasionally forgot that others were not quite so sprightly.

In the third Test Match at Melbourne in 1937 Australia set England 689 to make on the fourth innings to win the match. Walter, having made nought in the first innings, went in at ten minutes before the close of play on the fifth evening, with 534 runs still wanted and four wickets down. Maurice Leyland was still there having battled his way through an intensely hot day against a spirited attack. It was with great relief that Walter steered Bill O'Reilly's first ball through the gully and was off like a whippet from the trap. He was back for a second in a flash and, seeing no fielder in the vicinity of the ball, set off for a third. Half way there he was aware of a figure by his side. It was

Maurice whom he had lapped.

At once Walter turned back and Maurice plodded on to safety where, in a cloud of steam and sweat, he literally 'sat on the splice', blowing like a grampus. As Walter advanced to make his apologies Maurice tottered out to meet him. 'Take it easy lad,' he gasped, 'we can't get all these roons tonight.'

27 March 1979   **Ian Peebles**

At the Steroid Games

For the fatalists among us there is too much talk around the Rosicky Stadium in Prague, where the twelfth European Championships begin today, and the university complex in which the competitors are housed next door, about the racing certainties of the six days of competition.

Steve Ovett, Sebastian Coe and Brendan Foster are the names mentioned more than any others. They are contenders for some of the most popular titles, the 1500 metres, 800 metres and 10,000 metres. Nothing could be better of course for British athletics if by Sunday evening this trio and a few others from the team were the dominating personalities of the championships, but one suspects that while they may make some impact, the theme of the championships will be the power of East Germany's women and the growing feeling that this part of the athletic world is becoming divided even more by the use of anabolic steroids.

There are sixteen gold medals to be won in the women's events and ten of them are likely to go to the German Democratic Republic. It could be more. While Britain works hard to stamp out anabolic steroids, the body building drug, there is no evidence that testing goes on in Eastern European domestic meetings. 'Have you seen Udo Beyer? (East Germany's leading shot putter.) He's enormous. He must have put on a stone around his face,' said Geoff Capes, Britain's exponent who almost refused to come to these championships because he felt that testing was inadequate in Eastern Europe.

Someone who is not normally moved to speak on the subject,

Sue Reeve, Britain's women's captain, expressed her amazement about Vilma Bardauskiene, the new Russian world-record holder for the long jump who has just cleared 23 ft 2½ in. 'I smashed her in the European Indoor Championships when she did 20 ft 1½ in, and she didn't look like a class jumper to me. That was in March and she has not competed outside Russia. I was surprised when she did 22 ft 3¾ in, but this world record . . .'

Of course people do come out of the blue, because no one has suggested that Bob Beamon had any illegal uplift for his record take-off in the long jump at the Mexico Olympic Games. But when a Russian girl improves by that amount and Beyer (another stay-at-home athlete) comes to Prague with a four feet advantage over his nearest rival, it is no wonder that other competitors express their suspicion and frustration.

There will be testing, but it is fairly well known that if you come off the pills three weeks before competing then that phial of urine will not expose you as a cheat. One day the scientists are going to catch up and a lot of offenders will be caught. But not, I suspect, in Prague.

29 August 1978   **John Rodda**

Victorian artist hits the jackpot

David Roberts, one of the more commercial of Victorian masters, would no doubt have rejoiced that his pictures were still making money in the Middle East 114 years after his death. He would probably have been less flattered to learn that, while he was the best-known British painter in the Levant, he was almost forgotten at home, meriting barely a dozen lines in the encyclopaedias, and that since his work was long out of copyright there was nothing in it for his heirs.

Roberts's life reads like a nineteenth-century folk-tale: Born in 1796 at Stockbridge, near Edinburgh, the son of a shoe-maker; apprenticed to a housepainter, studying art at night school; scene-painter in Glasgow, Edinburgh, Carlisle, and finally Drury Lane; exhibited at the British Institute in 1824, elected president of the Society of British Artists in 1831, full member of the Royal Academy ten years later; paintings commissioned by royalty, hung in national collections (still to be found in the Victoria and Albert); died suddenly in 1864 while working on a picture in St Paul's Cathedral.

But the Roberts revival, like much of the Roberts fortune, springs from the ten industrious months he spent touring Egypt, Palestine, and the Lebanon in 1838 and 1839. Roberts, depicted in a contemporary portrait as a plump, Bohemian alderman, travelled like a gentleman, well-read, and well-furnished with letters of introduction.

At Alexandria he was welcomed by the British consul, who guaranteed him every facility. He sailed up the Nile with a captain and crew of eight 'to protect him from interruption or insult while sketching'. In Cairo he was the first non-Moslem allowed to draw inside a mosque, on the single condition that he did not use hog's bristle brushes.

From Egypt, Roberts and two English companions rode through the desert in Arab dress to Petra, the rose-red ultimate in exotic lost cities, an arduous month's journey following the route of the Israelites across the Red Sea and Mount Sinai.

After five days of sketching in Petra, Roberts was driven out by local tribesmen, apparently in collusion with his Bedouin guides for whom the Nabatean fastness had less allure.

Crossing into Western Palestine, Roberts was barred from Jerusalem by an outbreak of plague, but put his time to good use in Hebron, Gaza, Ashkelon, and Jaffa, ascending to Jerusalem through the Judean hills when the quarantine was lifted.

On Palm Sunday he went with 4000 Christian pilgrims to Jericho and the place of the baptism in the Jordan. From there he worked his way north and west through Samaria to Tiberias and the Mediterranean port of Acre, crossing the Lebanese mountains to Baalbec and Beirut.

Despite the harsh conditions and bouts of fever, Roberts returned home with hundreds of sketches, delicate, evocative and precise, catching the flow of the landscapes, the heat, languor, and stagnation of the Holy Land, the torpor of the Nile, the bustle of Cairo. His work was romantic – it sometimes looked as if he carted a broken Corinthian column in his knapsack – but never cloying.

Others were to follow, but Roberts had more dash and sense of place than Woodward and Fenn, the illustrators of Sir Charles Wilson's scholarly *Picturesque Palestine*, more professionalism than the Rev W. H. Bartlett, who drew the pictures for his own *Walks About the City and Environs of Jerusalem* and more stamina than Edward Lear, who painted Middle East scenes twenty years after Roberts.

Back in England, Roberts invested ten years exploiting his sketch books. He painted Jerusalem in oils and water colours. The British Ambassador's residence near Tel Aviv has one of the former, Teddy Kollek, the mayor of Jerusalem, one of the latter.

In collaboration with the lithographer Louis Haghe, Roberts published his handsome collection of *Sketches in the Holy Land and Egypt*, with a commentary based on his travel diaries. They were reprinted in the 1840s, 1850s and 1860s.

In London's Charing Cross Road last year a dealer told me that a Roberts volume would sell for £2500 if only he could lay his hands on one. The daughter of an antiquarian bookseller in Jerusalem said she had refused £3500 for a set of the de luxe Royal Subscribers' Edition, preferring to break them up and sell the plates at £125 each. Later editions fetch anything from £20 to £50 a print from an Arab picture-framer in the Old City of Jerusalem, the arty gift shop at the Intercontinental Hotel in Amman, and a French bookshop opposite Groppi's coffee house in Cairo.

23 December 1978   **Eric Silver**

Daughters of the Green Revolution

We are in Garian, fifty miles south of Tripoli where the fertile coastal strip ends and mountains mark the beginning of the desert that stretches a thousand miles down to the border with Niger. It's only an hour and a half by communal taxi from the capital, but already worlds away from the urban boredom of young men with new Volvos, stereo cassettes and nowhere to go, the sarcasm of journalists and film-makers freeloading on oily money while grumbling at room service, and the more serious disenchantment of the bourgeoisie who lost land and property when the Green Book advocacy of the essential freedom of owning your own house but no one else's was carried out.

It's the ordinary people of Libya like Salema, her husband Shaban and their eleven children who have benefited from Gadafy's ambitious programme to get the entire population housed, educated, agriculturally self-sufficient and industrially productive before the oil revenues dry up. Until a few years ago they, like most of the Berber peasant population of Garian, lived in the troglodyte underground dug-out houses beloved by conservationist Western historians and by the eldest son who picked up some European nostalgia while studying at Aston University. For the rest of the family the old house and its courtyard is fit only for chickens.

The move up and out had started before the revolution, but then the shacks and shanties were cleared and the new houses built with grants and interest free loans of about fifteen thousand pounds. No contracts and tenders here – each house is an individual interpretation of the traditional North African design: blank walls to the outside world, a guesthouse in the first courtyard, and then another gate to the house and inner court: Salema's realm.

Salema's ways are basically as traditional as her house, a reminder that when Gadafy came to power Libya was among the most conservative Islamic countries: the white Peugeot outside, running water, the bathtub and gas cooker have eased her life, while the colour TV keeps her in touch with the propaganda of the revolution, and Gadafy's photograph has joined those of the family.

She still greets strangers accepted into her house by killing the fattest chicken and ekeing it out over three days with delicious transformations of couscous, rice, chick peas or lentils. And when startled by the outside world she still automatically grabs for her veil – shocking pink or multi-flowered to Berber taste – and covers up her mouth and the parallel lines of tattooed dots that run up her chin and over her lips to the gums. Both she and Shaban know that times are changing, but he admits that he would be troubled to think of her exposed to other men's eyes.

214

POST OFFICE

Royal visit to Saudi Arabia Commemorative issue

On Sale here

14 February 1979

For her teenage daughters Assma and Eman it will be different. By the time they marry the rejection that is still the privilege of working city women will be common, hastened by alarm at the regressiveness of Khomeini's attitude to Iranian women.

In Libya, Gadafy has moved gradually and carefully on this issue, allowing time for the Islamic aspects of the Green Book to be transformed in the minds of the people into a new brand of socialism that respects tradition and varying need while insisting on the principle of equality. Increasingly of late he has insisted on the need for women to decide to stand beside the men in work, politics and if necessary in war, and their role will be the subject of the third volume of the Green Book due out in September.

The message is reinforced in the schools. In Garian, 800 girls aged between sixteen and twenty-two, some of them there for teacher training, conduct their own morning assembly over the public speaking system that discourages shyness. A couple of sentences on democracy from the Green Book, a phrase from the Koran, a quiz question about culture in the Arab world, and then a joke about marriage that makes the ranks break in laughter, shared by the twenty-five married girls. A word or two from us, the unexpected foreign visitors, then the Green Flag is run up and lessons begin.

Learning is dynamic in a country where ten years ago there were only fourteen Libyan graduates. Now seventeen per cent go on to the two universities. The history teacher has just graduated from one, El Fatah in Tripoli. It's a lesson on the causes of the revolution. She poses the initial question and lets the seventeen-year-olds take it from there.

They begin with the colonial repression of the Italians who treated their parents worse than animals and enforced the veil for women who had fought alongside men in 1911. Then on to the American imperialists who used the country as a military base, and the British – with apologetic glances at us – who exploited the oil. An Egyptian girl adds that the people of a country should not be confused with its government.

Students and teachers come from all over the Arab world, and in each school there are Palestinians, Egyptians, sometimes Sudanese and Polisario too. To the quotes from UN statistics of the early fifties on illiteracy (ninety per cent) and classic Third World stagnant poverty, a Palestinian girl adds a reminder of the need to help all struggles for liberation. This lesson could go on and on. They want to discuss how the Popular Committees were set up, but the physics master has already been waiting outside for half an hour.

Before we leave we ask the girls what they want to do. Our question is mildly corrected by the answers. Self does not come first. One says she hopes the Jamahiriya (the word coined by Gadafy to describe the first 'country of the masses') will last forever so she can become a doctor. Another extends this to peace and unity in the Arab world so she too can study to be a doctor, and a third takes it still further to world peace, since medicine, like science and engineering, are studied in English in American and British universities. The teacher is amused. Only five years ago the favoured profession was teaching, and everyone used to say 'God willing'.

216

Shaban collects us from school. He has taken off his white robes and skull cap, and is now a jovial soft-bereted policeman, underemployed because crime is virtually non-existent in Libya, except among the foreign workers. He puts that down to drink and insecurity. He drives us out into the stony semi-desert to show us a friend's farm in the new settlement of Scihdel Faras, a traditional house newly built, fifteen hectares of land planted with fruit trees, ploughed and ready to catch the two annual rainfalls.

All this was prepared by foreign tenders, then handed over with tractor and watering truck as part of the dream of the Green Revolution to make 1.5 million acres of desert fertile. After twenty years it will belong to the farmer and for the first five years, until the land is productive, he will be paid a salary. 'God willing and water lasting,' says Shaban, 'you will come back when my daughters are doctors and these lands are green with wheat.'

15 May 1979   **Caroline Tisdall**

The Lady from the Sea

Michael Elliott's season of plays from the Royal Exchange about obsessive protagonists who are prey to supernatural solicitings comes to a climax with Ibsen's *The Lady From The Sea*. Though I have some doubts about the extension of the play's watery images into the set itself, it makes a totally absorbing evening and boasts a performance by Vanessa Redgrave for which one has to dust down all the critical superlatives.

The play itself is a fantastically complex blend of the real and the symbolic. Dramatically it hinges on the choice confronting its strange, amphibious heroine, Ellida Wangel. On the physical plane, she is the second wife of a small-town doctor who has virtually bought her as part of a business deal. On the spiritual plane, she belongs to a long-vanished sailor with whom she once entered into a pagan compact in which they threw their rings into the sea. When the sailor arrives to reclaim her, she is torn not only between two men but between two worlds and it is only when her doctor-husband gives her the freedom to choose that she is able to accept her land-locked marriage.

As Agate used to say, Ibsen's plays exist on a ground-storey of realism and upper-storey of symbolism and the wonder of this play is that it moves so freely between the two floors. But by staging it in a set that looks a little like the lagoon scene from *Peter Pan*, I feel that Mr Elliott makes the play's symbolic content almost too explicit. The actors have to negotiate rocks and landing stages all surrounded by pools of stagnant water. But this strikes me as about as helpful as staging *Brand* in real snow. It physically slows down the action and it undercuts Ellida's feeling of physical confinement and her almost mystical hunger for the sea.

But, on the psychological level, the production works superbly. 'Can any actress,' C. E. Montague once asked, 'overcome the difficulty of making the Nereid or Venus Anadyomene side of Ellida fully effective?' Vanessa Redgrave triumphantly can. It is not only her startling first entry in bathing towel and dampened hair but her rapt inquisitiveness at all the marine references. 'You loved the sea?' she enquires of the youthful, consumptive Lyngstrand, and you see her instantly fixing him with her glittering eye. She also conveys superbly the feeling of a woman who is trapped and confined on land. She constantly points an admonitory finger at her confining husband and, when he embraces her, her body goes rigid and her fists instinctively clench. It is an enthralling study of a woman who is literally out of her element.

It is also backed up by some very good supporting performances. Graham Crowden as her doctor-husband is no dry old stick but a mature man desperate to reclaim his wife and enjoy his full conjugal rights. Terence Stamp in his two brief scenes as the mysterious Stranger also supplies a gauntly handsome presence and a sense of magnetic attraction. As Bolette, the daughter who also longs to escape from small-town Norway, Sherrie Hewson cannot quite efface memories of Miss Redgrave herself in the part eighteen years ago but John Franklyn-Robbins as the middle-aged tutor, who offers her marriage as her only chance of flight, has just the right desiccated desperation.

In short, an extraordinary evening. One that in seeking to free Ibsen from the supposed shackles of realism actually, in my view, limits him by over-insistence on the play's hydrophilic content. But one that also charts exactly Ellida's psychological crisis and that leaves you grateful for Miss Redgrave's overdue return to the London stage.

17 May 1979 **Michael Billington**

Pope throws caution to the winds

It is hard to know whether the Polish leadership, the Kremlin, or the Church hierarchy are the most disturbed by the Pope's crusading zeal, his evident determination to throw political caution out of the window, and his ability to communicate warmth, spontaneity, and vigour capable of finding an instant, devoted, and probably lasting response to the vast crowds which surround him.

After his 'homily' in Gniezno on Sunday, where he not only made his politically explosive commitment to promote the spiritual unity of Christians in Eastern Europe, but also added an unscripted plea for their right – even in Czechoslovakia and Russian Lithuania – to hear his message and see him on television, his first day at Jasna Gora, Poland's most sacred religious shrine, was less controversial.

Nevertheless, the informality of his first mass here again showed his determination to dispense with the constraints of the Papacy. At one point, he departed from his text to introduce some of the foreign bishops present, adding with a laugh that he might have forgotten a few hidden from his view under the white umbrellas shading them from the heat.

In a more serious allusion to his evident determination to work for more than superficial religious freedom for the people of Eastern Europe, he told his huge audience that many Vatican aides still had much to learn about the Slav world. The people responded by clapping and even interrupting him with religious songs in which he joined and sometimes led.

In remarks that will please other Christian churches, the Pope promised to work for unity and 'to meet in a more mature way our brothers in faith with whom so many things unite us, although there is still something dividing us'. He promised 'to meet all human beings and peoples who are seeking God and wishing to serve Him in the way of different religions'.

But there were no outstretched arms for non-believers, or Marxists. Instead, he issued a plea for 'peace, justice, and respect for the rights of people and of countries'.

The Pope arrived at Czestochowa yesterday morning, and will remain in Jasna Gora monastery until he goes to Krakow tomorrow morning. The painting of the Madonna in the monastery is considered, and is addressed as, the Holy Mother of God, and Queen of Poles and Poland. It is the Polish Church's most cherished possession and the subject of deep veneration.

Every block of flats and almost every house here is festooned with papal and Polish flags. Some also have photographs of the Pope illuminated at night. But the Communist Party has responded far more pointedly than it did in Warsaw, with big rival banners proclaiming the thirty-five years of achievement of Poland's Socialist republic. The poster war seems typical of an election campaign.

The authorities limited access to Czestochowa, and only locally-licensed cars are allowed into the town. Others are being stopped twelve miles outside, and there is no public transport, except for the limited numbers of parishioners with authorized invitations.

The church authorities are more upset by this, since the Government has not relented on its decision to permit only limited television coverage of the Pope's visit. Only the events of his first day in Warsaw were allowed to go out live on the country's first channel, which can be seen throughout Poland as well as in parts of Russian Lithuania, Czechoslovakia, and East Germany.

The channel will also show the Pope's visit to Auschwitz later this week, and his departure from Poland on Sunday. But other events are being shown only on local television, with the main evening news carrying brief accounts.

On Sunday after the Pope's day in Gniezno, the evening news led off with fifteen minutes on the opening of a children's centre and was followed by only a couple of minutes of the Pope. Polish cameramen apparently have instructions to focus crowd shots on the elderly, and not the young – though they appear to be in a majority almost everywhere.

Yesterday's mass at Jasna Gora provided great theatre. For Polish Catholics it is traditional to pray before the Madonna and vow, through her, fidelity to Poland and the Church. Pope John Paul, who was often here as priest, bishop, and cardinal, did not forget to recall yesterday, and indeed complain, that Poland's leadership refused Pope Paul VI permission to come to Poland when he had wanted to make a pilgrimage to the Madonna.

Jasna Gora monastery stands on a hill, and the fields lined by heavy trees provided a dramatic amphitheatre for the open-air service. With its church and the chapel holding the Madonna behind him, the Pope in full white splendour sat on his improvised throne or stood to address the bishops, priests, nuns, and ordinary pilgrims around and below him.

He was mobbed by nuns as he arrived, and leaves nobody in doubt that he enjoys the unconventional applause, even inviting it by the dramatic delivery of his thoughts.

His actor's training stands him in good stead. But it is his sincerity that is most remarkable. He appears genuinely moved as the people sing for him or when, as they did yesterday, they bear simple gifts of bread, flowers, ears of corn, and paintings of the Polish countryside.

5 June 1979   **Hella Pick**

Your fortune's my face, sirs, she said

Lawyers representing Marilena Innocenzi, aged twenty-one, are to file a suit against the Governor of the Bank of Italy, accusing him of having violated Miss Innocenzi's rights to her own face, which she claims appears on the 50,000 lire notes which have been in circulation in Italy for more than a year. Her lawyers are also asking that all the bank notes be impounded.

The artist who designed the new 50,000 lire notes (which have a nominal value of about £30) is Guglielmo Savini, a retired railway employee. He denies that he even knows the woman and says that his portrait had been idealized from the faces of many women, and in particular from a portrait done by Sebastiano del Piombo.

The bank note shows a woman whose features appear to have been carved out of granite by an artist of the Fascist or even Soviet school.

Miss Innocenzi's story and her background appear to bear out at least part of her claim. She is from the village of Roviano, outside Rome, which is next to the village of Anticoli Corrado, famous in the Renaissance, and again in the nineteenth century, for having produced more artists' models than any other. Peasants living there, after years of in-breeding, all have faces which look like portraits. Even today, Anticoli Corrado is chosen as the summer residence of many amateur painters.

Miss Innocenzi said the painter was brought to her parents' house three years ago. 'He had some of mother's fettucini (a pasta) and asked if I would pose for a portrait, which I did. My hair was blonde then, as it is on the bank note. He has never let me see the portrait, or even given me the photograph he took for his work. I would settle for the portrait, but he says that banking secrecy is now involved, and that if the portrait was stolen counterfeiters could use it.'

Miss Innocenzi also says she has suffered other damages. Her fiancé of five years has left her. 'Perhaps people began to talk, saying things like I've ended up on the streets, and calling me Miss 50,000 Lire,' she said.

17 November 1978   **George Armstrong**

Head and hands: the restorer's art

It took just a few seconds of vandal's work to ruin Poussin's Adoration of the Golden Calf – half a million of National Gallery property, give or take, put to the knife – and six months' hard slog by one man to restore it. That man is Arthur Lucas, the gallery's chief restorer, who picked up the five pieces of the slashed painting and now presents it, whole again, for inspection by the eagle-eyed press today and the public tomorrow.

It was the most badly damaged painting he has worked on in thirty-one years of National service, and to return the mended article now is a nice high to end on – Lucas retires at the end of the month.

He and his staff of six work in a skylit eyrie under the gallery roof, reached by a high narrow lift that will take a 13 ft 6 in painting (there's another nearby that will take a twenty-footer – old masters thought big). A committee that pondered restoration policy in the late 1940s found that between 1900 and 1933, just thirty-two of the National Gallery's paintings had been cleaned and restored. Now, about twenty major paintings a year take that lift journey to the roof. And some of them have brought even bigger headaches than the Poussin.

Like Giambatista Cima's The Incredulity of St Thomas: 'It's been flaking since the day he painted it,' says Lucas. 'He made a technical error in preparing the ground, so the paint has never stuck to it. It's my Moby Dick.'

Cima painted it in the sixteenth century, when 'all the boys were trying technical innovations, including the great Titian himself'. And Cima was no Titian. His innovation, like many since, came unstuck. The painting has been in and out of hospital ever since Lucas arrived at the National Gallery.

The treatment of Sebastiano del Piombo's Raising of Lazarus was shorter – three years – but much more painful; the most worrying piece of restoration in Lucas's memory. Lazarus is 14 ft by 13 ft, painted around 1517. In 1770 a French restorer found that most of the ground was too powdery to hold the film of paint, so he removed most of it and transferred Lazarus from its original wood base to canvas.

But the canvas shrank. By the time Lucas and his restorers got to it, 'we had more paint area than ground to put it on; it was foaming up like an earthquake.' It had also, in the intervening one hundred and eighty or so years, been relined with further layers of canvas.

Lucas's plan was to strip three of the four canvas layers off, then stretch the fourth to make room for all that dispossessed paint. Only when they had stripped the first three layers, they found that the fourth was not canvas at all. It was mock canvas, made from paper that had rotted right through.

What Lucas then faced each morning was a film of paint 14 ft by 13 ft and about one hundredth of an inch thick, lying face down on a huge board, and held together simply by a backing of tissue paper. As sixteenth-century Venetian masterpieces go, it was very sick. Lazarus simply could not be raised. He could not even be turned face upward.

The routine tests – carried out on tiny areas of about a square millimetre on the corners of paintings – had brought even worse news. Piombo's four-hundred-year-old paint was sensitive both to heat and to water. So there was no chance of making a new backing stick to the paint by ironing it on or by using water-based glues.

The answer was to dissolve wax in white spirit and brush it on in extremely thin layers. The spirit evaporated, leaving a fragile skin of wax. This was repeated until the wax was about a quarter of an inch thick. Then they could sandwich the film with its wax backing between the board it lay on and another they screwed down on top. They turned the sandwich over, reinforced the front of the picture with several layers of tissue paper, and turned it face down again to work on the back.

They treated the back with mastic, and put on a new ground 'using rabbit skin glue and oil'. (Lucas mentions exotic adhesives, the unguents of his healing art, like other people might mention Sellotape.)

Lucas was not content with a mere repair-and-clean job. It was still a very dark painting, and observation under strong photographic lights showed that there was a lot of Piombo that, in ordinary gallery lighting, would never be seen. He wanted to put a new, bright, white ground on the back, so that it would shine through the paint and raise the tone of the whole picture, revealing those hidden depths. That meant getting permission (duly granted) from the board. The Piombo got its new ground of brilliant titanium white, lifting the whole picture.

'That's why I think it's very important for a restorer to be a painter too, so that he understands about the effects of different grounds. I'm a colour-ground man myself, because of all these old masters I deal with, so one can make a pretty good guess at what the effect is going to be.'

Lucas began to draw and paint during the periods of his

boyhood when he was too ill to go to school. At eighteen, he got as far as part-time tuition at the Camberwell School of Art. But during the war, when his brother had to leave the family laundry business, Arthur Lucas had to take over the job. His father, he says cheerfully, 'was in a very near type of business . . .' Even in the laundry, one heard about solvents and soaps – both important in cleaning paintings.

By the time he was able to go back to painting, he had met his wife, and the principal at the Clerkenwell, William Johnstone, suggested he should go and work with Fritz Pollock, a refugee from the Nazis who had set up shop in England as a framer and restorer. 'It was work that very few people did, and Johnstone said I'd be able to make a living rather quicker than by painting. I don't think he thought much of my ability as a painter anyway.'

And what about his qualities as a restorer? What qualities do you need? 'Well, blowing me own trumpet, I've got very sensitive hands, connected to me brain. My eyesight's not too good. When I was younger, I was very skilful at puttying up holes in paintings. But sometimes I think I'm the worst picture restorer in the world, because I do it so many times to get it right.'

In the vertical light of his office, it is the head you notice rather than the hands. The beard is whiter than the hair: a Rembrandt burgher in cheerful mood, or one of Van Dyke's more benign patrons. He chuckles often. But the would-be restorer who – though warned three times – still failed to secure her work firmly to the easel, got the boot. Accidents and the possibility of accidents are not allowed.

There are still a few people who believe that what Lucas and his restorers do is sacrilege. But he clearly thinks the great debate – to clean or not to clean – is over. It was pretty muddled anyway.

The National's policy was attacked by people who believed that favourite paintings had never been cleaned before, 'whereas we knew they'd been cleaned several times.' Attacked, too, by people who confused glazing with varnishing, and thought that the solvents used to get the varnish off would also affect the paint (they don't). Varnish is simply a protective layer over the paint. Glazing is standard painting practice.

For instance, says Lucas, you would underpaint carmine with

iron oxide or vermilion, then put the glaze – a thin, semi-translucent layer of paint – on top to produce a marvellously deep colour.

'The problem comes with certain English painters of the eighteenth century like Reynolds, some nineteenth-century French artists like Delacroix, and some Germans, who put soft resins into their top glazes. If you have soft varnish in the glaze – which makes it go yellow – the solvent that takes the varnish off will take the glaze off too.'

He says that this work made him realize that even apparently coarse painters like Rembrandt – all that fleshy impasto – really worked with extreme delicacy. The restorer has to equal it. Fill the holes with the right colour putty; then ground paint; middle layer with the ground paint glowing through it; glaze.

Techniques and materials have improved, of course. Flake white, which the painters often used, becomes more transparent with age, changing the colour of anything it is mixed with. Now restorers can use titanium white, which is very stable. The acrylic and other plastic varnishes do not bloom or go yellow like the old, natural resin varnishes.

So he reckons the paintings he has restored should be good for a couple of centuries, 'and that's a pessimistic estimate. Some paintings that were *well* restored in the late eighteenth century are still good – and they haven't had the advantages of air-conditioning or modern techniques.'

But after thirty years, surely there are paintings that now need doing again? 'Blowing me own trumpet again, no there *aren't*.' He produces the answer with justifiable bravura, like a genial conjurer whose trick has come right. 'One picture is now being cleaned again after thirty-eight years, but I didn't do that one. By putting on non-discolouring varnishes, using permanent pigments, and the right colour build-up, the colour change will be incredibly slight. If a painting gets a bit grubby, you can now take the grub off with very weak detergents.'

But future restorers, he thinks, are going to have problems with the new old masters. Huge paintings in acrylic on cotton duck, on stretchers that are a bit too small because they are very expensive – all the characteristics of recent painting bode ill for their preservation. Cotton duck is not really suitable for acrylic paint, and cracks form.

'That kind of crack may be acceptable on a Van Dyke, but it isn't acceptable on a painting five years old. All we can do is to paint the cracks out with a oo brush.'

No one at the National Gallery is going to have to worry too much about that for a while – though they've dealt with some such paintings already, there are none in the gallery. And Lucas in retirement will be concerned more with his own 'not very good' paintings.

They are, he says, enormously influenced by the old masters he works on. 'My colours change. For instance, I've been repairing the Poussin, and I've been noticing some very interesting oranges and yellows against blue in it. When you're face to face with a picture for six months or so, that's bound to happen.'

13 December 1978   **Hugh Hebert**

Defying the ghosts of Polstead Rectory

Polstead Rectory, with its perturbed spirit which screams like a fox in the chimney, shoves women out of bed and ages wallpaper in a trice, was bought yesterday by an unabashed coin dealer who has a spiritualist mother-in-law.

The allegedly most haunted clerical abode on the books of the Church Commissioners was sold for £74,000 after years of rather troubled incumbency. The mother-in-law, Mrs Anita Wright, said: 'The ghost probably needs a little understanding and affection. It won't need to frighten people any more. I can't wait to hold a seance there.'

The purchaser, Mr John Hayward, aged forty, who plans to live there with his wife, son aged fifteen and daughter aged ten, said: 'The ghost, if there is one, is welcome to stay. Such things hold no terror for me and my family. I believe we have all had previous existences. We are all ghosts of a kind.'

In the small Suffolk parish, it was felt that the new secular owners might be taking the affair too lightly. Although the local archdeacon, the Venerable Jeremy Walsh, believes that Mr Hayward is approaching the move responsibly, he said last night that an exorcism would be 'very seriously considered' if the family asked for one.

The 400-year-old mansion, with its four acres of gardens and paddocks, has already been unsuccessfully exorcized twice – once in the early nineteenth century and once in the 1960s, by one of the most experienced demonologists in the church.

Its atmosphere drove its last rector, Rev Hayden Foster, out after only five nights only a year ago. He and his wife said they saw their newly-painted bedroom wall 'turn to peeling, damp old wallpaper, just as it might have looked twenty or thirty years ago', and heard screaming like that of a child.

Mrs Jones, who felt suffocated or strangled, was 'trying to say the Lord's prayer but couldn't get it out because of this overwhelming force'. But the experiences of the two previous incumbent families reminded the church that haunting is not always a simple horror story.

Mrs Mary Neads, widow of the 1963 to 1976 rector, felt 'unusual but not unpleasant spiritual activity'. The wife of her husband's predecessor, the Reverend Paul Biddlecombe, told the *Church Times* last year: 'I used to feel I was being pushed out of bed. My young daughter used to wake up screaming, sobbing that there were foxes in the chimney.'

But yesterday, Mr Biddlecombe said: 'There were strange things, as there are in many old houses. But we were extremely happy there and loved the house very much. In fact members of my family tell me they would like to have bought it now if they could afford it.'

The previous odd happenings came to light only as a result of the Fosters' flight.

By then the house was already due to be sold because it was too big and costly for modern church use.

Mr Walsh said yesterday: 'I certainly hope Mr Hayward is doing the right thing. Because we believe as Christians that we have a spiritual dimension to our lives we must not be surprised if we find spiritual forces occasionally breaking through.'

26 April 1979   **John Ezard**

Black as Hell

The effect of *Black As Hell And Thick As Grass* (BBC-2) was physical. My palms puddled and my skin goosepimpled. As Job remarked when a spirit passed before his face, 'The hair of my flesh stood up.'

Kenneth Griffith first went to South Africa playing a spirit, Oberon. You would have thought Bottom, but apparently not. Mr Griffith is television's marvellous one man band. He not only wrote this account of the Zulu wars but played a regiment, Disraeli, Gladstone, several assegais, 'whizz, rip, rip', and must, with difficulty and diplomacy, have been dissuaded from having a go at Cetewayo, King of the Zulus. 'A very fine man in his native costume or rather no costume,' as Queen Victoria put it.

There are few purer joys left to the poor viewer than the sight of Mr Griffith turning bright red and cracking consonants with his teeth. A hundred years ago at the time of Rorke's Drift, he would have been in a pulpit while a congregation gave a hymn hell and he gave them hell. I have not seen that sort of furious assurance since Bevan or rather since Mr Griffith's last piece when he played Napoleon. Naturally. Passion is out of fashion so his work, if not banned, tends to be transmitted as, in the BBC's hand-washing words, 'a highly personal view'.

From where I sat the view was marvellous. In a mac of poor pedigree which could have been no great use in South Africa except that he could turn up the collar and *crouch* or let it swing and *swirl*, he acted out the massacre of Isandhlwana and the defence of Rorke's Drift. These battles were lost and won by the 24th, a Welsh regiment. His treatment of the poor, bloody infantry was tender. It was a celebration of the soldier Zulu and Welsh but not necessarily of soldiering. 'Where we had to sleep was a very uncomfortable place among the dead bodies all night tell Harry not to enlist for God's sake for he will regret it.' Crosser direction would have lingered on one face among the soldiers singing in Brecon Cathedral where the colours of the 24th hang now. He was coloured.

A sort of proxy poshness was given the story by themes borrowed by the forthcoming film *Zulu Dawn*. A saucy novelty. It would, perhaps, have taxed even Mr Griffith to convey 40,000 Zulus in full battle array. But little miracles were achieved with very little: smoke, slow motion, the sound of bees, the colour of fire, and what you might call the little O of Mr Griffith. He is slightly on the circular side.

29 January 1979   **Nancy Banks-Smith**

A country diary: Kent 2

Should you be travelling in Kent at the time of the May festivities do not be alarmed if you encounter the most remarkable of its medieval mysteries, the Hooden Horse. In the eastern half of the county near the original landing site of the Germanic invaders, Woden was especially powerful, leaving his pagan presence in village names. He also left his horse, a bizarre wooden beast, a large head on a long pole, possibly a relic of the early Teuton sacrifice of the horse at the winter solstice. Now the beast makes its appearance at other times of the rural year, including the spring festival, garlanded with flowers, bedecked with ribbons and accompanied by hand bells. According to local experts the horse sometimes assumes female guise, adopting names like Mollie or the Old Woman, so the Hooden Horse gets mixed up with witches and broomsticks, a confusion of images typical of folklore. The most conspicuous feature of the horse is its mouth which clanks open and shut with ferocious intent, the teeth being made with large hob nails, giving it yet another local name of Hob the Nob and another link in the ritual chain with the hobby horse. Interpretations flourish with every festive brew, especially along the banks of the Stour where an inn proudly bears the Hooden emblem. As the horse clanks in procession it seems that Hengist and Horsa have only just landed and the invasion of the old gods is imminent. Its intent now is purely one of good will though it reputedly frightened one lady to death and drove another from her invalid chair, cured by panic. Today it seems as innocent as the Morris Men and children dance in its wake.

5 May 1979   **John T. White**

Trying to understand a pigeon's English

An officially sponsored £17,000 project was announced yesterday to explore the frontiers of a pigeon's intelligence, in the hope that it will solve a problem which puzzled Wittgenstein and still gives indigestion to the most elaborate modern computer.

The mystery – as Wittgenstein put it – is how human beings manage to understand and obey vague commands like 'Stand roughly there'. The great man remarked that some other philosophers would regard such an order as meaningless. Yet human beings in their everyday lives usually had no trouble grasping the unstated assumptions behind the words. Similarly, if a mother asked her daughter, 'Go and buy a piece of cheese,' the daughter would normally know how much cheese and what kind to buy. Not so a computer. 'A computer would come back and ask a lot of tedious questions about how large and what kind,' Dr Stephen Lea, of Exeter University psychology department, said yesterday.

If you told a computer how to draw the letter A on graph paper by instructing: 'Start from a point nearby co-ordinate 075, turn by about 150 degrees . . .' it would be thrown by the words 'nearby' and 'about'. In the trade, this was known as a 'fuzzy' programme. Yet if you made the order more precise you would be equipping the machine to draw A in only one typeface instead of the several typefaces for which the original instruction was designed.

It is this conundrum which has given birth to Dr Lea's three-year Science Research Council-backed project on 'Mechanisms of Polymorphous Discrimination by Pigeons'. For Dr Lea has discovered that pigeons – which are not rated as particularly bright, even among birds – can be taught 'fairly easily' to recognize the letter A, regardless of the typeface or handwriting in which it is shown to them.

American psychologists have already shown that pigeons can learn to differentiate between people and scenery on colour slides and even to pick out individuals. One experiment set out to get them to pick out Charley Brown from other Peanuts cartoon characters.

Dr Lea said: 'That one never got published and I believe it did not work. You need a sense of humour to work in this kind of thing.'

But his work with letters poses the sternest test yet of pigeon intelligence. One hope is that detailed analysis of the bird's way of handling information will produce a technique which is simpler than that of human beings and can be built into computers so that they can imitate it mechanically.

So far, by feeding three birds if they press the right switches with their beaks, he thinks he has taught them to distinguish between sets of letters randomly selected from the alphabet. The features which appear to give them most help in 'remembering' or forming a concept of a letter appear to be straight lines, closed loops, the height of the centre of gravity of the letter, and the presence or absence of oblique lines.

Closed loops have turned out to be the most important feature in pigeon learning. They are also one of the features thought to be most vital in child learning. The similarity could be a step on a path towards giving computers some of the creative quirkiness of a human race which – as Wittgenstein also remarked – fully understands the difference between 'fruit' and 'vegetables' without being able exactly to define it in words.

9 January 1979   **John Ezard**

Communication-wise

Christmas is the season of statutory goodwill, though at least it is limited to four or five increasingly irritable days each year. Journalists, however, do not escape so lightly. Goodwill and communications reach them in larger dosages than any other drugs, and what is more the drug levels are always rising.

Banks, insurers and building societies have been communicating frenziedly all year. At best communications is advertising with a human face, and usually, alas, the more companies communicate the less they say.

The Building Societies Association set the ball rolling. After some official pressure, wives who earn more than their husbands now receive the same financial treatment as couples where the earning powers are reversed.

'Societies should consider couples in this position like two married men living together, but not married to each other,' were the words in which the point was rammed home.

Communication ensures that a certain solemnity attends the simplest thought. One bank chairman announced at a press lunch that he hoped to make a particular decision soon. How soon? 'It will not be long on a historical time perspective' was the reply. No more than sometime with a public relations finish.

The situation reached epidemic proportions in – to coin a phrase – overall communications and marketing strategy. The infection spread from press release to press release, like some linguistic Dutch elm disease. No noun walked the lines of a company statement alone and in safety. If it did, a situation would attach itself on behind, not to be dislodged.

It happened in conversation, too. One unit trust manager who had put all his funds into shares, rather than keeping some of the money in the bank, announced in the communications newspeak that he was in a 100 per cent investment situation. The only extenuating circumstance lay in the broker, to whom he was talking. He was, he said, in an investment advisory position, the whole exchange representing the workings of Gresham's Law where bad English drives out good.

When many a noun is double barrelled, one upmanship demands three upmanship, or so one bank chairman believed. His group had not installed cash dispensers, which spit out money at the drop of a computer card, but he was not going to admit that lack of money was the reason.

It had not happened, he announced, because 'our customers are attached to the interview type situation', and he went on to analyse their psyches further. They would not like terminals, 'because they did not wish to interface with machines'.

233

I interface, thou interfacest, he, she, or it interfaces . . . Concealing himself in the thickets of computer jargon did not prevent anyone from seeing or seeing through the argument. But the word gave him a certain polysyllabic dignity, even if it did not mean anything.

And so communications onwent . . . on and on and on – and doubtless they will ongo triumphantly into 1979. The language, well used, provides a verbal deodorant against any nasty corporate smell. Prices do not rise, they escalate. President Nixon, like George Washington, never told a lie – his statements became inoperative.

But the prize for communication must go to the group whose chemicals destroyed all the fish in a river. Dead fish? Well, the company had actually met with a one hundred per cent mortality response.

The phrase is chilling. But communications' alter ego in advertising can make even funerals a fun experience, to use the language. The perfect example came in the chorus of happy, highstepping American morticians said to have sung their own jingle on American television.

> Chambers coffins are just fine
> Made of sandalwood and pine
> When your Loved One has to go
> Dial Columbus 390.
> When your Loved Ones pass away
> Speed them on the Chambers way,
> Happy Customers all sing
> Death, oh Death where is thy sting.

The verse is so magnificently awful that it crashes through the taste barrier to become entertaining – the process by which kitsch becomes fashionable. British companies use their cosmetics more delicately, but they are there all the same. Everyone knows death insurance as life insurance, for instance, in the same way that permanent health policies are always concerned with the risk of perpetual illness.

Communications, for all its faults, is still a language people speak and most others can at least half understand. But Insuroglot, based on English and widely used in the City and among insurance brokers, is a different matter. Take out a life policy at twenty-five, and you are transformed into an assured aged twenty-six next birthday, who has affected cover. The contract is embellished with guaranteed sums assured, and the prospect of reversionary bonuses together with a final terminal bonus, as either you become deceased, or the policy becomes mature.

Why is Insuroglot still in use? If disputes arise, judges will know exactly what each phrase means on the basis of past precedent, or so the industry maintains. But a conspiracy theory is far more emotionally satisfying and contains more than a grain of truth. Insurance, even life insurance, is not that complicated, but many people – brokers and consultants among them – depend on a sense of awe-inspiring financial mystery for their living. Like the sexual phrases in the *Decline and Fall of the Roman Empire*, insurance details live on 'in the decent obscurity of a learned language'.

Insuroglot is admittedly under attack from several companies, and communications may die of obesity, collapsing under the weight of its own polysyllables. Other obscure languages have died before them. Before the war, for instance, companies were unlikely to thank you for a letter. They merely announced that yours of the ninth ult was to hand, but made up at the end by assuring you of their respectful attention at all times.

So everyone can live in hope. The Christmas spirit rapidly becomes the Boxing Day hangover, and if you need to vent your spleen usefully, you could always attack the first person to talk of situations and communicating.

Meanwhile, the greetings of the festive season – or Merry Christmas as we say in English.

23 December 1978   **Tom Tickell**

A long weekend in Outer Mongolia

Outer Mongolia is one of those countries at which the arriving beats the travelling hopefully any day of the week, although in point of fact you can only arrive on Fridays. It is 5100 miles away and it takes eleven hours' flying time, not counting the hanging about in the airports of Luton, Moscow, and the sombre Siberian settlements of Omsk and Irkutsk. At this last airport, Mongol Air takes over with a twin-propeller Antonov, and the most doggedly elaborate security check this traveller has yet experienced. (There being no X-ray equipment at Ulan Bator airport, they make the most of the one at Irkutsk.)

The plane flies south from Baikal, through the cloud and over the Altai range, where, according to Marco Polo, the lords of the lineage of Genghis Khan were buried, and as the mountains fall away, something splendid begins to happen. The skies clear, the snowy ranges fade to brown, and the silent marches of the Mongolian landscapes begin.

There are range upon range of hills of granite and sandstone, running roughly east to west, with light dustings of larch on the northern slopes, the southern slopes being utterly bare of all but a skim of light brown stunted grasses. In between, the river valleys have flood plains with perfectly marked river meanders and oxbows and here and there traces of fields, unfenced, and dottings of occasional herds of cattle, and even more occasional circular structures that turn out to be the *yurts* of nomads.

I have concentrated on the landscape because this, more than anything else, makes the most intense impact on visitors to the Mongolian People's Republic. I travelled with a party of twelve from Luton, one quarter of whom were heard to observe, even before they had completed arrival formalities at the airport (these last being conducted with a courtesy again outside my experience as a traveller), that they were going to come here again. This first, immediate affection for the place did not disappear although there are a number of things about the country which sort out the traveller from the mere holidaymaker.

First, although it occupies a large territory – the size of perhaps France and Spain combined – it is a small nation. There are fewer than 1.5 million Mongolians, and the capital, Ulan Bator, has a population of only about 250,000, half of whom still live in *yurts*, the traditional tents of felt on a wooden frame first reported by Marco Polo 700 years ago. For years the country permitted no foreign visitors at all: now they are arriving at the rate of about five thousand a year, and while the hotels are certainly clean and comfortable and the people courteous, Mongolia's tourist industry is – to put it at its most kindly – marked by a certain lack of commercialized slickness.

The jolliest example of this was in the business of souvenir-buying: like the Soviet Union, Mongolia welcomes foreign visitors because they bring hard currency, and will, in the normal way, sell only through special hard currency shops. The package visitors arrive on Friday evenings, and leave first thing Monday mornings, and the hard currency shop attached to the hotel is closed for the weekend. (On the obverse side of the coin, on learning that the visitors also wanted to send off postcards, the Mongolians arranged for the post office staff to come thundering down to the hotel at lunchtime on Sunday with sheafs of stamps and postcards, and I can't see that happening in the UK).

The other, more serious frustration is the blanket of restraint placed on tourists: the tourist who opts not to take the group tour arranged for that morning or afternoon or night is, in effect, a prisoner within the hotel. Foreigners may not stroll at large on the streets of Ulan Bator without their passports, and these are impounded on arrival at the hotel. There were other, minor restraints: one of which was the authorities' hesitation at allowing a visit to the only surviving Buddhist lamasery in the city (in the event, it proved easy enough to tag along with a party of Russians making the same visit) because it might give the impression that Mongolia was still a Buddhist theocracy rather than a modern socialist people's republic. As a nation, Mongolians are sensitive to foreign opinion.

It is not difficult to sympathize with this. There are just two men in Mongolia's history who have made enough impact on the West to become household words. One was of course Genghis Khan. The other was Attila the Hun. Thus Mongolian writers have according to one report, incurred official displeasure for failing to criticize Genghis Khan, or for writing too much about religion. The country keeps an uneasy eye on China to the south, east, and west (it spent more than 200 years as a province of the Manchu empire), and manifests a modest independence of the USSR by retaining its statues of Stalin, who has long been an unperson in the north.

All that said, the journey has the most extraordinary rewards; the landscape has an arid, unfamiliar beauty bathed in a light, sparkling air so pure it tastes as though it has never even been snuffed by a yak. It's possible to take a coach out into the hinterland for a considerable distance and see only the occasional herdsman with his cattle. The Gobi desert to the south and the mountains to the north offer a considerable range of wild life – leopards, wolves, Bactrian camels, and a bear that eats rhubarb.

The pleasures of the city (the tourist material reports warningly that there are no night clubs in Ulan Bator) include a circus and an evening of national song and dance (during which one can hear a band composed of what one assumes to be traditional instruments simply murdering Swan Lake) and visits to a Buddhist museum and a pre-Revolutionary palace.

It doesn't sound much, but it's fascinating. The people are more than usually unmenacing and the children are inclined to burst into shy giggles at the sight of the aliens from the West. The food tends towards the international (steak and chips or steak, egg, and chips) although if you put your foot down a bit you can enjoy a local meal of beef and meatballs baked under sheaths of fat, which is in fact delicious. So is the yoghurt.

The traditional way with tea is to serve it very weak with milk and butter (it tastes just like weak tea with milk and butter) and the local tipple (Marco Polo again) is still *koumiss*, or fermented mare's milk which is not available in winter, when mares are not in milk. Otherwise, settle for Russian style tea (delicious) or coffee (plentiful) or East European beer or mineral water. Hotel prices for drink are high, but one duty free shop was observed to be selling vodka at about 75p a bottle.

Practical advice: You will need a smallpox vaccination for Mongolia, and visas. And in what was reported to be an unusually mild November, the temperatures fell to minus 22C: this

238

is so cold that icicles form on the inside of your nose when you breathe. Take a heavy long coat (army surplus will do admirably), boots, woolly socks, scarf, hat with ear flaps, and a polo-necked jumper for when you step outside. You could go to Ulan Bator by rail from Peking, but until April 17 Thomson Holidays run a package tour (from Tuesday to Tuesday) which includes two nights in Irkutsk on the way and a night in Moscow on the way back, for between £295 and £326 depending on the date. You won't need a lot of extra spending money unless you want to buy something furry in Siberia.

Irkutsk is a town built originally by Tsarist exiles: on the whole it is rather unSiberian because of the amazing Lake Baikal, huge enough to contain about ten per cent of the world's fresh water and 70,000 seals as well as several hundred species unique to itself, and which exercises an oceanic influence on the local climate - leaving, you might say, a smile on the face of the taiga.

16 December 1978   **Tim Radford**

E. H. Carr's Russia

In Asia they revere old men, savouring their wisdom. In England they immure them in medieval colleges, ignoring for the most part their accumulated knowledge. One of England's greatest sages, still largely unrecognized at home, has lived in and about Trinity College Cambridge for nearly a quarter of a century, gradually unfolding the mysteries of the Bolshevik Revolution.

Now aged eighty-six, Edward Hallett Carr, historian, journalist, diplomat, has this year produced the final - fourteenth - volume of his monumental *History of Soviet Russia.** It is an astonishing achievement begun when he was well over fifty at a time of life when lesser men might have been contemplating retirement. As sprightly as men thirty years his junior, E. H. Carr has outlived most of his rivals and critics. He looks indestructible.

Nowadays the criticisms have mellowed, but time was when the person of E. H. Carr was a free fire zone for indiscriminate attack. After the last war, Randolph Churchill accused him of turning *The Times* newspaper into 'an apologist for the policies of the

239

Kremlin', while in a famous polemic against him published in *Encounter* in 1962, Hugh Trevor-Roper claimed that 'no historian since the crudest ages of clerical bigotry has treated evidence with such dogmatic ruthlessness'.

The most obvious characteristic of the early volumes of Carr's *History of Soviet Russia*, Trevor-Roper wrote, was 'the author's unhesitating identification of history with the victorious cause, his ruthless dismissal of its opponents, of its victims, and of all who did not stay on, or steer the bandwaggon'.

Why, I asked Carr, on a visit to his Cambridge retreat, had there been such virulent hostility? 'Partly, I suppose, because I have a slightly provocative way of saying things. Partly because, on the whole, this country – ever since about 1950 – has been moving steadily to the right.'

When research on the book was first begun, at the very end of the Second World War, the atmosphere in England, Carr recalls, 'seemed generally rather favourable to the Russians'. He was, he believes, 'to some extent influenced by this'. Yet, 'By the time I began to publish' – the first volume came out in 1950 – 'the cold war was on.' With a vengeance.

The *Manchester Guardian* sent the book for review to its old Moscow correspondent, M. Philips Price, who referred to 'the repulsion we all have against aggressive Communist Imperialism embodied in the State machine of Russia today'. He concluded with the thought that E. H. Carr had provided 'material which gives us much food for thought on how to fight the Russian Communist menace, and the correct weapons to use in so doing'.

'Dear old Philips Price,' Carr now recalls, 'I'd better be careful in what I say. Like most old people, he was a little apt to become a bore in his last years, but he was a remarkable man.'

I bought the first three volumes of Carr's mammoth history, called *The Bolshevik Revolution*, when I was a student, probably excited by the title. Dry and arid stuff it seemed at the time, compared with *Three Who Made a Revolution*, or *Ten Days that Shook the World*. 'Twenty-five shillings it must have cost you then,' says Carr with a twinkle, 'and that was the hardback. The last volume' – with a grimace – 'costs £20.'

But if the later volumes cost more, they are also infinitely more fascinating and valuable. The four central volumes, entitled

Socialism in One Country, began to show the true measure of Carr as a disciplined and resourceful historian, while the final six volumes, called *Foundations of a Planned Economy*, are certainly what he will be remembered for.

They are what he had really aimed to write about all along, for the earlier books are merely an introductory exercise, setting the scene for the extended discussion and illumination of the subject of state planning which is the kernel of the whole concept.

'Planning is, I suppose,' he says, 'the antithesis of *laissez-faire* – the idea that the state can sit back and let the economy regulate itself. Planning is the conception that the state has got to regulate the economy. In those very broad terms, I'm convinced of its necessity.' And in the pages of his history, the intense and dramatic debates that took place on the subject in the Soviet Union during the 1920s are given full rein.

Fascinated by planning, some critics (like Trevor-Roper) have insinuated that Carr is also obsessed with power – the winners in his tale tend to emerge more sympathetically drawn than the losers. In Russia in the 1920s this means that Stalin is given a three-dimensional role, emerging as a positive and comprehensible politician rather than as the archetypal ogre of Trotskyist legend. Perhaps it would be fairer to say that Carr is an honest realist. I put it to him that Stalin does in fact emerge from his pages as a rather more serious political figure than people are as yet prepared to accept.

'Yes, it becomes awfully difficult, you see, because you can't really in this country – or perhaps anywhere – extricate Stalin from the moral condemnation of what he did. You can't believe that a man who did these things played any positive role. But Stalin did play a positive role. In any case, whether it's Stalin or somebody else, something or other was done that was very important. Stalin was a politician of very, very great skill. He was very good at cutting through all the difficulties. He was a curious figure. I mean some of his judgements were correct – and some were very much misguided.'

And does Carr feel that Stalinism was inherent in Leninism? 'Now you're asking a very difficult question. Everything in history can be followed back . . . You can always trace back causes to the previous era. The roots of what happened in Russia were already present in Lenin's day, certainly they were. He would have had to cope with them. He would have coped with them in a different way from Stalin. But the problem existed.'

Would the same have applied to Trotsky? Often it seems during the debates of the 1920s that Stalin did one year what Trotsky had recommended the year before – and subsequently changed his mind. 'Yes, that seems to me rather characteristic of politics – that one party takes the policies of another. But Trotsky could never have become a leader. We are dealing here with things that didn't happen and couldn't have happened. He had so many qualities, but not that one. Trotsky was a genius, intellectually he was by far the most acute of them all. He was a wonderful orator and a wonderful writer, and he was a superb administrator. But he wasn't a political leader. That particular quality was lacking.'

But Carr's view of Soviet Russia is concerned less with individuals than with the broad interweave of politics, economics and society. He still sees the revolution as a potent force in spite of 'the blots which tarnished its credentials in Western eyes'.

The final volume ends optimistically: 'The Russian revolution of 1917 fell far short of the aims which it set for itself, and of the hopes which it generated. Its record was flawed and ambiguous. But it has been the source of more profound and more lasting repercussions throughout the world than any other historical event of modern times.'

Lesser men might give up after completing such a major task, but Carr has no intention of putting his feet up. He is now working on the 1930s. 'It won't be internal politics, it'll be international – the Comintern and all that sort of thing. What I'm interested in at the moment is the reaction to the rise of Hitler. The thing that comes out quite clearly is Stalin's own personal position. Stalin didn't think that any German would be conceivably so stupid as to incur hostilities on two fronts. He never believed this was possible. It was an absolute axiom to him that if Hitler was against the West he would be friendly with Russia.'

'What a mistake!' I interposed.

'A terrible mistake. But we all made terrible mistakes about Hitler, I suppose, if you come to think of it.' A. J. P. Taylor, I reminded him, had once described his book on international relations between the wars, *The Twenty Year Crisis*, published in 1939, as an apologia for appeasement.

'I see the point,' says Carr reflectively, as though he had been taxed with the question many times before, 'but it did after all suggest that we were not exactly blameless.'

For Carr the thirties were a pivotal decade. 'It was a period of great idealism – and also a great deal of blindness among intellectuals as to what was happening in Russia. At the beginning of the thirties the disillusionment with the capitalist system was very widespread – both among the Marxists and the Keynesians. The Keynesians thought somehow you could have a refurbished kind of capitalism, but they also condemned the old kind, and the disillusionment with the system was very, very powerful.'

The solution seemed to be planning. 'People said "We must plan. The Russians are having a plan. We must have a plan." This was, I think, the real background of the obsession about Russia which existed in the thirties. Of course, just at the moment when the purges were at their worst . . . this was also the moment when the intellectuals in this country were flowing into the Communist Party.' But he still thinks that the economic crisis in the early thirties was of crucial importance. 'It was certainly an important turning point for me – and I think it was for everyone else.'

At first glance, E. H. Carr's career looks impeccably Establishment. A brilliant classical scholar at Cambridge, winning all the prizes, he spent the First World War in the Foreign Office, and the Second World War as assistant editor of *The Times*. How had he managed to escape from this mould?

'Well, when I went into the Foreign Office I was a very, very young man. I was a little frightened, I think probably, or intimidated. I don't think that I developed in that period any ideas that could be called unduly unorthodox. In fact, you see, in a sense my progress – such as it was – came rather late in life. I ran on pretty orthodox lines right up to the end of the twenties.'

In the latter part of that decade, from 1925 to 1929, Carr was a diplomat in the Baltic town of Riga. 'We had a legation there. It was an independent country then – Latvia. There was not a great deal of official business to do, and I took an interest in Russia and in Russian literature.'

He went to Moscow for the first time in 1927. 'I stayed at the embassy, just for a few weeks. I also went to Leningrad, but in those days you couldn't travel around very much.' This was just before Stalin's break with Trotsky. Were people aware of what was going on? 'Oh yes, they had some idea, I think. I find it rather difficult to know now because now I know so much more about what happened then. I don't think they knew an awful lot – but something.'

It was in this period that Carr's ideas began to be shaken, 'first of all a little by my reading of the Russians. Not by the Bolsheviks. No, no, no. Not by reading Lenin or Trotsky. But by reading Dostoievski and Herzen. And then, of course, the real turning point was the economic crisis.' In 1936, aged forty-four, with books on Russia's romantic nineteenth-century exiles behind him, Carr abandoned the Foreign Office and accepted the chair of international politics at the University of Aberystwyth.

Perhaps his real hero has always been the Russian anarchist Bakunin. He published a biography of him in 1937. 'The book never sold, yet in a way I'd almost say it was the best book I ever wrote. He was a very interesting man. I'll always listen to anything about Bakunin. He has no following in this country. Even in the period when anarchism attracted a certain interest, it was always that very dull man Kropotkin.'

Carr went to Russia again in 1937 and wrote an account of his trip for *The Times*. 'I didn't stay in the embassy then, and I did travel around a bit. I must have been there just about the moment of the Tukachevski affair . . . but one couldn't know what was happening.'

Geoffrey Dawson, editor of *The Times* and leading appeaser, offered Carr a job, but he did not actually join the paper till 1941, when Barrington Ward had taken over and the line had changed. 'I saw eye to eye with Barrington Ward on the whole – it was a very curious relationship. I was assistant editor. What I did mostly was to write leaders and to some extent manage those articles that used to appear on the leader page. He was always tuning down what I wrote and saying "Yes, well, say that, but don't write it in quite such a provocative way".'

After the war, Carr left *The Times*, abandoned the professorship in Wales and settled down to full-time independent research. 'I was interested then in writing the history of Soviet Russia, and I suppose I'd got enough to live on by that time, and I wasn't pressed to take another job.' The first volume appeared in 1950, the second in 1952, and the third in 1953.

'After I'd been doing nothing for four or five years,' he says of this productive period, 'I became a little restless and then this offer from Oxford came up and for two years I taught in Oxford, from 1953 to 1955, and then I came back to Trinity.' He had been an undergraduate at Cambridge before 1914.

For more than two decades the volumes of Soviet history flowed steadily off the assembly line, with only a momentary pause to produce the Trevelyan lectures at Cambridge in 1961, entitled *What is History?* – the book that so provoked the ire of Trevor-Roper. Others were more enthusiastic. 'E. H. Carr and Joseph Needham,' wrote Geoffrey Barraclough, 'are the only two English historians of the present generation likely to receive first class marks at the hands of that inexorable examiner, Posterity'.

The Russians themselves say very little about E. H. Carr's version of their recent past. 'When they do say anything, they say, "Well, this chap, of course he isn't a Marxist, so he can't really understand what happened. On the other hand, he makes some sort of attempt to understand and gets some things right." A kind of patronizing view.' But Carr thinks that 'some of them read it, certainly with interest and with some approval and enlightenment. They learn things from it which they hadn't realized before. But of course if they write about it in public they must say that he isn't a Marxist.'

Politically, Carr has never been easy to classify. He is anxious to stick to his historian's cast. 'I'm not writing contemporary politics, I'm not giving advice to statesmen, I'm writing history.' But in a series of broadcast lectures in 1951, called *The New Society*, he once again emphasized his belief in the inevitability of economic and social planning.

Even today, he agrees ruefully, such an idea is not everywhere accepted. 'It's under attack from the right wing of the Conservative Party. It's the issue that's dividing the party. Only half the party understands that no government can possibly not regulate the economy.' And in 1951 a belief in planning was much less acceptable. One reviewer at that time described Carr as 'a futurist and a revolutionary'. Another wrote of how he tried to balance himself 'between his liberal mind and a heart that beats more like that of a radical rebel'.

The lectures, Carr recalls, 'created a certain amount of indignation in the Conservative Party because it was just on the eve of an election'. The Conservatives protested to the BBC because they were thought to be Labour propaganda. Roy Harrod was put up to answer them 'and he gave what was supposed to be a sort of counterblast – to salve the conscience of the BBC'.

But after so many years devoted to the activities of Russian Marxists, does Carr himself feel sympathetic to Marx? 'It's an odd thing that one has to approach a great figure of the past in this way. I'm neither sympathetic nor unsympathetic. At least I wouldn't put it in those terms. Marx was a great revolutionary thinker. He was one of the two or three people in the nineteenth century who changed our way of looking at the world – Darwin, Marx, Freud. It wasn't so much their doctrines as the fact that they changed our way of looking at things.'

But surely Marx is still less accepted today than Darwin or Freud? 'Well, Freud in a very garbled form has been accepted in America, but not so much in this country. People who don't like Marx generally don't like Freud either.'

On one point Carr is absolutely clear. The working class shows little sign of fulfilling Marx's predictions. He thinks that this was the great mistake of the Comintern. 'They were bound to get it wrong because they assumed that the western European working class was revolutionary and waiting for the revolution to begin. The working class is not revolutionary, except for moments of extreme excitement when there are signs of it - but it always dies down when things get rough.'

Does he believe then that the working class has been bought off by the profits of empire? 'No, not by the profits of empire, but by the profits of the capitalist system. The whole trade-union movement is integrated into the capitalist system. It quarrels with the employers within the system because it wants a bigger share of the profits. It doesn't want to damage the profits. It's not empire, it's exploitation of the consumer in the home market.'

And so far the system has continued to provide the profits,

contrary to what some comrades in the nineteenth century may have thought. I reminded him that more than twenty-five years ago he had written of the need for the political education, not just of the working class, but also of the middle class. 'The ruling class,' he corrected me. 'You see, we've passed on our sins of the past to the working class – and they're now just as bad as we were. They've now got this notion that the great thing is to make money – which they didn't use to have. They got it from the ruling class. It was a good Victorian principle. To make money used to be a sign of worth.'

He is not confident that much can be done in Britain. 'You can't save this economy without measures which nobody is prepared to accept. People prefer to drift along in this unsatisfactory way. Things get gradually a bit worse and more intolerable. But we get along somehow. They prefer this to the enormous upheaval which would be involved in doing anything about it. We can't really have all wages controlled by the state – how monstrous. We can't really have all prices controlled by the state – monstrous. You see? So we don't.'

Internationally, Carr believes that the American domination of the world is gradually being eroded, but he regrets in a way that Britain ever became so involved in the West. 'I think it would have been nicer if we could have been a Third World state, or if we had recognized that we're really now rather like Sweden or Holland and that we are out of the big league, so to speak. I regard all this military expenditure as quite futile. Wars are decided by somebody else and even if bombs are going to be dropped on us, this will all be decided by somebody else.'

Carr also thinks that belief in progress itself has been badly eroded. 'It doesn't exist any more. This is one of the troubles. Things you don't believe in, you cease to do anything about. You become frightened of change, and then you become backward-looking. We are looking back at the past and saying, "Ah well, that is what we used to have." I think this is probably an inevitable feature of our decline in the world. You may say that we don't mind having lost the empire, and probably we don't but the whole thing has affected our outlook.'

At the end of *What is History?* E. H. Carr expresses the view that the world is moving forward. Does he still subscribe to this optimistic view? 'I'm getting very old, I suppose, but I would say basically that I still believe the world is moving forward, but it does not always move forward at the same time or in the same place. I don't think *this* country is moving forward. I can't see this country being in the van of anything.' Carr thinks that we cannot envisage the future 'because the future's going to be so different from what we regard as the glories of our past'.

But E. H. Carr remains - at eighty-six, on a sunny autumn morning looking over Trinity Great Court to where the clock is striking midday - basically optimistic. After writing fourteen volumes devoted to one of the greatest upheavals in history, that is no mean achievement. 'I don't really share the view of those people who say the world is going to be bombed out of existence and all that sort of thing. But the decay of civilizations may be a necessary prelude to the start of something else.'

*Foundations of a Planned Economy, 1926-1929, Volume III, part three, *the completion of a* History of Soviet Russia, *by E. H. Carr.*

25 November 1978   **Richard Gott**

Index